# CRITICAL ESSAYS ON JANE AUSTEN

## CONTRIBUTORS

*John Bayley*
*Brigid Brophy*
*Denis Donoghue*
*Robert Garis*
*D. W. Harding*
*Gilbert Ryle*
*J. I. M. Stewart*
*Tony Tanner*
*Rachel Trickett*
*Angus Wilson*

# CRITICAL ESSAYS
# ON
# JANE AUSTEN

*Edited by*

B. C. SOUTHAM

*London*
ROUTLEDGE & KEGAN PAUL

*First published 1968*
*by Routledge & Kegan Paul Ltd*
*Broadway House, 68–74 Carter Lane, E.C.4*

*Reprinted and first published*
*as a Routledge Paperback 1970*

*Printed in Great Britain by*
*Compton Printing Ltd London and Aylesbury*

© *Routledge & Kegan Paul Ltd 1968*

ISBN 0 7100 6243 5 (c)
ISBN 0 7100 6904 9 (p)

# CONTENTS

ACKNOWLEDGEMENTS                                          *page* vii

SELECT BIBLIOGRAPHY                                              ix

INTRODUCTION *B. C. Southam*                                     xi

I     THE 'IRRESPONSIBILITY' OF JANE AUSTEN *John Bayley*         1

II    JANE AUSTEN AND THE STUARTS *Brigid Brophy*                21

III   A VIEW OF 'MANSFIELD PARK' *Denis Donoghue*                39

IV    LEARNING EXPERIENCE AND CHANGE *Robert Garis*              60

V     CHARACTER AND CARICATURE IN JANE AUSTEN *D. W. Harding*    83

VI    JANE AUSTEN AND THE MORALISTS *Gilbert Ryle*              106

VII   TRADITION AND MISS AUSTEN *J. I. M. Stewart*              123

VIII  JANE AUSTEN AND 'THE QUIET THING'—A STUDY OF
      'MANSFIELD PARK' *Tony Tanner*                            136

IX    JANE AUSTEN'S COMEDY AND THE NINETEENTH CENTURY
      *Rachel Trickett*                                         162

X     THE NEIGHBOURHOOD OF TOMBUCTOO: CONFLICTS IN
      JANE AUSTEN'S NOVELS *Angus Wilson*                       182

INDEX                                                          201

# ACKNOWLEDGEMENTS

'Jane Austen and the Moralists' by Gilbert Ryle was originally published in the *Oxford Review*, and 'Jane Austen and "The quiet thing"' by Tony Tanner is adapted from his introduction to *Mansfield Park*, published by Penguin Books Ltd. Thanks are due to the publishers for permission to reprint these essays.

# SELECT BIBLIOGRAPHY

This select Bibliography is a list of the most important critical studies, both books and articles, referred to in the essays collected here.

Bradley, A. C. 'Jane Austen', *Essays and Studies* 2 (of the English Association), 1911.

Cecil, David. 'Jane Austen' (The Leslie Stephen Lecture), 1935.

Farrer, Reginald. 'Jane Austen', *Quarterly Review* 228, July 1917.

Forster, E. M. In *Abinger Harvest*, 1936.

Garrod, H. G. 'Jane Austen: a Depreciation', *Essays by Divers Hands* new series 8, (Royal Society of Literature), 1928.

Harding, D. W. 'Regulated Hatred: An Aspect of the Work of Jane Austen', *Scrutiny* 8, March 1940.

James, Henry. In 'The Lesson of Balzac', 1905, reprinted in *The House of Fiction*, 1957, ed. Leon Edel. In 'Gustave Flaubert', 1902, also in Edel.

Kettle, Arnold. In *An Introduction to the English Novel*, 1951.

Lascelles, M. M. *Jane Austen and her Art*, 1939.

Leavis, F. R. In *The Great Tradition*, 1948.

Leavis, Q. D. 'A Critical Theory of Jane Austen's Writings', *Scrutiny* 10, June and October 1941, January 1942; 12, June 1944.

Mudrick, Marvin. *Jane Austen: Irony as Defense and Discovery*, 1952.

Scott, Walter. Review of *Emma*, *Quarterly Review* 16, October 1815 (published March 1816).

Simpson, Richard. Review of the *Memoir of Jane Austen*, *North British Review* 52, April 1870.

Trilling, Lionel. '*Mansfield Park*', *Partisan Review* 21, 1954; a revised version in *Pelican Guide to English Literature* 5, 1957. '*Emma*', *Encounter* 8, June 1957.

Whately, Richard. Review of *Northanger Abbey* and *Persuasion*, *Quarterly Review* 24, January 1821.

Wilson, Edmund. 'A Long Talk on Jane Austen' in *Classics and Commercials*, 1950.

Wright, Andrew. *Jane Austen's Novels: A Study in Structure*, 1953, revised edn. 1962.

References to Jane Austen's Works refer throughout to the Oxford edition by R. W. Chapman.

# INTRODUCTION

## B. C. Southam

MANY READERS find a strong and distinctive personality in Jane Austen's writing. For some it is a personality of warmth and charm, commanding their admiration and affection. For others it is a cold and spinsterish soul, holding them at a distance, even to the point of dislike, as with Mark Twain who could feel nothing less than an 'animal repugnance'. The contributors to this volume come into neither category. They were not invited as known admirers nor as critics notoriously unsympathetic to Jane Austen. Nor, to take a third possibility, are they writers who subscribe to any particular line of thought or critical theory. In contributing to this volume they were perfectly free to take topics of their choice and there was no editorial prescription for the individual essays or for the collection as a whole. It was never in my mind, as volume editor, to try to present an agreed or consistent view, and among the essays there is considerable variety and opinion, certainly nothing that can be fastened upon as stating a single collective position.

In this, at least, the volume is characteristic of Jane Austen studies at large, which have never been dominated by critical orthodoxies, or, on the other hand, split by the kind of major controversy that divided Milton studies for so long. As Lord David Cecil put it in the Leslie Stephen Lecture (1935):

> All discriminating critics admire her books, most educated readers enjoy them; her fame of all English novelists, is the most secure.

These words hold true today. They describe a situation that has remained little changed for nearly a hundred years. The view of Jane Austen as a 'great' novelist is presented in every history of English Literature and finds modern support in critics as far apart

as Professor Trilling and Dr. Leavis. Jane Austen is an acknowledged classic of our literature—studied, discussed and written about
as such.

This judgement is generally accepted. But to *arrive* at this judgement, along properly critical paths, is not altogether easy. It involves
reconciling the notion of literary 'greatness' with the modesty of
Jane Austen's achievement. Modesty, with its personal ring, is the
very word, because it draws attention to the author's self-imposed
and self-declared limitations (which we can find in her correspondence, particularly with the Prince Regent's Librarian, the Rev. W.
Clark). It also draws attention to the author's presence in the novels,
a personal stance in the grace and charm of her narration, in the
quietness of style, and in the affected incompleteness of the author's
knowledge and control over her characters' destinies. These are the
tactics of irony. There is modesty, too, in the limited range of subject-matter and treatment. And any critic convinced of Jane Austen's
greatness, of her claim to be considered alongside such writers as
George Eliot, James, Conrad or Lawrence, in the English tradition,
or Tolstoy, Fontane, Stendhal, Kafka or Proust in the wider
European scene, bears the responsibility of explaining the remarkable
phenomenon of such 'limited' greatness. On this, the Leslie Stephen
Lecture is exceptionally interesting, for among the admirers of Jane
Austen, Lord David is remarkable in defining the problem and
seizing it so boldly. In a perspective of European literature, he
argues, the novels are nothing less than 'works of major art': *Mansfield Park* 'expresses a criticism of life as comprehensive as that of
*Madame Bovary*'. Lord David contends that the novelist's limitations are to be accepted as a condition of her achievement:

> Nor does the limited theatre of its presentation impair the power of
> this criticism. On the contrary, it increases it. It gives it charm. The
> unique irresistible flavour of her work, its gay astringent buoyancy, its
> silvery commonsense arises from the unexpected combination of her
> realistic moralism with the delicate elegance of its setting. Moreover,
> the fact that she kept so carefully to the only world she knew thoroughly
> well, meant that she was not distracted by superficial idiosyncrasies, but
> could penetrate beneath them to perceive its more general significance.
> *Emma* is universal just because it is narrow; because it confines itself
> to the range of Jane Austen's profoundest vision.
> For it is a profound vision. There are other views of life and more
> extensive; concerned as it is exclusively with personal relationships, it

leaves out several important aspects of experience. But on her own ground Jane Austen gets to the heart of the matter; her graceful unpretentious philosophy, founded as it is on an unwavering recognition of fact, directed by an unerring perception of moral quality, is as impressive as those of the most majestic novelists.

This is not a solution everyone will accept. In this volume Angus Wilson argues to the contrary: that for Jane Austen limitation was a deforming constriction, not a creative discipline. Nonetheless, Lord David's lecture is remarkable in facing the issue at all; and that it needs to be taken up, at this time, is commented upon by John Wiltshire, reviewing three recent books on Jane Austen in *The Cambridge Quarterly* (Spring 1967):

> The reader sharing the bewilderment of Conrad who wrote to Wells asking 'What is all this about Jane Austen? What is there *in* her? What is it all about?' will find himself ignored—and even his readiness to hear Jane Austen's claims put forward vigorously not encouraged.

Over the last thirty years there has been a great increase in the number of books and articles dealing with Jane Austen both at the learned and popular levels. This development is part of a general rise of interest in the nineteenth-century novel. The emphasis has been on technical aspects—the form and structure of the novel, its narrative devices, its texture of dialogue and so on. The novels of Jane Austen have proved to be rewarding ground for such approaches. In the last few pages of *The Rise of the Novel* (1957) Professor Ian Watt has written finely of 'Jane Austen's technical genius'. But in the excitement of 'technical' exploration some critics have lost sight of the country through which they have blazed their individual trails. By and large, in our time, in the midst of all this activity, the substance of Conrad's question has gone unanswered.

This was not so in the pre-Jamesian period, especially in the period before 1870 (the year in which the first biography, *The Memoir of Jane Austen*, laid the foundations of the Jane Austen cult, touched upon here by Rachel Trickett). From the time of Scott's review of *Emma* in 1816, until Richard Simpson's great essay of 1870, the Jane Austen issue was clearly seen. For all its unsophistication, its whiggishness, its waywardness and extravagance, the best nineteenth-century criticism of Jane Austen was healthily radical. It recognized the author's superb technique, a masterful artistic economy in

the relation of means to an end. But, equally, there was a severe estimate of Jane Austen's subject-matter and range. As we see in the
letters of Charlotte Brontë, there could be violent opposition to the
promotion of Jane Austen into the ranks of the great, an objection to the notion of Jane Austen as a 'prose Shakespeare', a
title conferred by Macaulay and Lewes. Mrs. Browning put the
matter neatly in a letter to Ruskin in 1855, when remarking that
the novels were 'perfect as far as they go—that's certain. Only they
don't go far enough'. Such comments could be dismissed as rank
prejudice and contrary taste. Yet the same dismissive note sounds
more mildly and extensively in a number of mid-Victorian reviews;
E. S. Dallas, for example, in his notice of the newly-published
*Felix Holt* in 1866: George Eliot, he wrote,

> has to deal with subjects far more difficult than Miss Austen ever
> attempted, with wilder passions, with stronger situations, with higher
> thoughts. Miss Austen scarcely gets out of the humdrum of easy-going
> respectable life; she can therefore well afford to be calm and neat in
> arranging every thread of the narrative she has to weave.

Other critics made other comparisons, equally unfavourable. Their
terms of reference were unsympathetic. Around them was a powerful and 'engaged' literature, focused upon the problems of the age—
its new industrial poor, its political and social inequalities, its crisis
of belief, its uncertainty and restlessness in the face of progress. In
this perspective, Jane Austen's works seemed slight and faded pieces,
little more than period comedies, scenes from another age, perfect
in their own small way, amusing but lightweight, their intellectual
horizons restricted, their social focus narrowly domestic, their
tragedies and crises no more than the poignancies of young ladies
in love. Some Victorian critics even detected a note of callous disregard in a view of life which could so serenely ignore the sufferings
of ordinary people, which could treat the state of England and the
drama of Napoleonic Europe as if they were events off-stage. Could
this be great literature?

The stock answer was to remark on Jane Austen's artistic
economy, and upon her genius in character-drawing, the feature
that moved Scott and then Whately, Macaulay, Lewes and other of
her early admirers to invoke the name of Shakespeare. Later in the
century the emphasis changed. Jane Austen began to be seen as a
writer of unsuspected strength, as a satirist delicate yet severe, or,

as we meet her in the essay by Richard Simpson, a writer with powers of mind, an artist aware that the language and form of the novel could serve as the instrument of her judgement on society. As Simpson put it,'Jane Austen's sense of the writer's control gave her a superiority to her subject, which is one element in solving the secret of her wonderful power over it'. Simpson recognized a writer with an intelligence and a serious, critical purpose. But all this within limits. His recognition of Jane Austen's achieved qualities is balanced by a sustained analysis of the *unrealized* possibilities of her art. To take an instance particularly relevant to our modern interest in Jane Austen as a novelist of society:

> Of organized society she manifests no idea. She had no interest for the great political and social problems which were being debated with so much blood in her day. The social combinations which taxed the calculating powers of Adam Smith and Jeremy Bentham were above her powers. . . . Her clergymen even have very little of their calling about them; there is little attempt to delineate clerical manners as such. . . . there is no distinctive social force incarnate in them, nor does the official social weight they carry become interwoven in the web of their characters . . . public opinion. . . . It is an abstract notion, a word not a thing, an idea not a force. . . . She was perfect in dramatizing the combination of a few simple forces; but it never struck her to try to dramatize the action and reaction of all.

Whether or not we agree with this analysis, its procedure is not to be discounted. In defining Jane Austen's qualities Simpson states the limit of their performance. This is not the only principle of good criticism, but it is a principle which critics of Jane Austen have often disregarded.

Although I noted at the beginning of this Introduction that no common theme or position emerges from these essays, it is clear that several of the contributors share, to some degree, the kind of dissatisfaction I have expressed about the present state of Jane Austen criticism. The emphasis of this volume is critical rather than appreciative. But of course critical does not mean depreciative. When John Bayley compares Jane Austen with Tolstoy we have a properly critical placing, which in working to Jane Austen's disadvantage does not fail to give us an enhanced and more precise definition of her achievement. And Professor Ryle's essay is critical in the same way, through the force of historical illumination. With his essay before us we are now able to judge one of the directions in which

Jane Austen's intellectual and moral experience was informed; and how, working through the force of her imagination, it found creative expression in the structure and characterization of the novels. The identification of this 'intellectual' content does not require us to judge her the greater novelist thereby. But it helps to account for the density of meaning that is our experience in reading the novels, a weightiness so constantly belied by the delusive modesty of their tone and performance.

Professor Ryle's essay provokes us to ask how far the current interest in the technique of the novel is likely to help us on our way towards a balanced understanding of Jane Austen's art. It also makes us want to press Jane Austen's admirers to a fuller statement of their case, particularly those who, like Dr. Leavis, place so much emphasis upon the novelist's moral concerns; as Dr. Leavis puts it, 'Without her intense moral preoccupation she wouldn't have been a great novelist'. Such an inquiry into the organization of the novels, embracing the unity of form and content, might begin to answer Conrad's still-abiding question.

# I

# THE 'IRRESPONSIBILITY' OF
# JANE AUSTEN*

## *John Bayley*

---

No one would deny that the pleasures and perceptions Jane Austen offers her readers can be of a very complex kind. Each re-reading strikes us afresh with something newly significant, and some change in the perspective of our own world in relation to hers. The shock of this renewed relationship has stimulated most of the good things that have been written about her, even the unfavourable good things, like Professor Garrod's *Jane Austen: A Depreciation*. She bothered Professor Garrod: she got under his skin: in re-reading her he discovered something about his own outlook on life that made it urgently necessary to depreciate hers. And this is typical. Our reaction to her seems intimately, even alarmingly, dependent on our own history. In meeting her again we reflect to ourselves in something of the way that Leopold Bloom does in *Ulysses*. 'Me. And me now.'

This may seem Janeite nonsense, mere inability to separate ourselves from art which has become assimilated into the vocabulary of our own consciousness. But the point is that it is not the kind of assimilation to which some works of art are subjected by their exclusive and excluding admirers, but a real questioning or wondering, an apparent dialogue between our own intelligence and another's. We never quite know where we are with Jane Austen, as we know where we are with George Eliot, and even with Henry

* A part of this essay entitled 'Emma and her Critics' was given as a lecture to the Jane Austen Society in July 1967.

James. *He* may sometimes not have been quite sure what he thought about things, but then we can see him being not quite sure—Jane Austen's certainties are much more enigmatic. And might we not, on this kind of ground, question the assumption of Dr. Leavis, that a 'Great Tradition' unites her unmistakably with the high intelligences who dominate the later nineteenth-century novel?

The idea of that tradition takes for granted, above all, a complete and confident knowledge of the minds of the authors who represent it. George Eliot, Henry James, Conrad and D. H. Lawrence—we can know them fully as literary personalities, and this knowledge is not directly dependent on the quantity of our biographical information about them. We can *consider* them, even as they considered their material. But our relation with Jane Austen is not like this. In one way we know her too well to be so coherently aware of her: and in another way we do not know her at all.

This dilemma is reflected in the best of the critical writing about her. It was Macaulay, I believe, who first associated her with Shakespeare; and the best things about her do indeed treat her novels with the same freedom with which criticism had treated Shakespeare's plays, finding in them what gives critical perception its chance to be free, bold, and speculative.

> I do not write for such dull elves
> As have not a great deal of ingenuity themselves.

Her own facetious parody of *Marmion*, in a letter to her sister, has certainly been taken *au pied de la lettre* by her liveliest critics, who have exhibited a great deal of their own critical ingenuity. And their own sense of her up-to-dateness. A Polish savant, Professor Jan Kott, has recently written a study called 'Shakespeare: Our Contemporary'. 'Jane Austen: our Contemporary' would describe equally well the tone of recent discussion about her, a tone perhaps first heard in the title of D. W. Harding's essay—'Regulated Hatred: An Aspect of the Work of Jane Austen'. Criticism can see her now as satisfying our literary appetite even for the strongest emotions.

It was not always so. She was once enjoyed—even by her greatest admirers—as almost a period piece, a sunlit refuge from the cares of the reader. But though the Shakespearean scholar A. C. Bradley called her 'exceptionally peaceful reading', Reginald Farrer was remarking about the same time that *Emma* produced at each reading more possibilities to ponder on; that it was far from being—in the phrase Dostoevsky used to describe *Anna Karenina*—an 'innocent' book. Edmund Wilson has since opined that much of its theme lies below the level of overt treatment—a line of argument to which the talk about *Hamlet* has accustomed us. And Professor Ryle not unreasonably wonders—as the philosophically inclined have wondered about Shakespeare—whether Jane Austen did not share something of his own interest in abstract problems; whether, for example, a reading of the philosopher Shaftesbury might not have led her to embody in Emma a complex moral concept which might be labelled 'Solicitude', as she embodied in other fictions the more straightforward concepts of 'Sense and Sensibility' and 'Persuasion'. Professor Trilling, who has written two of the most interesting essays of recent years about Jane Austen, has been as valuably speculative, perceiving in *Mansfield Park* something akin to his own preoccupations with the nature and style of a contemporary morality; and, in *Emma*, a sustained imaginative inquiry into how a society ideally works through its members; how it gains, and keeps, its virtues.

The Shakespeare parallel reveals in these cases a paradox which has a certain irony. For the more the modern critics write about Jane Austen as if she were Shakespeare, the more they tend to find in her novels what they find in George Eliot's, in Proust's, in Henry James's. The fact is that the more the novel comes to commit itself unreservedly to the lonely intellect, the less we can feel ourselves in a familial relation to those who profess and practise its art. It is the penalty of such an intellect that in holding forth, with whatever degree of sincerity and subtlety, it relinquishes that peculiarly immediate and yet equivocal attitude towards its experience that challenges and fascinates us in Jane Austen. With George Eliot, as I have said, we know exactly where we are—she leaves us in no doubt about herself and her convictions. She knows what she thinks, and she lets us know, for everything—or almost everything—that she creates has been raised to the level of cogitation and exposition.

I say 'almost everything', because it is notorious that in George Eliot's novels there is some material, and particularly certain characters, who seem to be left outside her penetrating, often humorous examinations—those figures and situations 'deeply studied and elaborately justified', in Henry James's phrase—which are her fine achievement. In the same context James goes on to say that her characters, however 'deeply studied and elaborately justified', are 'not *seen* in the irresponsible plastic way'; and here he reveals the great division which seems to me more important than the 'great tradition'. Jane Austen, with Shakespeare and Tolstoy, are on one side of it: George Eliot, and James himself, on the other.

If this is true, it shows us why there is this unacknowledged contradiction at the heart of even the most perceptive Jane Austen criticism. Her critics, like those of Shakespeare, find in her what most interests themselves, but having found it they assume in it a hard 'unplastic' significance, an intellectual absoluteness which they would also find in George Eliot or Henry James. They write of Emma, or of Mary Crawford, as if their cases were as masterfully documented and as firmly exposed as those of Dorothea Brooke or Rosamond Vincy. 'Plasticity' in Jane Austen is not charity, but it is the result of a familial recognition, the unspoken admission of a necessary kinship. This may strike us when, in one of the most concise and perceptive recent studies, we read the following:

> Both Darcy and Elizabeth are flanked by figures who parody their basic tendencies: in Mr Bennet the irony of the detached observer has become sterile, while Lady Catherine de Bourgh represents the worst side of aristocratic self-consciousness.... The Gardiners stand as a rebuke to Darcy's social prejudices and aristocratic pride, an example of natural aristocracy.... The marriage of Elizabeth and Darcy is, as Mark Schorer has pointed out, a kind of economic and social merging, an accommodation of traditional values based upon status with the new values personified in the Gardiners.[1]

The tone of this would be perfectly just in an analysis of *Daniel Deronda* or *The Bostonians*, but it does not seem quite suited to the world we actually enter in *Pride and Prejudice*. It is perfectly true, of course, that Jane Austen herself in her earlier novels delights in a certain sort of definition. Mrs. Bennet 'was a woman of mean understanding, little information, and uncertain temper'. Yet there is an immense difference between definition of this sort and the Olympian analysis of, and commentary on, society implied by the passage quoted above. Indeed, definition in early Jane Austen is surely almost a humorous abdication of the majesty of justice—its exasperation asks not for any measured agreement from us but for our sympathy as fellow-sufferers, as members of the same large family.

In these comments on Mr. Woodhouse by another critic we seem even further away from Jane Austen.

Mr. Woodhouse—after long years of invalidism, of being coddled by his daughter, of scarcely stirring from his house or seeing a new person —is an idiot. He is quite incapable of thought or judgment... When Emma, in a rare mood of almost irritable playfulness, tries to point out the contradiction between his respect for brides and his dislike of marriage, she only makes him nervous without making him at all understand... His tenacious clinging to Emma, to his acquaintances, to the seen boundaries of his world, comes to resemble the clinging of a parasitic plant, which must be now or sometime shaken off. Mr. Woodhouse is the living—barely living—excuse for Emma's refusal to commit herself to the human world.[2]

I confess to total puzzlement, which I feel Jane Austen might have shared, about the meaning of the word 'human' in this context. It is surely a wholly different fictional outlook which finds some human beings more human than others? And though the critic is entitled to his own assessment of Mr. Woodhouse, is it fair to assume his creator felt the same way? Doesn't he ignore Jane Austen's character-istic and 'irresponsible' sharing of Mr. Woodhouse with us? Jane Austen, and we with her, enter into Mr. Woodhouse as Shakespeare enters into Falstaff and Shylock, or Tolstoy into Stiva Oblonsky; and it is moving, liberating, and illuminating to be enabled to feel in this way how other people feel; to relax inside their limitations; to acquiesce briefly in the bonds of their temperament; to surrender for the moment our own modes of judging, perceiving, and desiring. This is a primal experience in literature, and one essentially different in kind from our being invited to contemplate the character as a portrait, and to assist in the analysis of its composition. Of course with Jane Austen we can do that too, but a kind of identification comes first, and profoundly modifies our ensuing appraisal. It is from his critical vantage-point outside that Professor Mudrick calls Mr. Woodhouse an 'idiot'. Jane Austen in life might herself have called him that in a moment of exasperation, and so can her reader; but it would be an exclamation from inside a community, not a verdict from outside it.

It is a vital premise of *Emma*, as a novel, that we have to live inside such a community, as Jane Austen enables us to live inside the individuals who compose it, and so we have to take the consequences of such an exclamation about one of its members, as Emma herself does after her unkindness to Miss Bates. The remarkable force of that event, and the directness of its impact upon us, proceeds from its summation of the whole tendency of the novel—its enveloping intimacy. No question but that both author and reader share in Emma's guilt. Jane Austen's art puts us and herself into a community from which there is no withdrawing; a community in which we are entitled to malice, to misunderstanding, to levity, to thoughtlessness—to anything except the right to detach ourselves and contemplate with our author from outside. The seeing and creating irresponsibility of the 'plastic' artist is an aspect of this total involvement: to Jane Austen, and hence to us, it is what 'that very dear part of Emma, her fancy,' was to Emma.

In using against Mr. Woodhouse the contradiction his daughter points out between 'his respect for brides and his dislike of marriage' Professor Mudrick is also surely missing a true Austenian complexity of some significance. Mr. Woodhouse's lack of his daughter's quick perception of individuals is indeed exquisitely ludicrous. 'Considering we never saw her before', he observes to Emma of Mrs. Elton, 'she seems a very pretty sort of young lady; and I dare say she was very pleased with you'. Mrs. Elton, as we know, was no more pleased with Emma than Emma was with her. But when Emma gets on to tease him for being 'no friend to matrimony but so anxious to pay your respects to a bride', we catch a glimpse of the reason why he is, for all his tiresomeness, so much loved and appreciated in the community.

'No, my dear, I never encouraged anybody to marry, but I would always wish to pay every proper attention to a lady—and a bride, especially, is never to be neglected. More is avowedly due to *her*. A bride, you know, my dear, is always the first in company, let the others be who they may'.

'Well, papa, if this is not encouragement to marry I do not know what is. And I should never have expected you to be lending your sanction to such vanity-baits for poor young ladies'.

'My dear, you do not understand me. This is a matter of mere common politeness and good-breeding, and has nothing to do with any encouragement to people to marry'.

Emma had done. Her father was growing nervous, and could not understand *her*.

(ch. 32)

Good manners require that we behave towards people not as we feel about them as individuals, but as their position or predicament in life dictates. Mr. Woodhouse does not know that he knows this, but he grows nervous when his daughter questions his unconscious acceptance of it. Emma is rude to Miss Bates because she forgot (we might say that her unadmitted resentment of Jane Fairfax willed her to forget) the impoverished spinster status, and thought only of being witty at the expense of the boringly garrulous individual. The intimate impact is that Jane Austen and ourselves have often done the same kind of thing, and have afterwards (one hopes) been ashamed of it. In reading Jane Austen (as in reading Shakespeare and Tolstoy) we both do the deed and rue it. The *outlook* of George Eliot may admit this kind of imperfection in the author and reader, but does her *art* ever enclose it? Isn't fallibility confined, by her outlook and method, to the characters themselves? If so, it may be the reason why our participation in the world of Jane Austen changes and shifts its emphasis with each re-reading; while our understanding of George Eliot's, already fully enlightened and satisfied when our sense of the problems she treats is still youthfully theoretical, does not do so.

Although Mr. Woodhouse could not have separated the two ideas —Miss Bates as impoverished spinster and Miss Bates as bore—he could never have been guilty of his daughter's offence. The most instinctive good manners, we might infer, are usually found in those with the smallest powers of lively individual discrimination; and this would be a typically wry Austenian inference, for neither Emma nor her creator, nor we if we who are enjoying them, can ever aspire to *that* summit of good-breeding!

Emma and her father cannot understand one another, but this is no bar to their affection. Harmony, even intimacy, can exist in a community without mutual understanding—indeed must do, for we must live as we can. And this acceptance of misunderstanding is surely the keynote of *Emma*, rather than—as has often been said —the confrontation of reality with a series of self-deceptions and misapprehensions.[3] Emma is Emma still, as Lydia—at the end of *Pride and Prejudice*—is Lydia still. Most things, like Harriet's partiality for Robert Martin, 'must ever be unintelligible to her', as similar things must be to us all. We cannot contemplate Emma's awakening to understanding, because neither we nor Jane Austen can profess to know what such an 'understanding' is. That pretension must be left to a later race of novelists. But we do know what her society is like, because like Emma and her friends we live in it as we read, and it is Jane Austen's achievement to leave us sharing rather than judging. Our judgements, like hers, are contingent on the inability to escape from the society in which she is writing, the boat—as it were—in which we and the other Highbury inhabitants are tossing together on the sea.[4]

The saving irresponsibility of Jane Austen is her freedom, as the prisoner of that society, to say what she likes about it. It is astonishing to me that the prejudice should still linger that she is a constricting and censorious writer, a writer claustrophobically preoccupied with the right and the wrong thing. In fact it would be more accurate to see her works as a peculiar kind of liberation from morality. This was surely sensed by D. W. Harding in his notable essay, and also by Professor Litz, who quotes from the philosopher Shaftesbury this extremely significant sentence. 'The natural free spirits of ingenious men, if imprisoned and controlled, will find out other ways of motion to relieve themselves in their constraint.'

And yet the critics seem reluctant to admit the consequences of this relief, this freedom, and how it affects Jane Austen's whole creative method, particularly in the last three novels. I have tried to illustrate by quotation the misleading tightness of patterning which the critics imply when they exhibit the significance of contrast and relation in her novels. The patterns that criticism sees—and often illuminatingly sees—can none the less mislead unless we recognize that they are used by the author in order that she may escape from them. She uses the rigidity of society as a means of liberating her fancy and her creative joy, whereas for later novelists the society they create is the product of their own interpretative and meaning-seeking vision.

This would be a way of saying that society as portrayed by George Eliot and Henry James is in many ways a visionary and *imagined* society. The town of *Middlemarch* is as much George Eliot's own construction—a realm adapted by and used by her imagination—as is the Florence she portrays in *Romola*. (It could equally be said that the London of *The Princess Casamassima* and of *The Golden Bowl* have their unique and fascinating existence only in James's mind.) For the social novelists at the end of the nineteenth century this must be so, because they cannot surrender themselves to society without sinking into a paralysing triviality. No social milieu holds them so closely that 'their natural free spirits' must find 'other ways of motion'. Society has become too vast and vague to be a prison, and the novelist cannot incarcerate himself voluntarily—that would be no substitute for the real thing. Any constraint must come from elsewhere, and it comes therefore from the novelist himself, from his involuntary abnegation of the 'plastic' and the 'irresponsible'. Patterns of relation and of morality must now *really* mean something. They must stand up on their own, and they must support the imaginative structure of the whole work.

At the end of his essay on *Emma* Professor Trilling observes, almost as if it were self-evident, that Highbury does not correspond to anything real in the England of the time, but has an ideal, an imagined status; that it is, in fact, Jane Austen's vision of a social unit, conceived in the interest of her social and moral purpose. Of course Jane Austen 'made up' Highbury, as all novelists make up their fictions, but it was also the world she lived and had to live in —if it was not we could not live in it as we do and ask the questions about it that we do ask. Highbury is a real place, as in their different ways Middlemarch and Henry James's Mayfair—even his Boston—are not; and its reality depends on its inescapability. George Eliot's places, we might note, are created either by meticulous and affectionate detail—she herself compared it to Dutch *genre* painting —or by an equally painstaking process of factual accumulation and research. Often the two are combined. Highbury is known by Jane Austen as Emma knows it by standing at the door of Ford's the draper. Though 'much could not be hoped', still 'she ... was amused enough, quite enough still to stand at the door. A mind lively and at ease can do with seeing nothing, and can see nothing that does not answer'.

Highbury, we might say, is real because it does not have to be explored and because there is no alternative to it. Sanditon, it is true, might have been created by a more adventurous and less instinctual process, though the tentative fragment of Jane Austen's last novel is hardly enough to build any supposition on. What we do know is that she declined to attempt the creation of a world as the historical novelist attempts it: she declined to attempt giving the Saxe-Coburgs a local habitation and a name—that kind of imagined world was not for her and never would have been.

Although some of the most perceptive discussion of Jane Austen's world has come from America, it may be that the American mind does have difficulty in taking for granted the reality of Jane Austen's social units. Nothing in America is quite real in her way—perhaps because there is always an *alternative* to it. It may be that because

American society is basically nomadic it is always in the state of becoming, of an idea about to arrive, and is never a fact. Henry James suggested something like this in a famous passage about the world in which Hawthorne grew up, and it is certainly true that American fiction has always remained visionary, dominated by conscience, concept, and dream. We can see this even in popular contemporary slogans like 'building the Great Society'. And indeed where these kinds of attitudes and assumptions are concerned we might be said to be all Americans today.

Class, in our modern world, is of course even less real than place. And it may be this that leads Professor Trilling to assume not only that Highbury doesn't exist, but that Emma herself—in her attitudes to the world she lives in—is a snob, 'a dreadful snob'. The two assumptions certainly go together, for snobbery—as we know it today—is essentially a visionary activity, an undertaking of the fantasy. As such it may be doubted whether it has any true place in Jane Austen's world. Sir Walter Elliot is not a snob in our modern sense but a ludicrously self-complacent Narcissist, as vain of his complexion as he is of his baronetcy. Mrs. Clay is not a snob but a woman who knows her own advantage, and Mr. Collins is the same: to get on with the great is for them quite literally their meat and drink. Mrs. Elton gives herself absurd airs, but is so little a snob that she doesn't even realize there is anything in society for her to feel snobbish about. Her insensitivity is far too great for her to aspire to the title! For snobs are not only sensitive people but imaginative people; they are obsessed with their standing in relation to society, but to an idea of society which they themselves have created. Jane Austen was extremely interested in the large society that she knew, and in all the distinctions that it incontrovertibly contained: but she did not create her own picture of it, she did not *imagine* it; neither do her characters.

Emma has her fixed and acknowledged place in society. No snob has. Indeed today very few of us do. Hence our preoccupation with the idea of snobbery, and our guilt about it, which has to a very large extent replaced, as has often been pointed out, feelings of shame and guilt about sex. Jane Austen's views on both matters were robust enough, but about class particularly so. I suspect she would have been both surprised and amused at the note of positive agitation in Professor Trilling's tone after he has quoted Emma's pert comment on Robert Martin: 'A farmer can need none of my help, and is therefore in one sense as much above my notice as in every other way he is below it'. 'This is carefully contrived by the author', Professor Trilling assures us, 'to seem as dreadful as possible; it quite staggers us, and some readers will even feel that the author goes too far in permitting Emma to make this speech'.

The irony of the speech, surely, is that it contains a core of common sense which Emma doesn't act on. It is the case that Emma has nothing to say to Robert Martin and his family—why should she have?—and they on their side are in no need of her help and advice. She and they are and should be quite independent of each other. But in fact she *does* interfere with them: she meddles by proxy in her relation with Harriet and in turning Harriet against them. Vain and vivaciously opinionated as she is, she ignores the soundness of her own instinct, the instinct of her own assured position. Mr. Knightley, who knows better than to meddle, would have endorsed the underlying sense of her remark, though he would have deplored the unbecomingly pert way in which she makes it. But what is really revealing about Professor Trilling's attitude is his assumption that Jane Austen, as if she were George Eliot, is intent here upon showing up Emma in the most 'carefully contrived' way she can. Equally significant—because it implies a contradiction—is the note of apology on her behalf ('some readers will even feel . . .') in his comment that here perhaps Jane Austen has gone too far.

Of course she has gone too far! She, and we, are always doing so—in life, and in our mutual relation in a novel which is so like life. Jane Austen is not Emma, but equally she is not manipulating and showing up Emma: she is participating with unmistakable relish in the outrageous vivacity of her heroine. And so are we. Professor Trilling's hesitancy gives the clue to the way in which we read Jane Austen, and *Emma* in particular. We do not watch her expose her heroine: we share with her and her heroine—and what a privilege it is to do so—our common lapses into superiority, complacency, bad taste; and we also share the sense that we can know these things in ourselves for what they are, that we have an idea of what is right and 'know how to prize and respect it'. Professor Trilling himself makes this point wonderfully well when he suggests that the relation between ourselves and Emma is 'a strange one—it is the relation that exists between our ideal self and our ordinary fallible self'—and that 'bad as her behaviour may be, we are willing to be implicated in it' —but he cannot forbear returning to the contemplation of Emma as a social phenomenon, a sister of later heroines like Emma Bovary and Isabel Archer, a heroine with a false and fantastic view of society and of the place she should occupy in it.

If Emma were really a snob in the modern sense, she might, as I have suggested, be such a heroine. And the same would be true if Jane Austen, as Professor Trilling feels, had a view of society to which Emma does not conform. But Emma, whatever else she is, is not a romantic. She knows exactly where she stands in her society and what it can offer her. And snobbery in the nineteenth century was to become a social aspect of romanticism, the most widespread one. It is the role played by Madame Bovary, and in their more flagrant ways by the Veneerings and the Verdurins and Trollope's Mr. Crosby—even by Julien Sorel, for the figure of the snob in his heyday is related, unmistakably though, if we like, ignobly, to the figure of the dandy and the romantic solitary. All those romantic heroes in society are on their own.

And Emma is not on her own. Totally individual as she is , she is none the less a part of a community, and her existence depends upon the part she plays and will play in it. Her very mistakes arise from her dependence on it; her spirited sense of herself from her complete acceptance of the way it works. That sense of herself is as different as could be from the egocentric isolation of an Isabel Archer or even a Dorothea Brooke. It is because of that isolation that the creators of those heroines can contemplate them as 'cases' as they do, and as they invite us to do. The fictional method of George Eliot and Henry James acquires its veracity from the historical isolation of the figures that they study in their society. Jane Austen's method depends on a very different sort of society, and a correspondingly different relation between author, character and reader.

An odd paradox here is that the author who imagines his *society* tends to fall back on real life for his *characters*. Caleb Garth is much more George Eliot's father than any father figure in Jane Austen's novels is hers. Henry James's Miss Birdseye, in *The Bostonians*, was immediately—and, as his brother felt, scandalously—recognizable, in a way that Miss Bates could not possibly have been. It is significant that Miss Birdseye, who might on the face of it seem to resemble a figure from Austenian comedy, in fact owes much to the model of Dickens; and Dickens, as we know from Mrs. Nickleby and Miss Mowcher—to name only two—habitually drew his comics from the life.

It is because she did not need to invent her world that Jane Austen truly invents her characters. And the admirable studies in her craftsmanship and creative method by Miss Lascelles and Mrs. Leavis have made it plain over what a prolonged and painstaking period of development the inventive process can extend. We can see it, for instance, in the line that may connect Lady Susan, through Mary Crawford, with Emma Woodhouse—the evolution of a type from a book into a completely self-sufficient individual. On a more trivial level we can see it in the perfect accord between the personality of Louisa Musgrove and her comedy accident in the Cobb at Lyme, an event which in its small way perfectly exemplifies the truth in Henry James's dictum: 'What is character but the determination of incident? What is incident but the illustration of character?' Person and event match one another exactly, because a careful artistry of thoughts and second thoughts have been at work. Jane Austen's first notion for Louisa was probably a carriage accident, but two of her own acquaintances in real life had been hurt in them—too much reality: and they might happen to anybody—too much randomness.

But the real significance of Jane Austen's total invention of her characters lies elsewhere. It lies in the fact that her female heroines are imaginative realizations of herself. Is this fact—a very commonplace one where heroes and heroines are concerned—compatible with the claim to total invention? In her case I think it is, and the clue to how it is so is contained in the quotation from Shaftesbury. Such characters are 'ways of motion' to relieve her constraint. Are they not in the case of Charlotte Brontë and George Eliot and a hundred others? Not exactly, The big difference between self-characterization as we have it in Jane Austen, and as we have it in later novelists, is that 'constraint' for Jane Austen is the condition of life—accepted, uncomplained of. Her self-projections have thus a true grace of irresponsibility—they are at once a humorous indulgence and a spiritual exercise.

It is because she says: 'Life has not put me in this position'—that she can make the figure she creates in it so endowed with herself and yet so separated. High pride in perception, and in beauty and wit; mockery; even cruelty;—these are some of the dangerous and spirited attributes—the sort that Yeats would have admired—which she exercises through her major figures. Particularly she indulges the fantasy of uninhibited display, and exchange with intellectual equals or with social superiors, the triumph of argument and the poised vigour of an expository *aria*. But equally she can indulge quite a different order of projection: the naïve simplicity and native good taste of Catherine Morland; the devout passivity and principle of Fanny Price; and—most moving of all—Anne Elliot's fidelity to an image of love which seems to have no prospect of renewal.

It is surely this relation to her characters which gives them their freedom and their capacity to surprise us. Emma is not a snob and Fanny not a prig because—apart from any other considerations— each of them can surprise us by being a little like the other. In the chagrin of her Portsmouth experiences, her devotion to her brother, her underlying toughness, Fanny is not unlike Emma. In her obstinacy, her defensiveness about Jane Fairfax, her tears after the Box Hill outing (which has a significant parallel with the theatricals in *Mansfield Park* in its revelation of the too much *tried for*, the overacted social effort) Emma has some kinship with Fanny. Were *Mansfield Park* a morality and *Emma* an idyll (as they have variously been found) we could not have this freedom, for the denizens of each could only be permitted their appropriate range of response. Once more we are back with the all-important premise of Jane Austen's art: the fixity, the humdrum actuality of society, and the contrasting liberation of type into personality which depends on it.

Of the *romantic* presentation of the self in post-Austenian fiction we can note two important points. First, the author is emphatically *not* confined to a given position in society, nor resigned to one. Second—which follows from this—the projected character who carries outward and upward the dreams of his creator for excitement, love, fame, and so forth, must have his environment, his expanding world, dreamed up in the same way he has been dreamed up himself. One fantasy leads to another: a Jane Eyre to a Mr. Rochester, a Dorothea Brooke to a Ladislaw, an Isabel Archer to a Ralph Touchett and a Gilbert Osmond. Emma's dreams, like her author's, do not go outside the society she knows: hence the reality of the figures Jane Austen summons up to meet them. Moreover Jane Eyre, Dorothea and others are constricted, as personalities, by the imagined world into which they are projected. They are too busy responding to a created environment to have a free and irresponsible mental life.

Startlingly enough, the heroines who do seem to me to exhibit something of an unexpected and untrammelled freedom of mental life are the two Catherines in *Wuthering Heights*. And the reason may be the same as in Jane Austen. In projecting them, Emily Brontë has not moved outside a wholly known and accepted environment of which she was as much a part as Jane Austen was of hers. If, as I feel, there is a great divide between Jane Austen and her successors, rather than the line of a great tradition, she may have more kinship across it with Emily Brontë than with George Eliot or with Henry James.

In pairing Jane Eyre and Dorothea Brooke I have of course laid myself open to a misinterpretation. Both are, it seems to me, romantic self-projections of a kind radically different from Jane Austen's. But then a further distinction needs to be made. Jane Eyre has no pretensions to be other than herself. But what is subtle and distinctive about the projections of George Eliot, as of Henry James, is their claim to an almost scientific objectivity. From imaginations of the self they have been converted into portraits which conceal their personal origins in the claim to a generalized social significance. They represent the self-analysis of their creators turned outward and developed into a portent, an exemplary type; and this can only occur because their creators' vision of society is as personal, as original, as they are themselves. Neither Flaubert, nor George Eliot, nor Henry James can be said to belong to a society: if they did they would not be the sort of great writers that they are. They create the Madame Bovary image; or the figure of the 'modern Saint Teresa'; or of the new female egotist 'affronting her destiny': and it is in the nature of these great creations that they cannot be other than social and psychological portents. They cannot, as James well knew, be 'plastic' and 'irresponsible'. Were Emma to be, as Professor Trilling implies she is, an embodiment of this created type, a spirited girl setting herself against Jane Austen's Tocquevillian vision of the wise give-and-take in English society, she would indeed join these great conceptualized characters. She would indeed be 'deeply studied and elaborately justified'. But however many times we read the novel and find—as Reginald Farrer claimed—more in it with each reading, we cannot find this version of Emma.

We cannot find her because Jane Austen lived with her characters in a fashion analogous to the way in which she lived with real neighbours; only with the compulsion of that actuality transmuted into the freedom of creation. It is because of this that she can imply without compunction or apology her lack of understanding of what does not concern her daily existence. So, strangely enough, did Tolstoy, but he proclaims it openly, indeed defiantly. In the preface to *1805*, the first, unpublished, version of *War and Peace*, he anticipated a possible charge of omitting much in the Russian society of the time by writing that 'the lives of officials, merchants, theological students and peasants do not interest me and are only half comprehensible to me'. Though he did not print this preface in *War and Peace*, it is as true of the completed novel as it was of the abortive one. By writing about the lives of the kind of people who were 'comprehensible, interesting, and dear to me', as he put it in the same preface, Tolstoy—like Jane Austen on her smaller scale—is not showing us something but living it for us, and with us.

The world of Tolstoy, like that of Jane Austen, seems complete because of his confidence that it' was so: both have the confidence of insiders. And this gives to her world something of the Tolstoyan power of effortless expansion, the negligent authority of a world that is possessed without being contemplated. Not so with George Eliot: indeed it is difficult not to feel that E. M. Forster made what is in some respects a misleading comparison when he suggested in *Aspects of the Novel* that *Middlemarch* is the closest English equivalent to *War and Peace*. Its scale may suggest an analogy, but it is surely very different in spirit and in method. Far too scientific and comprehensive an interest is shown in the creation and examination of Middlemarch as a society for it to resemble Tolstoy's, or Jane Austen's, societies. Because the intellectuals—George Eliot as much as Henry James—are outside life, they are interested in everything that life has to offer to their contemplation—an omnivorous interest is laid upon them as a sacred duty.

Jane Austen's affinity with Tolstoy appears even more striking if we consider the theme of *Anna Karenina*. There the relation of Anna and Vronsky to society is as categorical as that of Jane Austen's heroes and heroines. It is when they leave society, assuming that they can continue to be the same persons outside it, that we are led by the author's process to perceive them indeed from the outside, to contemplate them as cases, self-deceived and self-defining. Stiva, Anna's brother, who for all his shortcomings does not and cannot go outside the social world of the novel, is never seen in this defining way. Like Mr. Woodhouse he is a vessel of grace in spite of himself; and Tolstoy's creative insight, almost unwillingly, admits him as such.

In a doggerel poem, D. H. Lawrence claimed that Russian society 'might have been saved' by 'a pair of rebels like Anna and Vronsky'. Hardly. It is the pair themselves who are destroyed, not because society rejects them, but because their voluntary exile from society compels them to realize how much they are a part of it, and how much they owe to it their existence as the individuals Tolstoy had shown them to be. Had Emma, like 'Miss Churchill of Enscombe', been guilty of so great an unawareness of her dependence on the society she knew, she would cease to be the Emma we know. She also would have been seen from the outside as Miss Churchill—'who wanted at once to be the wife of Captain Weston and Miss Churchill of Enscombe'—is seen from the outside.

It goes without saying that Jane Austen could not in the nature of things have performed Tolstoy's massive feat of sustaining a deep inner acceptance of society—with all it adds to the vitality and certainty of his characters—together with an external vision of it, and of them when they have put themselves outside society. His ruthless comprehensiveness, his masculine freedom, could conjecture and continue to the bitter end where she could not. Her power to suggest and explore stops short at the boundaries within which she lived and wrote, but in her greatest novels the very act of stopping short is a peculiar tender of significance and illumination.

We can see this in the case of Jane Fairfax. Emma's coolness towards Jane Fairfax, and the reasons for it, is one of the best realized things in the novel; and, like Miss Bates's style of talk, it aquires dramatic resonance as the novel proceeds to its climax. We find its dramatic centre in the novel's most pregnant single phrase, when after the Box Hill expedition Emma has gone to see Miss Bates and Jane, and Jane has avoided her. Emma 'sat musing on the difference of woman's destiny'. Her own she can await openly and eagerly, and the contrast with Jane Fairfax's muffled, uncharted resignation is perhaps the author's deepest as it is her least emphatic theme. The drama involved is in Jane Austen's own unmistakable attachment to Emma's feelings about Jane Fairfax, and how these feelings are not dispelled but cease to count in the revelation of the innerness of Jane Fairfax's feelings and situation.

The situation folded by Jane Austen into her treatment of Jane Fairfax is most fully realized in the treatment of Sonia in *War and Peace*. It has pained many of Tolstoy's admirers that he should seem to regard as so eminently natural and right the latent hostility that both Natasha and her mother instinctively feel towards Sonia. At bottom it is the involuntary antipathy of those whose destiny it is to fill a place in society, and to 'be themselves', against those who have no place and who cannot be. Both Tolstoy and Jane Austen understand it perfectly, and accept it as they accept the society of which it seems an inevitable part. Neither author attempts to get inside the character thus muffled by society; neither give a voice to those who have not one of their own. All the more remarkable is Jane Austen's success in revealing Jane Fairfax's sense of her own position, for this is not done through her own speech or consciousness but through Emma's, and Emma's realizations about 'woman's destiny'.

Tolstoy's grand allotment of fates in *War and Peace*—fates which turn out to be 'inevitable' because he and society have allotted them —has something in common with Jane Austen's undercurrent of interest in the necessities of resignation, necessities which in her last three novels may be said to collide with her instinct for a proper fictional *dénouement*. How she resolves, or fails to resolve, the difficulty provides the most striking insight of all into the peculiar freedom and intimacy of her art to describe which I borrowed James's term 'irresponsible'. In *Mansfield Park*, for all its virtues, no resolution is achieved. The situation of Fanny, the perception of her divided feelings about Mansfield Park and Portsmouth, and of her half-admiring, half-hostile relation to Mary Crawford—a relation which carries a hint of Jane Fairfax's with Emma—these instance the real pressures conceived and conveyed in *Mansfield Park*. There are many more of the same quality, but none of them harmonize with the arbitrary winding-up of the plot. Fanny's triumphant marriage is not earned nor even indulged by anything crucial in the presentation of her; and the Crawfords, with the younger Bertrams, simply collapse into limbo. 'Let other pens than mine dwell on guilt and misery . . .' This is not the irresponsibility we can prize and participate in with her, but mere abdication, more elegant and light-hearted than it would be with professionals of a later date, but no more satisfying.

In *Emma* and in *Persuasion* the case is very different. It seems to me that the harmony established in both between a deep and serious acknowledgement of the unrecorded, unremitted sadness of things, and the never impossible *peripeteia* of joy and surprize, gives them a unique status as fictional masterpieces. Jane Fairfax's destiny, we feel, *was* to disappear as a governess into the limbo which Jane Austen imagines with such quiet but terrible realism. Frank Churchill saves her from it, but even so it remains psychologically a part of her—the irony of his insensitivity and frivolity is that they parallel the insensitive carelessness or kindness of an employer 'not quite of human flesh, but of human intellect.' Emma's happy fate is very different; it will lead her into that world of 'intelligent love' which Richard Simpson so eloquently spoke of.[5] But this solution of ideality and light would not be complete without its obscured and patient opposite. Tolstoy exhibits a kind of fictional diplomacy, not dissimilar in the effect it leaves with us, at the end of *War and Peace*. The good of life, so lyrically summed up in the married dialogues of the Epilogue, does not distract us from but rather draws our attention to its varieties of suffering and deprivation, things which were beginning to haunt Tolstoy in ways which had little to do with art and fiction; but which, in his great work, combine with the joy of its ending, and continue in our minds beyond the ending.

The contrast, and the harmony, are as successful in *Persuasion*. Mrs. Smith may be a mechanism in its plot, but she is also a deeply moving figure, and the more moving because of Anne's realization of her, and of what her life must be like. Anne herself combines in one character the roles of both darkness and light, of both Jane Fairfax and Emma. We feel that we do not see all her mind in the same gay and open way in which we see Jane Austen's other heroines, because the discoveries of resignation and cheerfulness are suggested below the surface by more muted means; and her story is as much about living without a future as it is about the grace of unexpected happiness.

Jane Austen had learnt, as her last two novels show, the strange secret of allowing a part of her subject its own slightly eerie freedom, while not in any way disassociating it from the logic and pattern of her plot. It is the fruition of the aim which she may have consciously set herself in *Mansfield Park*, but which cannot there be said to have been quite successfully realized.[6] When it came it did so, as in so much great art, without apparent consciousness and volition. Tolstoy's 'irresponsibility' is a massive affair: he sees 'in the irresponsible plastic way' even where he disapproves, perhaps all the more where he does so. Jane Austen's is more subtle, more imponderable; but it leads her art along the same paths and towards the same fulfilments.

# NOTES

1. A. Walton Litz, *Jane Austen. A Study of her Artistic Development*, p. 105. Professor Litz, I should add, goes on to say that 'any attempt to establish rigid patterns leads to absurdity', but the tone of his analysis has already suggested, not rigidity, but certainly characters 'deeply studied and elaborately justified'.

2. Marvin Mudrick, *Jane Austen: Irony as Defense and Discovery*, p. 196. In 'A Long Talk on Jane Austen' (*Classics and Commercials*), Edmund Wilson referred to Mr. Woodhouse in similarly uncompromising terms as 'a silly old woman'.

3. The clearest and most forceful statement of how an illusion/reality pattern dominates her books is C. S. Lewis's 'A Note on Jane Austen' (*Essays in Criticism* October 1954).

4. The ship as an image of her kind of social unit seems to have appealed to Jane Austen. Her enthusiasm for the Navy often strikes one as being more than just a family affair.

5. I owe to Professor Trilling (who himself acknowledges a similar debt to Professor Joseph Duffy) my acquaintance with this remarkable appreciation. I should add that in spite of my differing with Professor Trilling's views on the points mentioned earlier, I admire and concur with the conclusion of his own essay on *Emma*, in which he refers to the *North British* reviewer's comments on the ideal of 'intelligent love' in the novel.

6. Criticizing *Pride and Prejudice* in a letter to her sister Cassandra in 1813 she remarked that it 'wanted shade', and commented on the advantages to a novel of 'something unconnected with the story; an essay on writing, a critique on Walter Scott or the history of Buonaparte...' (*Letters* (1952) pp. 299–300).

# II

# JANE AUSTEN AND THE STUARTS
*Brigid Brophy*

WE ARE all deposed kings.

At three months old, we were monarchs absolute and arbitrary. Courtiers gathered round us, singing (often literally) our praises and cajoling us to smile on them. If, instead, we felt like raging at them, we did so; no one shouted back or even asked us to account for our caprice. Every adult within earshot was in our domestic service. A yell would more instantly than a pasha's handclap fetch a servitor to wait on our bodily wants.

Growing up is one long fall from majesty, education the process supposed to reconcile us to it. We are compensated by gaining independence, becoming able to do things for ourselves; but that, under a certain disenchanted aspect, means only that other people are no longer willing to do them for us.

It was under such an aspect, I surmise, that Jane Austen was considering the process of growing up and being educated, a process she had herself barely finished, when, at the age of fifteen, she satirically wrote *The History of England*.

In one item Jane Austen's *History* itself exercises an infantile caprice and unaccountability. A history of England is cutting a notably arbitrary slice of national life when, without explanation, it starts at the accession of Henry IV and leaves off with the death of Charles I.

The arbitrariness of her chronological limits is, of course, all part of Jane Austen's joke, along with the arbitrariness of the historical judgements passed by the—as she declares herself in the title—

'partial, prejudiced, and ignorant Historian'. The judgements, however, are at least pinned to her satirical purpose—though the satirical purpose itself is by no means all there is to the *History*.

Although it is not a formal parody with a single specific target, the *History* does direct some accurate side-swipes at some specific targets, the chief of which seems to be Oliver Goldsmith.[1] It is what she took to be Goldsmith's anti-Stuart bias that Jane Austen reproves by the satirical mechanism of proclaiming a still more impassioned and unreasoning—in fact, a ludicrous—bias in the opposite direction.

The randomness of her slice of history, however, is not a hit at Goldsmith, whose *History of England* proceeds with perfect orthodoxy 'from Earliest Times to the Death of George II'—to, that is, the latest monarch's death before the publication (in 1771) of Goldsmith's work. Even Goldsmith's *Abridgement*, at which Jane Austen has a specific tilt in its own right,[2] is not so abridged as to omit everything before Henry IV. Jane Austen's other most likely exemplar is David Hume[3] and he, it is true, published the volumes of his *History of England* out of chronological order; but well before Jane Austen was born he had filled in the gaps and produced a chronicle running unexceptionably from the Roman invasion to James II.

Presumably, therefore Jane Austen's arbitrariness was not a specific and historical but a general and literary joke. And as a matter of fact several others of the juvenilia record, by way of satire, her annoyance with ill-thought-out literary construction of the kind which starts a narrative merely at whatever point chanced to stray first into the Author's head. (And of course just as the juvenilia satirize getting the starting-point wrong, Jane Austen's grown-up novels constitute six superb examples of getting it exactly right.) To recount 'The History of England from the reign of Henry the 4th to the death of Charles the 1st' is essentially the same joke as the surreal irrelevance of the opening of *Jack & Alice*, the burlesque novel Jane Austen wrote probably in the same year (1791) as the *History*: 'Mr. Johnson was once upon a time about 53; in a twelvemonth afterwards he was 54, which so much delighted him that he was determined to celebrate his next Birthday by giving a Masquerade to his Children & Freinds'.[4]

A non-fiction critic of haphazard narratives has merely to call them haphazard. A critic who, like Jane Austen, criticizes by means of satire has to call on his own invention. If Jane Austen was to castigate random story-telling, her own fantasy must supply her with a gobbet of fictitious material which she could then stick on to the start of her own story with a randomness equal to the randomness she was criticizing. The satirist, because he makes demands on his own fantasy, is subject to the rule discovered by Freud,[5] that, when it is a human mind which is supplying it, there is no such thing as a random instance. Cast about for a number—any old number—to serve in a mathematical example, or summon a proper name—any proper name—to serve in an anecdote, and the gobbet of material that offers itself, though it will be truly random and non-significant when placed in the intellectual context of the sum or the anecdote, will have very precise determinants indeed in the mind that supplied it.

What determined that, for an irrelevant opening to *Jack & Alice*, Jane Austen should pick on a Mr. Johnson who was about 53, I can only guess; and the evidence that might have corroborated or queried my guess has probably vanished. I suspect that the fictitious Mr. Johnson borrowed the name of a real one, whom Jane Austen mentioned—as, simply, 'Mr. Johnson', which implies that the family had at least heard of him before—in a letter[6] written some eight years after *Jack & Alice*. In that letter, which is of 1799, Jane Austen tells Cassandra Austen that their first cousin[7] Edward Cooper is to become rector of Hamstall-Ridware, Staffordshire, where the living is 'vacant by Mr. Johnson's death'.

This real Mr. Johnson is identified, in R. W. Chapman's Index to the *Letters*, as the Rev. Augustus Johnson, who had become rector of Hamstall-Ridware in 1791. In other words, Mr. Johnson became rector at a time very close[8] to the composition of *Jack & Alice*.

Immediately before Mr. Johnson was appointed, the Hamstall-Ridware rectorship must have been vacant. The living seems to have been in the gift of Mrs. Austen's family, the Leighs.[9] The Austens might well expect it to go to one of their own family, either the Edward Cooper[10] who did get it eight years later or another of the numerous Austen clerical brothers, cousins and connections. Instead, it went to Mr. Johnson. I surmise that the younger and more ruthless Austens at once began speculating how old Mr. Johnson might be now, with a view to calculating how long a relation of their own might have to wait before stepping into his pulpit, and that *Jack & Alice* was written, partly in reflexion of that, soon after Mr.

Johnson's appointment in 1791. When Jane Austen describes the fictitious Mr. Johnson as 'about' 53, she is perhaps recording her uncertainty of the exact age of the real one. How old he in fact was in 1791 I have no means of knowing, but 'about 53' is at least plausible, for in that case his death in 1799 would have come when he was 61.

To drag the fictitious Mr. Johnson into *Jack & Alice* under the real name and presumed real age of the genuine one was, I imagine, a conscious and deliberate family joke, which Jane Austen probably shared with her brother and dedicatee Francis. However, her unconscious, liberated by writing acknowledged fiction, was able to take the joke a little further. Jane Austen might permit herself consciously to calculate the likelihood of the real Mr. Johnson's dying soon, but she would hardly let herself express a wish that he should. In fiction, however, the wish can be acted-out. The bustling opening sentences of *Jack & Alice*, whose literary purpose is to satirize openings of out-of-breath irrelevance, accomplish that purpose through fictitious material which hustles Mr. Johnson towards his grave. At the beginning of the first sentence he is 53; by its end he is 54; by the second sentence he has 'attained his 55th year'—which Jane Austen, still imperfectly educated, seems to have thought (since she speaks of this as his 'next Birthday' when he is already 54) meant being 55. The cruellest stroke of all was no doubt wholly unconscious except in so far as it was struck by a sure-handed literary technique. Mr. Johnson opens the story in the role of an irrelevance. That was Jane Austen's implied comment on the man who had so inappositely drifted into the living she destined for a relation of her own.

If my reconstruction is correct, the seemingly nonsensical and non-significant beginning of *Jack & Alice* is a fantasy act of revenge (by hurrying him towards death) against a man who had done the Austens out of something they felt they had an hereditary right to. With only the alteration of the family concerned, precisely this is the declared theme of *The History of England*, whose *raison d'être* is to vindicate the Stuart family—which had been done out of something *it* believed *it* had a right to, namely to exercise absolute monarchy from the throne of England.

The ludicrously extravagant partisanship satirically assumed by the 'partial, prejudiced' historian takes for its centre Mary Queen of

Scots, 'this bewitching Princess whose only freind was then the Duke of Norfolk, and whose only ones now Mr. Whitaker, Mrs. Lefroy, Mrs. Knight and myself'.[11] The impassioned historian declares that her 'principal reason' for writing the History is 'to prove the innocence of the Queen of Scotland . . . and to abuse Elizabeth'. Yet she espouses the cause not just of the Queen, but of the whole family; the mana has been passed on to the Queen's descendants; there is one argument, the historian maintains, by which she is sure of convincing her readers of the innocence of Charles I '— and this Argument is that he was a STUART'.

Indeed, so extravagant is the historian that she contrives to extend the mana of Mary not merely on through time and the Stuart line but backwards, so that it actually ante-dates the appearance of the Stuarts in English history. By a stroke which brilliantly sends up the monomania of historical partisans, the historian remarks that Lord Protector Somerset might with reason have been proud to have his head chopped off had he known in advance that such would be the fate of Mary Queen of Scots.

Yet Mary herself is only the culminating-point of the historian's indignation. This historian is on every losing side. She is for all ousted families and deposed monarchs. She maintains the innocence of various of Henry VIII's discarded or beheaded wives. Lady Jane Grey, slapped for showing off about her Greek, is found inferior to 'her lovely Cousin the Queen of Scots', yet she comes in for approval precisely as a sort of inferior Queen of Scots. The historian is against the usurping Lancastrians and for the defeated Yorkists. She is inclined to acquit Richard III of murder ('as he was a York, I am rather inclined to suppose him a very respectable man'); she will even at least affect to entertain the notion that Perkin Warbeck was really Duke of York—and, if so, she continues, carrying her predilection for unsuccessful pretenders into the realm of nonsense, 'why might not Lambert Simnel be the Widow of Richard'.

The content of the Lambert Simnel joke is incidentally interesting because it suggests rather more awareness of homosexuality than most people would offhand attribute to Jane Austen. The History confirms this further on, in the scathing 'sharade' on James I's favourite Carr. The History seems to suggest that Mary Crawford's pun in Mansfield Park about 'Rears and Vices' was anatomically intended. It is symptomatic of the strong conflict in Jane Austen's psychology—a conflict whose happy ultimate issue was the absolute classicism with which, in her writing, severity of form is pitted against the upsurge of the imaginative material—that the only one of her novels where verbal indelicacy breaks through should be the only one where the tone and tendency of the narrative are quite tyrannically repressive towards indelicacy.

The Lambert Simnel joke is also the only bit of the *History* whese actual content touches nonsense. Formally, however, the *History's* chronological limits are also nonsense: the *History* takes a non-sensically arbitrary stretch of time. But this random example of randomness is, like the one in *Jack & Alice*, only formally random. The limits Jane Austen picked on are such that their actual content sums up and reiterates her cardinal theme of fellow-feeling for deposed monarchs. Naturally she ends with the death of Charles I, a death which constituted as signal a deposition as a king can suffer. And though she opens with the accession of Henry IV, this in practice obliges her to open with the deposing of his predecessor Richard II. A monarch is ousted from the throne in her very first sentence. Her entire *History* runs from 'one heinous article, Containing the depos-ing of a king' to another.

And indeed, though the *History* refers the reader only to the Henry plays, I think Jane Austen may have been half-consciously remember-ing[12] the text of *Richard II* when she wrote her cardinal mock-rhetorical passage about the execution of Mary Queen of Scots. That they permitted Elizabeth to perpetrate it is her great reproach against Elizabeth's ministers: 'this blot, this everlasting blot', she calls it, 'upon their understanding and their Character'. And that 'heinous article', Richard II says, 'is mark'd with a blot, damn'd in the book of heaven'.

We are all deposed kings, but we don't all write satirical histories at fifteen. I believe there are—over and above the pre-requisite of a literary talent already fluent by adolescence—several discernible lines of motive in Jane Austen all converging on the result of the *History*.

There is first the simple psychological fact that a girl is likely to feel herself deposed from the infantile throne with a worse jolt than a boy. The crude fantasy-theories of childhood usually explain the bodily difference between boys and girls by the supposition that a bloody mutilation has been practised on the girl, and at adolescence that fantasy is likely to be reanimated, at least in the unconscious, by the start of what may seem a ritual monthly bleeding in commemoration of the original wound. There is a straightforward castration symbolism in Jane Austen's self-identification with the wronged Queen who was bloodily beheaded.

In the world Jane Austen had just grown up into when she wrote the *History*, the physiological dethronement of girls was endorsed by their social situation. Jane Austen submitted to education—whereby one learns self-control, with the implied promise that one will emerge at the end independent enough to control one's own life: but by the age of fifteen she must have discovered that the promised reward was a very limited affair for a girl, especially if she contrasted herself with her midshipman brother, who was less than two years older than herself. The social backgrounds and asides in the juvenilia show that Jane Austen early grasped that, for women, independence was conditional on inheriting or marrying money.

Moreover, as her own mature novels display, the social rules were doubly unfair. It was the young woman without a private income who most needed to marry well, but it was the young woman without a private income or the intangible asset of a title who was least likely to marry at all. I cannot doubt that Jane Austen was realist enough to predict correctly that the Austens' want of money would diminish her own and Cassandra's chances in the marriage-market which, at the time of the *History*, she was preparing to enter.

Her true situation and prospects no doubt seemed to Jane Austen a cruel come-down after both her personal and her family past. She had tumbled from the social absolutism and inherent narcissism of childhood straight into the realization that she was dispossessed also of what she might have expected from her ancestry. In her mother's family there was both a baronetcy and an estate. Neither was to be passed on to the children of George and Cassandra (Leigh) Austen, whose daughters must come unendowed, if at all, to marriage and whose sons and nephews could not even count on the patronage of relations with livings in their gift.

It is hard enough to take a social nuance when it is contemporary. Here it has to be read through the protests and, perhaps, concealments of the next generation on, since much of the evidence is in the memoirs by, respectively, Jane Austen's niece and her nephew. From those it looks to me as if, in Jane Austen's generation, the Austens were distressed aristocracy. Jane Austen and her siblings perhaps did not experience any very stringent financial pinch—or, at least, there is no documentation to that effect—until their father's retirement and the sale, whose results again disappointed Jane Austen's expectations,[13] of their goods at Steventon. But after the father's death, they must have felt an almost literal pinch in living in the cramped cottage at Chawton.

Caroline Austen[14] is at her most revealingly protestant on this subject—her motive less, I surmise, snobbery than to rebut any suspicion that Edward (Austen) Knight had behaved meanly towards his widowed mother; Caroline Austen emphasizes that he had offered his mother the choice of two houses and that she settled for Chawton. And in general many of Caroline Austen's emphases seem designed to distract attention from other things. In the *garden* at Chawton she emphasizes, 'you did not feel cramped for room', and she expands on the delight the garden and extensive outbuildings held for children. Inside the house, she has to admit, '*some* bedrooms' were 'very small' and '*none* very large', though she insists there were plenty of them and maintains that the house as a whole 'was quite as good as the generality of Parsonage houses then'. She attributes the low and 'roughly finished' ceilings to the house's being in the Parsonage-type 'old style'. However, she makes it clear that, quite apart from servants, the regular complement of the house was four adult females and one child. A visit to Chawton makes it clear in turn that that *must* have been cramped —not intolerably so, and not, indeed, in comparison with the living quarters of most English people at the time, but in comparison with the milieux of Jane Austen's novels and with what, it can be legitimately guessed, Jane Austen herself had originally expected of life.

For item after item in Jane Austen's letters seems to anticipate that horror of a transposition from grandeur to poverty which, in *Mansfield Park*, she ascribes to Fanny Price on her return from Mansfield to her family home in Portsmouth. 'My father'—about the time of his retirement—'is doing all in his power to encrease his Income by raising his Tythes &c., & I do not despair of getting very nearly six hundred a year'.[15] 'Yesterday morning we looked into a house in Seymour St:'—this during the search for a home in Bath—'... the largest room downstairs, was not much more than fourteen feet square'.[16] 'My mother looks forward with as much certainty as you can do,'—this during the preparations for moving to Bath—'to our keeping two Maids.'[17] But two maids were not in themselves enough to guarantee the gentility of their employers. Even the squalid Prices at Portsmouth keep two maids,[18] one

'trollopy-looking', the other 'whose inferior appearance informed
Fanny, to her great surprise, that she had previously seen the upper
servant'. Jane Austen, in her own real life, entertains hopes of add-
ing a manservant to the establishment, but she does so in a nonsense
fantasy—'We plan having a steady Cook, & a young giddy House-
maid, with a sedate, middle-aged Man, who is to undertake the
double office of Husband to the former & Sweetheart to the
latter'[19]—which probably indicates she feared it was nonsense to
suppose they could afford one.[20] As for the small rooms she would
not contemplate living in at Bath, they closed in on her indeed at
Chawton—as they do on Fanny Price at Portsmouth, where 'The
smallness of the house and thinness of the walls brought everything
so close to her, that . . . she hardly knew how to bear it.'

Writing after the two youngest of Jane Austen's brothers had
restored the fortunes of the family and brought a new title into it,
J. E. Austen-Leigh in the *Memoir* seems to patch over the period—
Jane Austen's period—when the family was only just hanging on
to upper-class status. He is at pains to emphasize to his Victorian
readers—which is not to say he was wrong on the point of social
observances—that such habits of the Austen sons as breakfasting in
the kitchen before hunting were perfectly genteel at the time. In
places he *seems* to take an anti-snob line, rebuking Sir Egerton
Brydges—though taking care to quote him—for bothering to record
that Jane Austen was, through her mother, great grand-daughter to
the sister of a duke.[21] But it seems not unfair to guess that what
Austen-Leigh really wanted to gloss over was not the high ancestry
but any suggestion of a fall from it. What would truly distress him
would be if his readers were surprised to hear Jane Austen was
related to a duke. In her writing, he remarks, 'she is entirely free
from the vulgarity, which is so offensive in some novels, of dwelling
on the outward appendages of wealth or rank, as if they were things
to which the writer was unaccustomed'.[22] Under the euphemism
'some family troubles'[23] he hides the bankruptcy of Jane Austen's
brother Henry and the disappointment of almost the whole family
in the will of Mrs. Austen's brother. He is anxious to keep his readers
from actually visiting Chawton, telling them that it has now (1870)
'lost all that gave it its character' because, after Cassandra Austen's
death in 1845, 'it was divided into tenements for labourers'.[24] Thus
Jane Austen's nephew managed, perhaps, to keep curious persons
from seeing with their own eyes the tiny dimensions of the cottage,

but in explaining how promptly it had tumbled into working-class use he disclosed how perilous its upper-class status had been. Caroline Austen managed to turn the occasion better to the Austens' glory by recounting that the house which had accommodated one genteel family 'was divided into habitations for the poor, and made to accommodate several families—so I was *told*—for I have never seen it since'.[25]

When she wrote the *History* Jane Austen had not yet experienced the crampingness of Chawton, but she could predict it from the social *datum*. Like Fanny Price at Portsmouth, she felt present exigency in contrast to previous grandeur: but in Jane Austen's case the grandeur existed less in real life than in imagination and not quite expectation but, rather, sense of entitlement. She had a strong sense that her whole family had been dispossessed of something they had a right to—a feeling bitter enough to make her take a lethal fantasy-revenge on Mr. Johnson. And this notion concentrated itself, I incline to think, in a feeling that her sister Cassandra had been wronged—for Jane Austen probably early came to think of herself as compensated by her literary genius.

Jane Austen's championship—in her own *History* and in the margins of her copy of Goldsmith's[26]—of the Stuarts, the most wronged and dispossessed upper-class family of all, reflects her notion of her own family's fate. Her cardinal identification with the chief Stuart, Mary Queen of Scots, proceeded, I surmise, by way of identifying herself with Cassandra Austen, whom Jane first identified with the wronged Queen. It even seems probable that Mrs. Austen had an unconscious inkling (which she might have picked up from watching make-believe games played by the two girls) of the beheaded-queen fantasy her younger daughter entertained in relation to the elder; for Austen-Leigh quotes Mrs. Austen as remarking 'if Cassandra were going to have her head cut off, Jane would insist on sharing her fate'.[27]

The identification of wronged Austens with wronged Stuarts was a simple step in any case, and all the simpler because there was an easy stepping-stone in the pro-Stuart policy of Mrs. Austen's family, who had sheltered Charles I at Stoneleigh Abbey (and had been prepared to shelter Prince Charles Edward).[28] Indeed I suspect that Mrs. Austen, like several of her kin, incarnated pro-Stuartism in her children's names. Mr. Austen bore the Hanoverian name George.

But for their eldest son the Austens chose the pointedly Stuart name (which was also that of Mrs Austen's brother—they may have been already angling for the legacy the family was eventually disappointed of), James. The second son was named, whether by reversion to the Hanoverian cause or simply after his father, George. But this was the 'suppressed', never mentioned, presumed defective Austen child. As if his parents took his naming as ill-omened, they avoided, for the four further sons they had to christen, the least touch of Hanover; and out of the total of six sons four had first names of Stuart associations, James, Edward, Henry and Charles. The girls were named not for Stuarts but at least for pro-Stuart Leighs: Cassandra was the name of their mother, Jane of their mother's sister. And chance thereby reinforced Jane Austen's ousted-queen fantasy, inviting her to identify herself, the second Austen girl, with that second-best Queen of Scots, Lady Jane Grey.

When she wrote a history of England containing the deposing of kings and queens in as high a concentration as she could contrive, Jane Austen was simultaneously writing, in metaphor, a history of her family and a history of herself to date.

In the second, she was pursuing a metaphor perhaps invented and certainly shaped by the gothick novelists and presently taken up by romantic writers. Probably most ages have acknowledged an age of heroes; but the idea of costume-drama, set in a glamorous but vaguely-dated 'history'—the mental climate which can use 'period' as an adjective without specifying *which* period—this seems to have been largely an eighteenth-century invention. If one accepts Horace Walpole's claim to be its originator, then the invention was born with the equation written into it of 'the historical past equals my infantile past', for Walpole's gothick flummery is readily deciphered into a rather *Hamlet*-influenced account of the Oedipus situation;[29] and the monkish chills and ghostly thrills of later High Gothick are disguises not very hard to penetrate for the pleasurable wickedness of breaking the infantile sexual taboos. It took a great romantic poet to re-assemble the gothick bric-à-brac of knights and hauntings into *La Belle Dame Sans Merci* and tell definitively under the costume-dramatic metaphor the true history of every human being's first and irremediable heartbreak in love.

Jane Austen was thoroughly conversant with the gothick metaphor. The *History* shows her deeply susceptible to the equation between one's own infantile history and an infatuation with 'history', in which 'history' is a throng of people in vivid—as if perceived by infant eyes—fancy dress, scarcely one of them, except for the necessary servants, below the rank of lords and ladies (thus, no doubt, fantasy presented to her the history of her Leigh ancestors), each in a small feudal way an absolute monarch to himself. 'History' in this sense ceases, of course, where Hume—no doubt from a different point of view—ended his *History of England*, namely with the establishment of constitutional monarchy. Likewise infancy ceases when education has made the individual constitutional monarch of himself and persuaded him finally to abdicate the divine right of babies.

Yet, susceptible though she was, Jane Austen was also the world's great resister of her own romantic fantasies. In *Northanger Abbey* she sent them sky high. Catherine Morland is leading with her chin when she muses 'An Abbey! Yes, it was delightful to be really in an Abbey!' And perhaps in *Northanger Abbey* Jane Austen is pounding to bits (the first fissure had perhaps been opened by her attendance at the Abbey School) her own infatuation with the family home Stoneleigh Abbey. Only Fanny Price among Jane Austen heroines is allowed to get away with propounding the gothick view of history seriously: 'there is nobleness in the name of Edmund. It is a name of heroism and renown; of kings, princes, and knights; and seems to breathe the spirit of chivalry and warm affections'. Fanny, perhaps, is allowed to salvage a little of Jane Austen's adolescent romanticism because her repressive priggishness has, by direct moral disapproval, written out of existence another infatuation of Jane Austen's childhood. Fanny has killed by priggishness not only the amateur theatricals that went on in the Austen home at Steventon but Jane Austen the child playwright, whose works the adult Jane Austen loved enough to keep them, in fair copies, all her life.

It is in the *History*, however, where Jane Austen most strongly expresses her infatuation with absolute kings and her infant self, that she also makes her cleanest cut across her own infatuation. Hume stopped when the struggle against absolutism was won. Goldsmith stopped at the end of the reign before the one he was writing in. Jane Austen, in stopping with death of Charles I, modelled her procedure on, I think, Goldsmith's. She implied she was writing under the Commonwealth. In metaphor she announced her education completed, her babyhood over; she declared there was now no monarch.

Some of Jane Austen's funniest sarcasms are against babies. It was a peculiarity of that most rational woman that she held it against babies that they were not rational. More bitterly still, she held it against mothers that they showed an irrational adoration of their babies, an adoration entertained on an argument as poor as that on which Jane Austen had bidden her readers succumb to Charles I, merely that he was a Stuart. 'Mary grows rather more reasonable about her child's beauty, and says that she does not think him really handsome';[30] 'I saw their little girl ... Harriot's fondness for her seems just what is amiable and natural, & not foolish'.[31]

Primarily, I don't doubt, Jane Austen was countering her own irrational adoration of her irrational infant self. But speculation is harmless providing one labels it speculation, and I speculate whether Jane Austen knew of the existence of her 'suppressed' brother (how could it have been concealed from her? was she, perhaps, told when she reached adolescence?) and whether his defect was that he remained permanently a baby. Was Jane Austen in protest against some special irrational fondness for him—all the more special, probably, through guilt in letting him be put away—on the part of their mother? Indeed, was the mother's ill-health, which her daughters recognized,[32] and her long life seems to demonstrate, not a genuinely somatic ill-health, a self-punishment for repudiating her second child? Was there, most likely of all, an over-compensation in the singular loyalty of the Austen siblings to one another and their emphasis on family obligations? Did they feel they had put away one brother for the sake of the rest—to improve the boys' chances of careers and the girls' of marriage, and to keep the whole slipping family on the right side of respectability—and that the guilt they had incurred must be continually cancelled out by a more than customary intensity of love towards the brothers who remained?

Jane Austen subscribed to the eighteenth-century faith in education. She even concurred in the eighteenth-century faith in solving political problems by educating monarchs; such tiny faults or foibles as she will admit in Mary Queen of Scots are written off as 'Imprudencies into which she was betrayed by', *inter alia*, 'her Education'—which is just the Enlightenment tone in which, in her memoirs (the tone remains authentic even if the memoirs aren't), Madame du Barri ascribes the vices of her royal lover to *his* poor education.

The adult Jane Austen, of course, stuck to her Enlightened faith. Each of her novels is a moral and emotional education to its heroine and, usually, its hero, too. In *Pride and Prejudice* she holds the differences in the Bennet sisters' education (Elizabeth reads, Lydia doesn't) accountable for the difference in their moral characters. Not without purpose does she consistently put bad grammar[33] into Lydia's mouth and letters. And education became the rational criterion by which Jane Austen matured her original irrational judgement that one must admire people in family or feudal loyalty, simply because they are Stuarts or Leighs. She thus arrived at her *moral* concept of 'good breeding', where the literal breeding-stock is no longer all important. Elizabeth Bennet can be better bred than her younger sisters, though all are of the same middle-class family, and Darcy better bred than Lady Catherine though both are of the same aristocratic family.[34] The contempt Jane Austen shows, in her treatment of Lady Catherine, for aristocratic absolutism was already developed when she wrote her juvenile works. Lady Catherine's upper-class insolence to Elizabeth is already sketched in detail in the third of the juvenile *Collection of Letters;* Jane Austen had already withdrawn belief from the principle of Stuartism.

Yet this systematic Enlightenment educationalist makes, in her *History*, literally a nonsense of a very important part of education. (History *is* a very important part of education.) She announces in her title that the historian is ignorant; she adds 'N.B. There will be very few Dates in this History'.

Partly, I am sure, she is in revolt against her own education, which seemed, as she grew up, to cheat her of the independence promised and to drive her back to the complete but illusory liberty of childish daydreams. Jane Austen's nonsense is often, like Mozart's, a rebellion against being schooled. In his case it was a rebellion against a too driving and pressing father-cum-tutor; in hers against the absence of prospects at the end of the educational tunnel.

But I think that in writing the *History* Jane Austen was also thinking of the educational process from the other point of view. Her supreme argument that Charles I was a Stuart will, she opines, convince everyone 'whose opinions have been properly guided by a good Education'—by, that is, being taken through a history course such as Jane Austen was writing. In other words, she is now seeing herself not as pupil but as tutor.

And this, I believe, is the ultimate message of defiance Jane Austen delivered by way of the nonsense and illogic of her *History*. At the end of her own education the promised independence narrowed itself into the chances of marriage. If marriage failed, there was only one other route to independence open to an impoverished but well educated gentlewoman—and the better she was educated, the more frighteningly open it was—namely, to become a governess. Jane Austen in her maturity showed what she thought of such a fate by making it, in *Emma*, impend over Jane Fairfax like a realistic version of a supernatural doom in a gothick novel. She thought no better of governessing when she was fifteen. Perhaps her pride was hurt earlier still by the fact that her father had to supplement his income by taking in pupils—and, indeed, more than her pride, if M. A. Austen-Leigh is right in suggesting that Cassandra and Jane Austen, at the ages of nine and six, were packed off to Oxford because the space at home was needed for their father's pupils.[35] Perhaps Jane Austen resolved not to become doubly the victim of the tutoring/governessing system. Her *History* implies this threat: if you force me to become a governess, *this* is what I will teach my pupils—ignorant history, history with very few dates, history which so far from teaching the pupil to govern himself will endorse him in his babyish principle of absolutism.

This, I guess, is the source of another curious symptom of an anarchical disregard of education in Jane Austen, her refusal to learn to spell. Not only did she decline to spell in conformity with conventional orthography—which, it is true, was only just settling into rigidity. She was not consistent even with obvious etymologies (she writes 'adeiu',[36] no doubt in mimicry of the English pronunciation —but she can hardly have thought the French for 'God' was 'deiu'). She was not consistent even with herself (within the same fortnight she writes 'beleive' and 'believe').[37] She was not self-consistent even in the matter of her own inventions, where she was the sole arbiter: she spells her own heroine Catharine (in the juvenile novel of that name) sometimes with an *er* and sometimes with an *ar*; and even after seeing *Pride and Prejudice* in print she can, in a letter,[38] spell one of her own Bennet family with a double *t*.

To be herself unable to master spelling was Jane Austen's perpetual insurance policy against being obliged to teach it to others.

Yet it was as an educationalist—but in the education of herself—that the adult Jane Austen preserved her adolescent writings in fair copies and even, to the surprise of later editors, amended their texts after she had grown up.[39] The juvenilia were her own education. It is easy to see how they served her technically: the technical faults she satirizes in the juvenile works, by the mechanism of exaggerating them to ludicrous intensity, appear as technical perfections in her grown-up books. The nonsense passages are reverse images of the absolute logic of her later plots. The juvenile *Frederic & Elfrida* whirls ludicrously through time. Captain Roger and Rebecca marry in one paragraph; in the next but one, 'Weeks and Fortnights flew away . . . the Cloathes grew out of fashion & at length Capt: Roger and his Lady arrived, to pay a visit to their Mother & introduce to her their beautifull Daughter of eighteen'. It is out of this as it were acorn in reverse that there grew the perfectly measured technique for expressing the passing of time that Jane Austen employed in *Persuasion*.

For if the young Jane Austen satirized the technical blunders of popular fiction, those were also her own blunders and weaknesses. And indeed, both in technique and content, the weaknesses of her own writing and of popular writing had a common source: daydream. The juvenilia satirize, and thereby overcome, the high-handed absolutism with which daydreaming technique abolishes the obstructions put in its way by time and logic. And in overcoming the absolutism of daydream technique Jane Austen overcame the absolutism of daydream itself and her own nostalgic tendency to go back through her own history and, as it were, re-enthrone the Stuarts. At fifteen, Jane Austen confronted the prospect of having to become a governess; she was tempted to retreat into a daydream in which the wealth and grandeur of the Leighs was restored to her; instead, she satirized her own daydream in the *History* and thereby sharpened the literary technique with which, in *Emma*, she punctured the daydream finally. In *Emma* the 'family romance', the fantasy of a high but undisclosed pedigree, is already objectified by being projected, by Emma, onto Harriet Smith; and when Emma is educated out of it, Jane Austen finally abandons her childhood dream of re-inhabiting the gothick and absolutist grandeur of the Leighs or the Stuarts.

# NOTES

1. See B. C. Southam, *Jane Austen's Literary Manuscripts*, (1964) p. 2.
2. B. C. Southam, *loc. cit.*
3. Both Hume's and Goldsmith's Histories were in Jane Austen's library at Steventon. See note to *Minor Works* (1954) p. 459.
4. *Minor Works* (1954) p. 12.
5. *Psychopathology of Everyday Life*, XII.
6. No. 18 in R. W. Chapman's editions, *Letters* (1952), 21 January 1799.
7. The son of Mrs. Austen's sister.
8. November 1791 is the latest possible date for *Jack & Alice*, which is dedicated to Jane Austen's brother Francis, 'Midshipman on . . . the *Perseverance*', a ship he left in November 1791. See *Minor Works*, p. 2.
9. When Edward Cooper did get the living in 1799, Jane Austen writes 'Mrs. Leigh has begged his acceptance' of it.
10. In 1791 Edward Cooper was only 21 or 22 and might not yet have taken orders, though he certainly had by 1793.
11. R. W. Chapman, assuming that Mr. Whitaker, like the others in the list, was a personal friend of Jane Austen, notes that he is not mentioned in the letters. I am indebted to Michael Levey for pointing out that the reference is surely to John Whitaker, 1735–1806 author of *Mary Queen of Scots Vindicated*, 1787.
12. 'No doubt one is familiar with Shakespeare in a degree', says Edmund in *Mansfield Park*, 'from one's earliest years . . . we all talk Shakespeare.'
13. E.g letter of 12 May 1801.
14. *My Aunt Jane Austen* (1952).
15. Letter of 3 January 1801.
16. Letter of 12 May 1801.
17. Letter to Cassandra Austen, 3 January 1801.
18. Jane Austen knew of a worse case in real life in the same town. 'Earle (Harwood) and his wife live in the most private manner imaginable at Portsmouth, without keeping a servant of any kind. What a prodigious innate love of virtue she must have, to marry under such circumstances!' (Letter, 27 October 1798).
19. Letter of 3 January 1801.
20. But even after Mr. Austen's death the Austens still contemplated keeping one. On 20 November 1808 Jane Austen reported to Cassandra that their mother was 'reconciled' to the idea. After her sister's death, Cassandra Austen had a manservant. (See *The Recollections of John White, 1821–1921*, published by the Jane Austen Society, 1952.)
21. *Memoir* (1870), ed. R. W. Chapman, (1926) p. 50.
22. *Memoir*, p. 18.
23. *Memoir*, p. 159.
24. *Memoir*, p. 86. The *Memoir* speaks of the death of 'Mrs. Cassandra Austen', presumably a slip for 'Miss Cassandra Austen'. Mrs. Austen died in 1827.

25. *My Aunt Jane Austen*, p. 4.

26. M. A. Austen-Leigh, *Personal Aspects of Jane Austen* (1920) pp. 26–8.

27. *Memoir*, p. 16.

28. *Personal Aspects of Jane Austen*, p. 15.

29. See my *Mozart the Dramatist*, (1964) X.

30. Letter, 8 January 1799.

31. Letter, 20 June 1808.

32. E.g. Jane to Cassandra Austen, 21 January 1799: 'It began to occur to me before you mentioned it that I had been somewhat silent as to my mother's health for some time, but I thought you could have no difficulty in divining its exact state—you who have guessed so much stranger things. She is tolerably well . . . She would tell you herself that she has a very dreadful cold in her head at present; but I have not much compassion for colds in the head without fever or sore throat.'

33. E.g. in the letter Lydia writes after her elopement, '. . . if you cannot guess with who'.

34. Darcy is said to look ashamed of, specifically, 'his aunt's ill breeding'.

35. *Personal Aspects of Jane Austen*, p. 21.

36. Letter, 19 June 1799.

37. 'Beleive' in letter of 19 June 1799 and 'believe' in letter of 11 June 1799.

38. Letter, 4 February 1813.

39. E.g. the surprise R. W. Chapman expresses (*Minor Works*, p. 1) that revisions in *Catharine* should be made, and a letter in *Evelyn* actually be dated, as late as 1809.

# III

# A VIEW OF MANSFIELD PARK

## Denis Donoghue

HENRY JAMES spoke of Jane Austen's 'light felicity', thereby patronizing a novelist whom he was happy to admire provided he was not required to take her too seriously. 'Light felicity' is a term of praise, in its way, but it does not accord with the image of Jane Austen which modern readers recognize and sponsor. 'Everybody's dear Jane', like James's mistress of felicity, has been replaced by the astringent figure outlined in D. W. Harding's famous essay, 'Regulated Hatred'. Professor Harding's Jane Austen is a systematic ironist, writing of a society which she accepts, but only subject to the critical rigour for which she makes, in her fiction, an assured place. She votes for the society when it is a question of voting, but meanwhile she insinuates general and specific critiques, brisk summaries of disenchantment; many of these hover on the edge of subversion. This view of Jane Austen is agreeable largely, I think, because it exemplifies a position in society which many of us would wish to hold. We want to participate in a social order while purifying it, privately, by mental reservations; and we want to feel that this way of life is intelligent, humane, and artistic, that it has a certain finesse, a meticulous propriety of conscience. Jane Austen discloses this happiness.

But, not, I think, invariably. The modern image of Jane Austen corresponds accurately enough to the narrative voice of *Emma*, for instance, where the formative vision of life is systematically ironic; but these are not the terms in which we would speak of *Mansfield Park*. In *Mansfield Park* the irony is local, a sharpening of the instrument now and again, rather than a constant imperative.

There is, for example, the announcement of Mr. Norris's death:

> The first event of any importance in the family was the death of Mr.
> Norris, which happened when Fanny was about fifteen, and necessarily
> introduced alterations and novelties. Mrs. Norris, on quitting the
> parsonage, removed first to the park, and afterwards to a small house
> of Sir Thomas's in the village, and consoled herself for the loss of her
> husband by considering that she could do very well without him, and
> for her reduction of income by the evident necessity of stricter economy.
>
> (ch. 3)

The critical voice is sharper here than generally in *Mansfield Park*,
but even here we are invited to attend not to the voice itself but to
the narrated facts, the events, almost as if they had not yet become
verbal. We can readily believe that Jane Austen disliked such people
as Mrs. Norris, and we are meant to register the parody of feeling in
the widow's consolation, but the narrative voice is as 'neutral' as
it can well be: it is content with an enabling role, it does not declare
itself as the object of primary interest. The relation between Mrs.
Norris's husband and the reduction of her income is a rhyme of
syntax, indisputably verbal; but as soon as we have taken the weight
of the juxtaposition, we are free to let the words go. This is to say
that the words do not insist upon themselves beyond the moment at
which the delivery of the 'facts' is made. But listen to the announcement of Mrs. Churchill's death in *Emma*:

> It was felt as such things must be felt. Every body had a degree of
> gravity and sorrow; tenderness towards the departed, solicitude for
> the surviving friends; and, in a reasonable time, curiosity to know
> where she would be buried. Goldsmith tells us that when lovely woman
> stoops to folly, she has nothing to do but to die; and when she stoops
> to be disagreeable it is equally to be recommended as a clearer of ill-
> fame. Mrs. Churchill, after being disliked at least twenty-five years, was
> now spoken of with compassionate allowances. In one point she was
> fully justified. She had never admitted before to be seriously ill. The
> event acquitted her of all the fancifulness, and all the selfishness of
> imaginary complaints.
>
> (ch. 45)

This is Professor Harding's mistress of regulated hatred. We are still
in clichés of feeling; the mechanical slide from tenderness to
curiosity, the automatic compassion, the provisional obscurity of
gravity and sorrow. Indeed the ironies, word by word, are dazzling;

we read this prose as we read the verse of the *Dunciad*. Clearly a much larger proportion of the effect depends upon the narrative voice in this case than in the paragraph from *Mansfield Park;* the ironist is listening to the sounds and relishing their brilliance. In the passage from *Mansfield Park* the dominant assumption is that the meaning, the human 'point', lies in the facts themselves, apart from any incidental force attributable to the voice of the narrator. But in the passage from *Emma* the locus of significance and value is far less in the 'facts' and far more in the voice of a narrator deemed to be superior to any facts. The voice is nearly everything; the facts, the events, are merely the occasion of its performance. It is like opera in a foreign language when the singing is magnificent.

We are already exaggerating. But a modest distinction is valid: the witty and superior voice of Jane Austen is the commanding presence of *Emma*, *Pride and Prejudice*, and *Sanditon*; but in *Sense and Sensibility*, *Northanger Abbey*, *Persuasion*, and *Mansfield Park* there is far less irony, far less 'voice', the meaning is entrusted to facts which largely speak for themselves. Jane Austen, indeed, wrote two quite distinct kinds of fiction. *Mansfield Park* is not an unsuccessful attempt to repeat the success of *Pride and Prejudice*; it is a different kind of novel and, in that kind, a masterpiece. The reader is free to prefer *Emma* or *Pride and Prejudice* but the preference counts for little until *Mansfield Park* is acknowledged as a major work in a different *genre*.

A common view of *Mansfield Park* is vigorously given in Marvin Mudrick's *Irony as Defense and Discovery*. The novel is the triumph of mere gentility. Fanny Price is a dull prig. Mary Crawford is so charming and vital that she threatens to overthrow the novel and compels Jane Austen to betray her in the end. 'In *Mansfield Park*', Professor Mudrick says, 'the most notable omission is irony'. I should deflect the blow a little by saying that it is not an omission; if *Pride and Prejudice* strives towards the condition of French classical comedy, *Mansfield Park* is cousin to the Morality plays.

Jane Austen knew that *Pride and Prejudice* was a masterpiece and something of a *tour de force*, but I think she felt that it was slightly operatic in its brilliance. In the famous letter to Cassandra (4th February, 1813) she says: 'The work is rather too light, and bright, and sparkling: it wants shade, it wants to be stretched out here and there with a long chapter of sense, if it could be had; if not, of solemn specious nonsense, about something unconnected with the story; an essay on writing, a critique on Walter Scott, or the history of Buonaparté, or anything that would form a contrast, and bring the reader with increased delight to the playfulness and epigrammatism of the general style'.[1] I think she felt something factitious in *Pride and Prejudice*, as if it were too dazzling to be true; and she was beginning to think a good deal about the nature of truth. In *Mansfield Park* she would propose a sterner discrimination, even at the risk of being, as she said, 'not half so entertaining'.[2] In *Pride and Prejudice* life allowed the novelist to declare the marvellous union of Wit and Wisdom, but this was one liberty in a thousand restrictions. The more general rule of life is that Wit and Wisdom are cut adrift and often in that severance Wit becomes corrupt and Wisdom a little dull; and if it must be a choice, then one must choose Wisdom, because (as Jane Austen wrote to Fanny Knight in November, 1814) 'Wisdom is better than Wit, and in the long run will certainly have the laugh on her side'.[3] This is more English than French; like Cowper's indigenous morality in 'Tirocinium' when he refers to 'wit's eccentric range'. *Mansfield Park* is written in the same idiom; it is concerned with Wisdom, with Truth, with the moral sense and the possibility of improving it or corrupting it.

We know what Jane Austen means by Wisdom; at least when she sets it off against Wit. We know that by 'Truth' she means, in human relationships, a direct correlation of speech and action. In the great argument between Emma and Mr. Knightley (ch. 18) about Frank Churchill's behaviour, Emma speaks for charm and wit, but Knightley will listen only to duty and truth. Several chapters later Emma adopts his idiom. Speaking to Mrs. Weston of Frank Churchill's secret engagement, Emma says: 'Impropriety! Oh!—Mrs. Weston—it is too calm a censure. Much, much beyond impropriety!—It has sunk him, I cannot say how much it has sunk him in my opinion. So unlike what a man should be!—None of that upright integrity, that strict adherence to truth and principle, that disdain of trick and littleness, which a man should display in every transaction of his life' (ch. 46). Each of Jane Austen's novels has at least one major occasion on which the demands of Truth are flouted: Frank Churchill's secret engagement to Jane Fairfax; in *Sense and Sensibility*, the secret trip of Marianne and Willoughby to Allenham (ch. 13), which mimes a marital relation to which they have no claim; in *Pride and Prejudice*, Lydia's elopement with Wickham; in *Persuasion*, the bland secrecies of Mrs. Clay; in *Lady Susan*, the sexual strategies from beginning to end; in *Northanger Abbey*, Isabella Thorpe's duplicity with Frederick Tilney; and in *Mansfield Park*, the chain of deceit which leads to Henry Crawford's elopement with Mrs. Rushworth and Julia's with John Yates. But *Mansfield Park* moves the issue into the centre of the novel; nothing less than Truth is at stake in the crucial chapters which deal with the amateur theatricals.

We first hear of the playacting in ch. 13. The notion is opposed by Edmund and, with natural silence, by Fanny. But the stronger party consists of John Yates, Tom Bertram, Maria, Julia, the Crawfords, Mrs. Norris and the indolent Lady Bertram. Edmund's argument is that 'In a *general* light, private theatricals are open to some objections', but 'as *we* are circumstanced', they would be 'most injudicious'. They would show a certain lack of feeling for an absent father: Sir Thomas would not wish his daughters to act plays; the business would be particularly imprudent now that Maria is engaged to Mr. Rushworth. Besides, the play itself, *Lovers' Vows*, is objectionable in detail. Edmund is rather vague in specifying the scandalous implications, and Fanny, of course, is silent, but as the arrangements proceed the issues become clear enough, although they are never debated. Private theatricals were a frequent amusement in the Austen home; acceptable enough, indeed, so long as their innocence was guaranteed by the privacy of the family. But privacy was always vulnerable. In 1787, for instance, Eliza de Feuillide, wife of a French aristocrat, arrived at Steventon. Soon she was taking part in the family theatricals. Some years later, when her husband was executed in Paris, she turned her thoughts again toward the Austen family; toward Henry, in particular, whom she married in 1797. Jane Austen's feeling on this occasion may have made its way into *Mansfield Park*, though there is no evidence of direct transcription. In any event, innocence did not hold when, as in *Mansfield Park*, the players included people who were likely to become emotionally involved with one another. Mary Crawford will not marry the infatuated Edmund because she despises penniless clergymen, but she is ready to make love to him, vicariously, by miming the part of Amelia in *Lovers' Vows*. Julia wants to play the part of Agatha, the lover of the Baron, played by John Yates—with whom she eventually elopes, in the 'fact' of the fiction. Edmund refuses to join, but when there is talk of inviting Charles Maddox to take his place, he objects that this will put an end to 'all the privacy and propriety'—his phrase—and to prevent this he agrees to play. But now he himself, within the play, is what he longs to become, 'outside', Mary's successful lover. Perhaps Fanny was justified in thinking of her hero's 'unsteadiness'. Maria, engaged to Rushworth, is in love with Henry Crawford: the rehearsals enable her to avoid Rushworth and to spend a lot of time with Henry. The implications are clear, the playacting is corrupt. If the great question in Jane Austen's fictive world is the relation between human feeling and the social forms in which it is certified or distorted, then the theatricals at Mansfield Park are corrupt because they obscure the forms and evade the ethical sanctions which the forms sustain. Above all, the theatricals are an offence against Truth. That is why Fanny will always associate Henry Crawford's behaviour during the rehearsals with his deceitful stratagems at Sotherton.

We are dealing with a stern ethic. Indeed, *Mansfield Park* seems to associate itself with those letters in which Jane Austen expressed an increasing respect for the seriousness of the Evangelicals. She had started off by simply not liking these people, and even in her later years she would remain cool to the idiom of Regeneration and Conversion, but there is a revealing letter in which she says, 'I am by no means convinced that we ought not all to be Evangelicals, and am at least persuaded that they who are so from Reason and Feeling must be happiest and safest'.[4] This is close to the spirit of *Mansfield Park*, a novel which dramatizes many of the leading moral issues from Shaftesbury to Adam Smith, Cowper, and Johnson. *Mansfield Park* is Jane Austen's most committed novel: the free play of irony is only one of its resources, and not the greatest. When the novelist said that her subject in *Mansfield Park* would be 'ordination', she was concerned to focus upon the bristling relation between truth, the moral sense, and the integrity of the self.

There are two great commitments in *Mansfield Park*: Edmund's choice of the priesthood, and Fanny's love for Edmund.

Of the first: Halévy's *History of England in the Nineteenth Century* gives many reasons for the low status of ministers in the Church; enough to show that Mary Crawford's contempt for the clergy was a common and sustainable view, however corrupt. But it was, indeed, corrupt. In *Sense and Sensibility* Edward Ferrars mentions (ch. 19) that he wished to become a minister, but that this profession 'was not smart enough for my family'. And his brother Robert laughs 'most immoderately' (ch. 47) at the vision of

Edward 'reading prayers in a white surplice, and publishing the banns of marriage between John Smith and Mary Brown'. We are to understand that when Edmund Bertram insists upon becoming a clergyman and taking up all the duties of rural ministry including that of residence, there can be no deeper commitment. William James, speaking of the consciousness of self, mentions the common situation in which we are compelled to choose, to stand by one of our empirical selves and relinquish the others. Edmund Bertram is in love with the fascinating Mary Crawford, and to be her husband is one of the 'selves' he most strongly wishes to achieve, but he stands by the greatest of these, his role as minister, and he eventually relinquishes the role which impedes this self. One of James's sentences happens to give the situation precisely: 'the seeker of his truest, strongest, deepest self must review the list (of selves) carefully, and pick out the one on which to stake his salvation'.[5] For similar reasons, Fanny commits herself to Edmund, once for all, despite the persuasions of Sir Thomas, Henry Crawford, Mary Crawford, and Edmund himself. Bishop Butler argues in his *Analogy* that personal identity is established by the similarity, on different occasions, of one's consciousness: through a multitude of whirling circumstances Fanny Price is conscious of loving Edmund, and this consciousness is inescapable. In *Persuasion* Anne Elliot's love for Captain Wentworth is of a similar order; and in *Sense and Sensibility*, Elinor's commitment to Edward. This is what Jane Austen means by 'Truth' in personal relations.

The two great temptations which lie across the path of truth in Jane Austen's fiction are 'charm' and selfishness.[6]

It is possible, of course, for charm to be good, as it is in the miracle of Elizabeth Bennet. But Jane Austen often felt, and particularly after *Pride and Prejudice*, that the dangerous people were those whose charm was at once irrefutable and corrupt. She would always relish charm, even in a Henry Crawford; there is a letter of March, 1814, in which she refers to her brother: 'Henry is going on with 'Mansfield Park'. He admires H. Crawford: I mean properly, as a clever, pleasant man'.[7] What she means is that we cannot ignore or despise the cleverness or the pleasantness of such a man. These virtues render his corruption the more lamentable, the more insidious. She would never have approved Lord Chesterfield's advice to his son, but she knew the force of charm, she relished it, and—I feel sure—feared it. Clearly she was afraid of charming, worthless, clever men like Willoughby, Wickham, Crawford, and Frank Churchill. She knew that charm in such men is notoriously beguiling; even Elizabeth was greatly taken by Wickham's charm in chapters 16 and 17 of *Pride and Prejudice*, and poor Edmund in *Mansfield Park* is so bewitched by Mary Crawford's charm that he forgets the civilities due to Fanny, especially at Sotherton. This is one of the great successes in *Mansfield Park*, Mary Crawford's charm; we are constantly aware of it, partly under its spell, even though the text is strewn wih hints of its corruption. She openly criticizes her uncle (ch. 6), comes very close to an obscene pun (ch. 6), boasts of knowing only Admirals (ch. 6), sneers at prayer (ch. 9), despises the clergy (ch. 9), takes London as her moral standard (ch. 9), makes unforgivable remarks about Maria's impending marriage (ch. 11), is quite insensitive to natural beauty (ch. 22), and changes her mind about Edmund when it seems likely that Tom will die and Edmund will inherit his father's wealth. Perhaps the earliest and strongest hint of Mary's character is in ch. 6, at Mansfield, when she demands a cart to bring her harp from Northampton and cannot understand the conditions of rural life which make this demand particularly unwelcome at harvest-time. But the charm persists and cannot be neutralized until at last it reveals its corruption to Edmund; when Mary speaks of the adultery of her brother and Mrs. Rushworth as mere folly: 'She saw it only as folly, and that folly stamped only by exposure' (ch. 48).

The second temptation in the path of Truth is selfishness. Jane Austen was not a pupil of Mandeville or Hobbes but she was sufficiently wry to acknowledge that selfishness, whatever the cause, is a common effect in human action. But if truth means commitment —so her argument would run—the movement of feeling cannot be self-engrossed, it must go out in full acknowledgement of other people. There are many versions of selfishness in Jane Austen's fiction, some deadlier than others; in *Sanditon*, Sir Edward Denham's plan to seduce Clara Brereton; Lady Susan's entire life; William Elliot's advances to Anne, in *Persuasion* (ch. 20); in *Sense and Sensibility*, (ch. 27) Marianne's rudeness to Mrs. Jennings; Mr. Bennet's systematic contempt, in *Pride and Prejudice*; Emma's snobbery. These are not morally identical. But they are all, in their differing degrees, reprehensible. In Jane Austen's fiction the rule is that extreme cases of selfishness must be punished, and the milder versions—since most of us exhibit them—must be neutralized and if possible transformed into love and wisdom. The greatest example of this conversion of force into style is Emma: her rudeness to Miss Bates, her repudiation of Robert Martin, her patronage of Harriet Smith; these must be neutralized, Emma must be brought to the point of saying, as she does towards the end of the book, 'It would be a great pleasure to know Robert Martin'. At this point force becomes style, which is energy without aggression. All the analogies now flow together to enrich the marriage of Emma and Knightley—the 'sweet' English landscape (ch. 42), Hartfield and Highbury rather than London, an ethic of principle and truth. But where selfishness has been extreme, there is no forgiveness. In *Sense and Sensibility* Lucy Steele is repudiated, by Jane Austen if not by Edward Ferrars. The same punishment is dealt to Isabella Thorpe in *Northanger Abbey*. In *Mansfield Park* the most extreme act of selfishness is Henry Crawford's decision to make Fanny fall in love with him. This is the culmination of a chain of selfish acts on his part, beginning with his remark at Sotherton (ch. 9), 'I do not like to see Miss Bertram so near the altar'. Thereafter he flirts with the engaged Maria, behaves like a boor towards Rushworth, and plays with the feelings of Maria and Julia. When he decides to make Fanny fall in love, it is to amuse himself 'on the days that I do not hunt' (ch. 24), and even when he is really in love with her, he continues to think of his emotion as a favour (ch. 30) and to exhibit what Fanny, despite her gratitude on other grounds, calls 'a want of delicacy and regard for others' (ch. 20). This being so, even in his finer moments he cannot speak the language of true grace. When Fanny is visited by her brother William and her happiness is clear to everyone, Henry Crawford is greatly taken by the picture:

> It was a picture which Henry Crawford had moral taste enough to value. Fanny's attractions increased—increased two-fold—for the sensibility which beautified her complexion and illumined her countenance, was an attraction in itself. He was no longer in doubt of the capabilities of her heart. She had feeling, genuine feeling. It would be something to be loved by such a girl, to excite the first ardours of her young, unsophisticated mind! She interested him more than he had foreseen. A fortnight was not enough. His stay became indefinite.
>
> (ch. 24)

There is a characteristic deterioration of feeling here. The first notes are of eighteenth-century weight and civility. They are Jane Austen's terms, and she is prepared to lend them to Crawford to the extent that he merits them; terms like 'moral taste', 'insensibility', 'the capabilities of the heart', and 'feeling'. This is one of the tests which Jane Austen imposes upon her characters; some will speak this language gracefully, and these are her saints. But Henry Crawford handles the words awkwardly and soon slips into the easier idiom of conquest and triumph. It would be 'something' to be loved by such a girl, he muses, but the 'something' has nothing to do with the higher 'value' sponsored by his moral taste; it is a public prize, the success of strategy. The 'interest' of the occasion is in direct proportion to the pride of victory. It is the kind of interest which Mary Crawford offers Fanny in the possession of Henry, several chapters later. When Fanny refers to the gallantries in which Henry has indulged himself, Mary points to 'the glory of fixing one who has been shot at by so many; of having it in one's power to pay off the debts of one's sex!' 'Oh, I am sure it is not in woman's nature to refuse such a triumph' (ch. 34). Henry shares this language of prizes, triumphs, debts, and—the word is now defined—'interest': like his sister, he is a capitalist of the sensibility. He may read Shakespeare well, and this is in his favour, but he has said so much in the language of fashion and power that he cannot bring himself to learn the idiom of truth and love. He speaks it as a foreign language, too recently acquired. At the end of the book he is still the same. When he meets Maria Rushworth and is received 'with a coldness which ought to have been repulsive', he becomes again a man of mere power, winning, and winning nothing. Jane Austen's last word is a blank cheque. We may fairly consider, she says, 'a man of sense like Henry Crawford, to be providing for himself no small portion of vexation and regret—vexation that must rise sometimes to self reproach and regret to wretchedness—in having so requited hospitality, so injured family peace, so forfeited his best, most estimable and endeared acquaintance, and so lost the woman whom he had rationally, as well as passionately loved' (ch. 48). In *The Beast in the Jungle* Henry James takes up where this sentence leaves off: John Marcher realizes, too late, when May Bartram is dead, that he has 'lived' 'in the chill of his egotism and the light of her use'. Fanny Price is preserved by Edmund, by Jane Austen, and by a chosen 'self' which demands nothing but its own small space. Henry Crawford is preserved, to the extent that he is preserved, merely by not being deemed worthy to suffer in John Marcher's way.

Clearly there is a problem. Jane Austen cannot allow her world to be divided between charming scoundrels and dull saints. She must discriminate between the charm of Wickham and the vivacity of Darcy, between the force of Frank Churchill and the style of Knightley. She must set up a rivalry of spirit between Mary Crawford and Fanny Price, letting Fanny lose the battles and win the war. The central question is the moral sense. What is it, and what is its function?

Jane Austen's treatment of this matter corresponds very closely to the position of 'orthodox' English moralists in the eighteenth century. She assumes the operation of a moral sense, an 'inner sense', a power deemed to be innate in every person, as Shaftesbury said, 'a first principle in our constitution and make'.[8] Hutcheson argued that the moral sense is universal and uniform because there are 'some actions or affections which obtain the approbation of any spectator or observer, and others (which) move his dislike and condemnation'. Furthermore (and this bears directly upon *Mansfield Park*) it is assumed that while the moral sense may be, as Burnet says, 'improveable into more distinct knowledge',[9] it may also be depraved, notably by 'Custom, Habits, false opinions, Company',[10] as Hutcheson says, or—in Shaftesbury's account—'from the force of custom and education in opposition to Nature'[11] or through 'licentiousness of practice'.[12] In Adam Smith's *Theory of Moral Sentiments* the idea of sympathy plays a much larger part than in the writings of moralists like Burnet, Shaftesbury, Butler, and Hutcheson, but it is all the more revealing that he speaks in similar terms 'of the influence of Custom and Fashion upon Moral Sentiments'. The following paragraph from *Theory* might almost have been written to prepare us for the Crawfords of *Mansfield Park*:

> Those who have been educated in what is really good company, not in what is commonly called such, who have been accustomed to see nothing in the persons whom they esteemed and lived with, but justice, modesty, humanity, and good order; are more shocked with whatever seems to be inconsistent with the rules which those virtues prescribe. Those, on the contrary, who have had the misfortune to be brought up amidst violence, licentiousness, falsehood, and injustice, lose, though not all sense of the impropriety of such conduct, yet all sense of its dreadful enormity, or of the vengeance and punishment due to it. They have been familiarized with it from their infancy, custom has rendered it habitual to them, and they are very apt to regard it as, what is called, the way of the world.[13]

Hence, in *Mansfield Park*, the importance of education, one of the leading themes of the novel.

*Mansfield Park* begins with arrangements by which Fanny Price is brought to Mansfield as Sir Thomas's ward, and it ends with similar arrangements in favour of Susan, Fanny's agreeable sister. The main difference is that Susan arrives under better auspices; Sir Thomas, who has been primarily interested in preserving the social differences between Fanny and his daughters, is now concerned only with the proper education of character, with what Jane Austen calls 'the sterling good of principle and temper' (ch. 48). The sins of Julia and Maria have been prefigured, from the beginning of the novel, by instances of their defective education. 'To the education of her daughters', we are told, 'Lady Bertram paid not the smallest attention' (ch. 2). As for Sir Thomas, he had handed over his daughters' education to Mrs. Norris. As a result, 'it is not very wonderful that with all their promising talents and early information, they should be entirely deficient in the less common acquirements of self-knowledge, generosity, and humility. In everything but disposition, they were admirably taught' (ch. 2). Julia's education was entirely superficial: Jane Austen speaks of 'the want of that higher species of self-command, that just consideration of others, that knowledge of her own heart, that principle of right which had not formed any essential part of her education' (ch. 9). Maria's education was even worse, giving her nothing but 'self-consequence' (ch. 48). Indeed, towards the end of the novel, when Sir Thomas's eyes have been opened, we are told that 'the anguish arising from the conviction of his own errors in the education of his daughters, was never to be entirely done away'. At this point, thinking of 'the most direful mistake in his plan of education', Sir Thomas has a meditative passage which begins with an extreme speculation and goes on to translate the tropes of eighteenth-century moral philosophy into his own experience:

> Something must have been wanting *within*, or time would have worn away much of its ill effect. He feared that principle, active principle, had been wanting, that they had never been properly taught to govern their inclinations and tempers, by that sense of duty which can alone suffice. They had been instructed theoretically in their religion, but never required to bring it into daily practice. To be distinguished for elegance and accomplishments—the authorised object of their youth— could have had no useful influence that way, no moral effect on the

mind. He had meant them to be good, but his cares had been directed to the understanding and manners, not the disposition; and of the necessity of self-denial and humility, he feared they had never heard from any lips that could profit them.

(ch. 48)

These sentences are in the idiom of English educational and moral theory from Burnet to Adam Smith. In considering the possibility that his daughters' moral sense may have been 'wanting' from the beginning, Sir Thomas questions the fundamental optimistic assumption of moral theory. This is the degree of his horror, beyond the issue of defective education.[14] Edmund's horror arises from the same fear in regard to Mary Crawford: when he has finally broken with her, he decides that 'hers are not faults of temper . . . hers are faults of principle, Fanny, of blunted delicacy and a corrupted vitiated mind' (ch. 47). Before this, he has assumed that Mary's faults are the result of bad education. In the middle of the novel, when he has been distressed by her contempt for the clergy, he still considers her 'disposition' faultless but that she has been educated in corruption by her aunt and uncle. Even at the end, when he blames the world for Mary's defects, he says to Fanny, 'This is what the world does. For where, Fanny, shall we find a woman whom nature had so richly endowed?—Spoilt, spoilt!' (ch. 47). The same explanation is offered to account for Henry Crawford; his education at the hands of a corrupt uncle. Finally, Fanny's love for Edmund is closely related to his share in her education: she thinks of him as having 'directed her thoughts and fixed her principles'. As early as Chapter 2, when Fanny has just arrived at Mansfield Park, Edmund becomes her guide and counsellor:

Miss Lee taught her French, and heard her read the daily portion of History; but he recommended the books which charmed her leisure hours, he encouraged her taste, and corrected her judgement . . .

This sounds formidably explicit, but we should not take these sentences as mere moral ballast for a smoothly running novel. The question of education figures in the book because Jane Austen is tracing the hazards of the moral sense when confronted by widely varying experiences. Education is an inextricable part of the story because it is 'added' to the moral sense: the addition bears immediately upon the nature of the chosen self and its probable fate in the world at large. It is at least as important as marriage. Jane Austen's account of this issue in *Mansfield Park* is remarkably deft; some of her most delicate moral perceptions ring the changes upon the theme and reverberate through the novel. I shall mention one or two.

When the play is first proposed, Edmund laughs it aside. Julia rebukes him, 'Now, Edmund, do not be disagreeable . . . Nobody loves a play better than you do, or can have gone much farther to see one'. And Edmund answers: 'True, to see real acting, good hardened real acting; but I would hardly walk from this room to the next to look at the raw efforts of those who have not been bred to the trade,—a set of gentlemen and ladies, who have all the disadvantages of education and decorum to struggle through' (ch. 13). The irony is Jane Austen's, not Edmund's; Edmund, after all, is only asking that these people assent to what they are; his tone is like Sir Henry Harcourt-Reilly's in *The Cocktail Party*. 'You must accept your limitations'. This prepares us to find the play-acting gauche and the participants silly, but the result goes far beyond this; the emotions released by the play-acting are corrupt, and the source of this corruption is the failure of education to engender a proper truth, a genuine decorum.

Education in *Mansfield Park* is such a crucial issue that we may expect to find it featured in practically all the situations involving change and progress. Two people, Fanny and Edmund, have chosen the ground of their characters; the others veer according to whim, pride, or greed. This is the structural figure of the novel. Jane Austen is concerned with ethical changes, so she presents several instances of changes which are casual or wild. Many of these belong to the same 'family' as the word 'education' itself. The most incisive example of this linkage is the topic of 'improvements'. Clearly there are many possibilities in juxtaposing one kind of 'improvement' against another: think of a passage like this from Humphrey Repton's *Fragments on the Theory and Practice of Landscape Gardening* (1816):

> In a House entirely new, Character is at the option of the Artistic Proprietor; it may be Gothic or Grecian, whichever best accords with the face of the country; but where a great part of the original structure is to remain, the additions should doubtless partake of the existing character.[15]

The terms of landscape-gardening are drawn from an aesthetic-moral world, implying that one's house and gardens have a 'character' corresponding to one's own, the character of one's moral choice. One cannot speak of 'improving' one's estate without implicating the analogy of moral education, an improvement of a much more fundamental kind. In English literature we find this implication in Jonson's 'To Penshurst', in Marvell, Goldsmith, Wordsworth, Ruskin: it is active in *Howard's End* and in Charles Tomlinson's *A Peopled Landscape*, to take examples at random. 'Improvement' is one of the crucial terms in those late seventeenth and early eighteenth century English moralists whom we have invoked, especially in optimists like Burnet and Shaftesbury. Locke's *Treatise on Education* is an important text in a sterner tradition, and naturally he will not use the term with such weight. But if, like Burnet, you posit a moral sense, 'a principle of distinguishing one thing from another in moral cases, without ratiocination', and if you admit that the moral sense in children is at first weak and obscure, then you must allow that it may be developed into full vision, as Burnet says, 'according to the Improvement that is made of it'.[16] Blake had this term in mind when, in *The Marriage of Heaven and Hell*, he derided the optimistic and prudential ethic which it implies: 'Improvement makes strait roads; but the crooked roads without Improvement are roads of Genius'. Jane Austen's code is more orthodox, oldfashioned. Like most people in 1813, she did not subscribe to the view that the tigers of wrath are wiser than the horses of instruction. Some of the most incisive local ironies in *Mansfield Park* arise from the concern of several characters with improvements of a superficial kind, at a time when there is room for considerable improvement in their principles and actions. This applies to the great chapters devoted to the improvements at Sotherton Court.

We first hear of these in Chapter 6. Rushworth has been visiting a friend who has recently had his grounds laid out by an improver. Rushworth 'was returned with his head full of the subject, and very eager to be improving his own place in the same way'. Maria advises him to hire Mr. Repton. Babbling on, Rushworth toys with the notion of cutting down some of the old trees at Sotherton, and Fanny remembering Cowper's lament in *The Task* pities their fate. The talk of improvements continues: Edmund, Fanny, Mary, Julia, Mrs. Grant, even Henry Crawford are drawn in. When Julia asks Henry whether he is fond of improving an estate, Henry, speaking of his own, answers:

> Excessively, but what with the natural advantages of the ground, which pointed out even to a very young eye what little remained to be done,

and my own consequent resolutions, I had not been of age three months before Everingham was all that it is now.

(ch. 6)

Julia's reply shows again how easily this idiom slips into the language of moral action. 'Those who see quickly', she says, 'will resolve quickly and act quickly'. At this point Henry's assistance is sought on Rushworth's behalf: the upshot is that the entire party will make a trip to Sotherton to enable Henry to see what improvements are desirable. Edmund 'heard it all and said nothing'. On the trip the deceptions begin. Julia and the engaged Maria conduct a silent battle over the possession of Henry Crawford. At Sotherton, when they are shown the chapel, and Rushworth's mother says:

> It is a handsome chapel, and was formerly in constant use both morning and evening. Prayers were always read in it by the domestic chaplain, within the memory of many. But the late Mr. Rushworth left it off.

(ch. 9)

Mary Crawford says to Edmund, with a smile, 'Every generation has its improvements'. Walking through the wilderness, Mary challenges Edmund on his decision to become a clergyman. Henry Crawford and Maria Bertram connive in getting rid of Rushworth, to whom Maria is engaged: the ambiguities of improvement allow Henry to make an elaborate pretence of caring for Maria. When she asks him what he thinks now of Sotherton, he says, 'I find it better, grander, more complete in its style, though that style may not be the best':

> 'And to tell you the truth', speaking rather lower, 'I do not think that *I* shall ever see Sotherton again with so much pleasure as I do now. Another summer will hardly improve it to me'.
>
> After a moment's embarrassment the lady replied, 'You are too much a man of the world not to see with the eyes of the world. If other people think Sotherton improved, I have no doubt that you will'.

Henry answers:

> 'I am afraid I am not quite so much the man of the world as might be good for me in some points. My feelings are not quite so evanescent, nor my memory of the past under such easy domination as one finds to be the case with men of the world'.

(ch. 10)

Henry and Maria are walking through Sotherton, discussing the improvements, but between the lines of the conversation they are indulging themselves in illicit emotions which will lead to adultery by way of the theatricals at Mansfield Park. This scene at Sotherton is one of the finest achievements of Jane Austen's art. It is like the second act of *The Three Sisters*, where the idiom of moral choice seeps through the surface of social convention. Indeed, if we respond to this in Chekhov it is not because we have been schooled in these epiphanies by Shakespeare and Strindberg but because we recognize them in the ostensibly casual progression of the novel; especially in Jane Austen and Henry James.

My argument is that we must receive *Mansfield Park* in the ethical idiom in which it is cast. Macaulay would have us approach it by way of *Evelina*, *Cecilia*, and *Camilla*, with a glance ahead at *The Absentee*.[17] This is sound advice, but there is a lot to be said for approaching *Mansfield Park*, *Sense and Sensibility*, *Northanger Abbey*, and *Persuasion* by way of the eighteenth-century English moralists. These are the sources of the great abstractions which Jane Austen places across the paths of her characters, pointing to centuries of judicious experience held in poise. If we look ahead we see on one side the continuity of the English novel and, on another, *Culture and Anarchy* and *The Education of Henry Adams*. Indeed, when Arnold in *On Translating Homer* rebukes Chapman and remarks that the characteristic virtue of English thought is force and its characteristic defect the want of lucidity, he makes the same point which Jane Austen dramatizes in *Mansfield Park*. The moral history of English force is written on her two inches of ivory. As for Henry Adams, the conversion of force into style was his great chimerical hope, a style of expressive equilibrium without naïveté or arrogance; a style like that of St. Thomas's Gothic where the equilibrium 'is visibly delicate beyond the line of safety; danger lurks in every stone'—as Adams said on the last page of *Mont Saint-Michel and Chartres*.

But in the meantime we have to put these matters back into *Mansfield Park*, to see how they are made to function not as inert blocks of morality but as values in a magnetic field of personal relationships. We need a scene which is all composition, if not composure, where the clash of values is all the more dramatic because of the formality, the minuet of the occasion which reveals them, and the noise of arms is audible only to some of the participants, and to the reader. One of the most revealing occasions is in Chapter 23, the card-playing at the Grants'. Two games are in progress: Whist, a sober square game played by Sir Thomas, Mrs. Norris, Dr. and Mrs. Grant; and at the round table there is Speculation, played by Lady Bertram, Mary Crawford, Fanny, Henry Crawford, Edmund, and William, Fanny's brother. William is an innocent player, with the resilient concentration which reminds us that outside the Parsonage and beyond the Park there is a world in which midshipmen hope for promotion. Lady Bertram is in the group to remind us that the Schoolmen describe the condition of vegetative being as having the powers of local motion and growth but nothing else. She is marvellously uncomprehending and silent, one kind of silence setting off the other kind, Fanny's, making Fanny's appear all sensibility, which it nearly is. The game is Speculation, which is based on two principles, the first, the purchase of an unknown card on the calculation of its probable value when known, the second, the purchase of a known card on the chance of no better appearing in the course of the game, some cards in the pack not being dealt. So already we have something to conjure with in the idiom of valuation, price, and competitive risk. This, in an almost Dutch interior.[18]

The games begin. At Speculation, Henry Crawford is in command, guiding Lady Bertram and Fanny, directing their play as well as his own. Like all card-games this one has an air of engrossment which can be used to parody genuine care or to cast a delicately respectful glance in its direction; it brings several people together to testify to the observances of their society. An artist can use the observances to show how different these people are, the limits of their community. Henry Crawford talks of Thornton Lacey, which is to be Edmund's residence when he is ordained. It must be greatly improved, or so Henry insists; the house must be turned to front the east instead of the north, there must be a new garden, and so forth. This is a splendidly brash performance, in the course of which Henry throws out a few remarks which we can pick up as we please. He says, for instance, 'I never do wrong without gaining by it', and again that he never inquires about anything, he always tells people. But Edmund has his own resilience, and tells Henry that in the matter of improving Thornton Lacey he has in mind something far more modest; he will make the house comfortable and give it 'the air of a gentleman's residence'; that will be enough. All this time Mary Crawford has been listening while playing her cards, and suddenly she disposes of William Price by taking his knave at an exorbitant rate, exclaiming, 'There, I will stake my last like a woman of spirit. No cold prudence for me. I am not born to sit still and do nothing. If I lose the game, it shall not be from not striving for it'. There is more, but this is enough for the moment.

The 'plot' of the scene is designed to set off Edmund's values against those of Henry and Mary Crawford; and indeed a few moments later Mrs. Norris will speak of the Rushworths in almost the same terms as those of the Crawfords, and the Crawfords will find it hard to recover from that infection. Later on, we will have to discriminate between Henry and Mary, giving Henry at least the merit of having been in love—to the limit of his character, and the most we can allow to Mary, apart from charm, is that she has a certain right to feel that Edmund has wounded her. Henry's speeches at the card-game are practically insolent, and it says a lot for Edmund's civility that he puts up with them; but Mary supplies a vigorous theory to endorse Henry's practice. She will stake her last like a woman of spirit. No cold prudence for her. Jane Austen knew as well as anyone how compelling this idiom is, how attractive and strong. Mary Crawford is a formidable person because she is the only one in the book who could use this heroic language without absurdity. At a later stage we reflect that she urges this spectacular way of life on others while fixing her own eyes on the main chance. If I lose the game, she declares, it shall not be from not striving for it. Yes, but Jane Austen's next sentence is: 'The game was her's, and only did not pay her for what she had given to secure it'. If this were our motto for the entire novel, we should add a gloss to the effect that heroic gestures are fine in playing cards, but in life they invariably take the form of trading on other people, and—Jane Austen would say—in these transactions the price is never right.

In the same scene there is more talk of improvements, and the conversation roams a little. In his sturdy way Sir Thomas supplies the answer to the moral questions we have been considering, questions about the priority of action, the sitting still and doing nothing, the staking all like a woman of spirit. What Thornton Lacey amounts to, in Mary Crawford's eyes, is a desire 'to shut out the church, sink the clergyman, and see only the respectable, elegant, modernized, and occasional residence of a man of independent fortune'. But Sir Thomas, now that his Whist is finished, joins the group at the round table and speaks of Thornton Lacey in quite different terms, offering a theory to support Edmund's quiet practice. 'He knows', Sir Thomas says, 'that human nature needs more lessons than a weekly sermon can convey, and that if he does not live among his parishioners and prove himself by constant attention their well-wisher and friend, he does very little either for their good or his own'. This is unanswerable. Life may be in some respects a game of cards, but some of the cards—as in Speculation—are not dealt, and there are certain respects in which the metaphor is simply an impertinence. When Sir Thomas speaks of a man's duty to his parishioners, the card-game comes to an end. *Homo ludens* is only part of the truth.

What stays in the mind from this scene is a wonderfully percep-tive art in which the movements of a social occasion provide, for some of the participants, all the meaning there is; and, for others, sufficient form to contain the visible feeling but not the turbulence. The two card-tables, the Parsonage, the rules of the game, the encounters; on these the waves of individual feeling break, declaring themselves, then falling back. This is the art of the thing. But it would be fruitless to effect a neat separation between this art and the morality which gives the composition its gravity and composure.


# NOTES

1. Jane Austen, *Letters*, edited by R. W. Chapman (Oxford University Press, second edition, 1952) pp. 299 foll.
2. *ibid.*, p. 317.
3. *ibid.*, p. 409.
4. *ibid.*, p. 409.
5. William James, *The Principles of Psychology* (Macmillan, 1907) i. 310.
6. Cf. Erich Fromm, 'Selfishness and Self-Love', *Psychiatry* (1939) ii. 507–23.
7. *Letters*, p. 375.
8. Anthony Ashley Cooper, Earl of Shaftesbury, *Characteristics of Men, Manners, Opinions, Times* (London, 1727) ii. 44.
9. Thomas Burnet, *Third Remarks upon an Essay concerning Human Knowledge* (London, 1699) p. 8. Quoted in Ernest Tuveson, 'The Origins of the "Moral Sense"', *Huntingdon Library Quarterly* (1948) xi. 241–59.
10. Francis Hutcheson, *An Essay on the Nature and Conduct of the Passions and Affections, with Illustrations on the Moral Sense* (London, 1727) p. xi.
11. *Characteristics*, ii. 45.

12. *ibid.*, ii. 46.

13. Adam Smith, *Essays Philosophical and Literary*, Part V, Ch. 2.

14. In *Billy Budd* Melville, to whom speculation on these matters is a natural activity, elucidates Claggart in somewhat similar terms: 'Now something such was Claggart, in whom was the mania of an evil nature, not engendered by vicious training or corrupting books or licentious living, but born with him and innate, in short, "a depravity according to nature"'. (Ch. 10.)

15. Quoted in R. W. Chapman's edition of *Mansfield Park* (Oxford University Press, 1953 impression) p. 351.

16. *Third Remarks*, p. 8.

17. Macaulay, *Works* (Longmans, Green, 1907) iv. 70.

18. For other implications in this scene, see P. R. Lynch, 'Speculation at Mansfield Park', *Notes and Queries* (January 1967) n.s. *XIV*. i. 21–22.

# IV

## LEARNING EXPERIENCE AND CHANGE

### Robert Garis

JANE AUSTEN's form is the comic drama of reason, in which the happy ending comes about not through the lucky disappearance of accidental impediments, but through a dramatic action in which one of the leading characters learns something important enough about reality and his own nature to experience a deep change of mind or heart. But she doesn't always succeed in making this learning process dramatic, or convincing, or significant; and it seems to me that some very plain and simple things remain to be said about when, how and why, and with what kind of character, she succeeds or fails.

Looking at the four middle novels as a group and taking it for granted that *Sense and Sensibility* and *Mansfield Park* are relatively unsuccessful and that *Pride and Prejudice* and above all *Emma* are magnificently successful, one sees immediately that pendulum swing between failure and success to which Marvin Mudrick has drawn attention, and one sees too that there is this same swing in Jane Austen's technique for representing the crucial learning experience. She succeeds when she is looking directly at the learning character and the learning experience, and seeing the rest of the action from this perspective, *through* this experience; she fails when this is not the case. This fairly predictable relation between cause and effect is worth some emphasis and attention when it's correctly identified as an index to a deeper distinction. For the decision not to put Marianne Dashwood's and Edmund Bertram's learning experience in the centre of the novel was no merely unlucky miscalculation of technique: in these novels Jane Austen was very deliberately busy elsewhere, busy giving insistent protection and support to Elinor Dashwood and Fanny Price who don't learn or change and who are emphatically praised for not needing to, but are nevertheless the leading characters, from whose point of view all the action is seen. We are dealing, then, with Jane Austen's deliberate refusal to give herself to the learning experience on which her drama of reason nevertheless depends; and she made this decision at considerable cost to her work and to herself. When she refuses to look at the learning process directly everything else in the novel suffers too, particularly the representation of the unchanging heroine. Insistent praise of Elinor and Fanny leads to distortions, falsities, failures of intelligence, tact and tone—in short, to unmistakable signs that Jane Austen is forcing her will rather than following her imagination. On the other hand, the decision to put Elizabeth Bennet's and Emma Woodhouse's learning experiences at the centre of the novel is an equally unmistakable sign that Jane Austen's sympathetic imagination was fully engaged with these characters; in consequence she gets everything else right. The learning experience not only works convincingly and accomplishes a major change of heart, but it also seems to happen of its own accord; and these two novels are also free from other signs of strain and falsity.

Learning brings all four characters closer to what Jane Austen means by her complex word 'sense.' The two chief meanings of this word are 'seeing well' and 'behaving well' and both meanings are in force in all the novels, but with different degrees of emphasis; once again we can see the pendulum swing. When in *Pride and Prejudice* and *Emma* the emphasis is on 'seeing well,' 'behaving well' seems to come about naturally. In *Sense and Sensibility* the emphasis on 'behaving well'—actually on 'behaving cautiously'—is so arbitrarily heavy, so resolutely blind to the instincts and interests it is suppressing, that 'seeing well' is not only slighted but deeply confused. In *Mansfield Park*, where 'behaving cautiously' is also heavily emphasized, Edmund does, in a convincing action, learn to see better, but this learning has almost nothing to do with learning about himself and produces no significant change, so that this serious and solemn novel is rather thin in meaning.

In *Sense and Sensibility* and *Mansfield Park* learning feels like losing something, giving up some hope or some possibility; after an unsuccessful gamble at freer living, Marianne and Edmund creep back defeated to the boundaries of sense. In *Pride and Prejudice* and *Emma* learning feels like gaining something positive, eagerly and energetically chosen once it is recognized. Elizabeth and Emma in fact *fall in love* with sense; Marianne and Edmund fall out of love into sense, which they then accept as the better way, though both characters are then of course alleged to fall in love again with habitués of this cautious world.

Finally, Jane Austen achieved her most brilliant drama of learning and change, in *Emma*, only when she at last brought the learning character into the range of her irony and when she reduced the learning experience to radical simplicity. These two decisions are virtually identical: Emma can be looked at ironically exactly because her mistakes are total and totally self-induced. But Emma's 'simple' comic self-discovery is paradoxically one of the most complex, most convincingly inevitable, most vividly rendered things in art. *Emma* is Jane Austen's masterpiece. The wonderfully beautiful *Persuasion* is the only work, and the masterpiece, of an essentially different writer.

To say that Jane Austen forced her will rather than following her imagination in *Sense and Sensibility*, is not to locate the source of the novel's failure in Jane Austen's praise of the will *in itself*. All of her novels take the necessity of the will for granted. The trouble with *Sense and Sensibility* is that it's a very *wilful* argument for the will. On almost every page we see the signs of Jane Austen's extraordinary intelligence, and on almost every page we see that intelligence distorted and defeated by a stronger force.

One of the few times this doesn't happen is when Jane Austen is giving a straightforward analytic account of Elinor's will at work. There is one most dangerous argument against the thesis that sense is preferable to sensibility: Marianne's suspicion that Elinor's self-control is valueless because she has no really strong feelings to control. At least once in the novel Jane Austen's powerful mind and firm sense of justice made her attempt an explicit rebuttal of this suspicion and the result is the extremely interesting and successful Chapter 22. In this chapter the image of the mind's operation is decidedly quantitative, spatial and mechanistic—unattractive words to modern ears. Chapter 22 concerns Elinor's discovery that Edward has for some time been secretly engaged to Lucy Steele. When she first hears the news her 'astonishment' would 'have been as painful as it was strong, had not an immediate disbelief of the assertion attended it': the point is that even Elinor might on this occasion have been unable to repress her feelings if the mind were not a receptacle which can hold only one strong emotion at a time. This argument lacks finesse, perhaps, and sounds too triumphantly ingenious as a defence of Elinor, yet the psychology seems to me perfectly convincing. When Lucy follows up her assertion with confirming evidence, 'disbelief' is gradually dispelled in a process which represents Elinor's mind as a set of scales, with disbelief on one side and the little pieces of Lucy's evidence gradually accumulating on the other until the balance shifts; again the image is convincing, and the inexorably gathering weight of the evidence makes a powerful effect. When the balance shifts, the mind is now emptied of disbelief and begins to experience pain, and Jane Austen's image for Elinor's way of handling this is unmistakably mechanistic: 'an exertion of spirits, which increased with her increase of emotion.' If this too is perfectly acceptable, the reason of course is that it is all but impossible to render the operation of the will in any other than mechanistic terms. Hence our modern distrust of the faculty. But Jane Austen isn't nervous about this, nor need she be; and historical imagination, if nothing else is available, can easily counteract any irrelevant modern uneasiness about this clear account of a psychological process that does in fact occur. (Whether or not it should occur is another matter entirely.) If the rest of *Sense and Sensibility* had the security and clarity of this chapter, all would be well. For Jane Austen's failure with Elinor isn't at all due to her legitimate admiration of the will. It is rather that in her own wilful contrivance of occasions on which Elinor can be praised for manifesting this element of sense, Jane Austen loses her own common sense.

Most of the troubles she invents for Elinor, in order to praise her correct handling of them, are simply hard to believe. The scene I have just described is an exception; it makes splendidly good sense that Elinor should use her will to control her painful emotions in front of a woman who is maliciously trying to make her suffer. But what lies behind the scene, Edward's engagement to Lucy, makes very little sense. Mr. Bennet's youthful infatuation with his pretty and hysterical wife isn't discordant with his rather trivially ironic kind of sense; Sir Thomas Bertram's marriage to the nearly subnormal Lady Bertram is perhaps even more convincing than Jane

Austen herself realized; but Edward's infatuation with someone as vulgar as Lucy Steele is out of key with everything we know about him. And Jane Austen's defence—he was younger in those days, she was prettier and she set her cap for him—is so weak that it actually underlines the obstinacy of will responsible for the whole contrivance.

The love-relation between Edward and Elinor is almost worse. One can accept the possibility of an *initial* conflict between Edward's love for Elinor and the sense of honour that forbids him either to break his engagement with Lucy or to tell Elinor about it. But one can't accept this conflict as an abiding and insoluble dilemma without falling into one or the other of two mutually exclusive conclusions which are both fatal to Jane Austen's scheme. One is the suspicion that Marianne voices: though caution, propriety and protocol matter more to us than they do to Marianne, even we can see that Elinor's and Edward's love must be a very poor business, hardly worth the name of love, if it can't give them any help whatsoever toward clearing up misunderstandings, doubts and depressions of such magnitude. But if we try dutifully to believe in their love, then we can't escape the equally awkward conclusion on the other side. Since even Elinor's unparalleled prudence cannot save her from such misery, then prudence seems in the major concerns of life to lack just the *practical* value that Jane Austen claims for it successfully in the minor concerns. What's the good of being the kind of person who gets the packing done and keeps the budget, if you have to depend on doubtful introspection to find out whether the man you love loves you, and on sheer luck to get married to him once you're sure he does? Marianne's indecorous directness would have done very well here, and would have amounted to very good sense indeed. Jane Austen really can't have her argument both ways, but she often tries to in this peculiar novel, and she seldom seems conscious that she is arguing against herself.

I hear a hint of such consciousness in the most egregious falsity of all, the trouble that Elinor gets into because of *her* vow to keep Lucy's secret. This perverse invention is a mild version of the kind of outrageous act with which the healthy part of a sick mind signals to the outside world that it needs and wants help. Here it is Jane Austen's good sense that is crying for help. There is no rational reason whatsoever for Elinor's having contracted in the first place to keep from her beloved sister and mother a secret which she never asked to be told: she ought simply to have refused. Her over-excitable mother and sister would have grieved excessively on her account and they might have expressed their resentment openly to Edward; but these seem minor ills compared with the betrayal of family affection which Elinor's silence amounts to. But Jane Austen's obsession with the need for self-control infects her heroine with a similar obsession, in which self-control becomes an end rather than a means:

> From their counsel, or their conversation she knew she could receive no assistance, their tenderness and sorrow must add to her distress, while her self-command would neither receive encouragement from their example nor from their praise. She was stronger alone.
>
> (ch. 23)

A repellent passage, and worse is to follow. For Jane Austen's obsession carries Elinor beyond silence into actual lies, which incite Marianne not only to splendidly just disdain but also to that unexampled secrecy about her own feelings and actions on which so much of the ensuing disturbance depends. It is one of the most complete messes in fiction; the betrayed imagination has rarely taken such vengeance.

Jane Austen's decision not to look directly at Marianne's learning experience makes for emptiness rather than falsity at the crucial junctures; but before these there have been plenty of falsities with Marianne too. She is supposed to be both very attractive and very foolish, but this works out well only in the parodistic writing early in the novel, when she is most self-consciously living up to the arbitrary code of sensibility. With Willoughby her behaviour is far more attractive than Jane Austen's scheme can support. Professor Mudrick has written with keen and spirited intelligence about this: Marianne's spontaneous love, courage and anger command more than affection and pity, they command admiration. The criticism of sensibility therefore depends solely on the consequences of this behaviour. But both sisters, after all, have been deceived by their lovers, both have *seen* badly, and if Marianne's suffering—the breakdown and the accompanying éclat—seems quantitatively greater than Elinor's drab depressions, this isn't a moral criterion which we can use with any dignity and it happens also to be contradicted by Jane Austen's explicit claim that Elinor in fact is suffering just as intensely, though more quietly. Nor does Elinor's trouble escape the attention of Mrs. Jennings and others. Both the practical and the moral issues are confused. Jane Austen is trying to work *indirectly* here, of course: the fate of Colonel Brandon's ward reminds us of the really high dangers to which Marianne's reckless impropriety might have led. But Brandon's embarrassingly theatrical narrative is flatly inapplicable. Dim as our understanding of Marianne is, we are positive that she would never get into this sort of trouble. Early in the novel, when Elinor questions the propriety of Willoughby's having taken Marianne to see Mrs. Smith's house, Marianne's argument comes straight out of the book of sensibility: "'If there had been any real impropriety in what I did, I should have been sensible of it at the time, for we always know when we are acting wrong, and with such a conviction I could have had no pleasure.'" (ch. 13). One sees the danger Jane Austen is arguing against—the danger of a standard of morality founded on sensibility, on taste, rather than on principles. But this episode is quite out of scale with the serious issues of sexual conduct, and no reader has ever considered the possibility that Marianne might have pursued her impetuous love for Willoughby to the point of entering into an illicit relation with him. Nor of course does the representation of Willoughby really alter this impression. Jane Austen's contemporaries would have been more sensitive to, and thrilled by, the echo of Lovelace in the characterization than we are, but the reason why we are not thrilled is that Jane Austen hasn't given us the wherewithal. The facts are there but the feelings are missing: Jane Austen fortunately wasn't interested in or capable of Richardsonian pornography about such a figure, but taste and good sense are here ironically misapplied, since they have the unfortunate effect of robbing Marianne's learning experience of any substantial meaning whatsoever. She learns that one can love twice, that Brandon isn't senile, that Elinor has been marvellous, but Jane Austen has made her simply immune to the really serious danger of confusing sensibility with morality.

But in this truly perverse novel, the truth will out in unexpected ways, and it is actually Elinor who for a moment—one of the most powerful in the novel—responds in dangerously sexual feeling to Willoughby's attraction:

> She felt that his influence over her mind was heightened by circumstances which ought not in reason to have weight; by that person of uncommon attraction, that open, affectionate and lively manner which it was no merit to possess; and by that still ardent love for Marianne, which it was not even innocent to indulge. But she felt that it was so, long, long before she could feel his influence less.

(ch. 45)

Jane Austen has at last found an extraordinarily interesting subject, somewhat late: and one can't of course seriously blame her for not having rewritten the three hundred and thirty two pages to bring them into line with it, 'that person of uncommon attraction, that open, affectionate and lively manner *which it was no merit to possess*'—the words I have italicized cry out for contradiction. It is as if Jane Austen had suddenly realized that her novel amounted to a sterile refusal to consider the mysterious complexities of the Gospels. For *Sense and Sensibility* is an argument against the story of Mary and Martha. I agree with Jane Austen that there is plenty to be said for Martha; but you can't say it justly, let alone interestingly, if you cannot frankly and openly see the point about Mary. Elinor's temptation shows how fearfully Jane Austen has refused to see it.

Her refusals in *Mansfield Park*, and the discords to which they lead, present of course a far more complex and subtle case, and one is always eager to read a new defence of a novel which contains so many of Jane Austen's best pages. But Lionel Trilling's remarkable essay—which contains so many of *his* best pages—is more faithful to all the other writers and issues he discusses than to his principal subject. On Mary Crawford he is very good, though I wish he had shown in a little detail that her speeches 'diminish in charm as we read the novel a second time'; and when he calls her the first example in literature of modern 'insincerity' he diminishes her significance somewhat. If Professor Mudrick's admiration for Mary's wit and energy is certainly too automatic and unquestioning, Professor Trilling suppresses important evidence when he ignores the baldly moralistic language in which Mary is actually denounced by both Edmund and Fanny. On the ideal of duty and the life of ceremony that Mansfield represents, Professor Mudrick is again somewhat automatic but he argues far more honestly than Professor Trilling, who mentions almost everything one objects to in the novel, but then doesn't add it all up at the end. His portrait of the meekly censorious Fanny Price is, in its quieter way, even more devastating than Professor Mudrick's, yet he claims to be defending the conception; and his account of the amateur theatricals makes us see the imbalances and strains of this episode more clearly even as he is trying to explain them away. It is a form of sleight of hand. The account of Sir Thomas, for instance, is at once very full and very illogical. Sir Thomas is the only father in Jane Austen 'to whom admiration

67

is given'; yet since he 'betrays the daughters of his blood', Mansfield is 'governed by an authority all too fallible'; but Fanny's judgement that everything at Mansfield is 'dear to her heart and thoroughly perfect in her eyes' is 'not ironical'; after this correct account of the conflicting elements, here is the summation: 'Fanny's loving praise of Mansfield, which makes the novel's last word, does glance at ironies and encompass ironies,' and the example given is Lady Bertram's 'unregenerate . . . life of cushioned ease.' Since Professor Trilling can't mean to be emphasizing superfluously Fanny's knowledge that Lady Bertram exists, he must mean that her view glances at *our* ironic view of her. But this is demonstrably untrue, and this sort of sophistry, which shows up in most defences of *Mansfield Park*, more than vindicates the animus of Professor Mudrick's attack on the novel's refusal to face its inner contradictions.

The action of *Mansfield Park* makes no sense whatsoever unless we feel that there are serious imperfections and gaps in the world of Mansfield, and at the beginning of the novel Jane Austen does in fact make us feel this strongly and see it clearly. Edmund's love for Mary stands for his longing for the qualities that are missing, or brutalized, at Mansfield. And when he forgets Fanny's need to ride for health in his excitement at seeing Mary ride for pleasure; when the groom amplifies the point by admiring Mary's skill and courage as a beginner and contrasting it inoffensively with Fanny's famous timidities and ineptitudes; when Fanny soon afterwards is exhausted to the point of illness by gathering roses in the sun and two walks to Mrs. Norris's house; when we see Edmund as Mary's eager and energetic companion, but as Fanny's affectionately dutiful, and in this instance guilty, protector; when we hear him praise Mary's playfulness, wit and amiable heart—when we follow this beautifully contrived dramatic action it is perfectly clear what Edmund longs for: a woman who shares his sisters' kind of physical energy and self-confidence without their mindless vanity and stolid insensitivity, and who shares something like Fanny's emotional sensitivity and clear mind without her poverty of body and spirit. Now the action in which Edmund discovers that Mary does not in fact represent what he longs for seems to me clear and convincing. It is not only that her speeches diminish in charm on second reading; it is not only that she is insincere; it is that we gradually suffer an almost physical loss of balance as we hear her genuine charm, good humour, wit and feeling for others so often and so disconcertingly contradicted by painfully cheap lapses in taste, tone, feeling and sheer intelligence. We ourselves, then, actually *experience*, along with Edmund, her lack of integrity, soundness, dependability. And though Edmund's and Fanny's language about her at the end is too grossly moralistic to match the subtlety of the characterization, it isn't irrelevant language. We are perfectly convinced that Edmund does come to feel, and rightly, that Mary is not the woman for him, and this is an important thing to learn.

But if he seems to take too long to learn it, that is because he is not at the same time learning anything about himself. What his love for Mary meant at the beginning of the novel has been silently discarded as a major theme, and at the end when his 'eyes are opened' all they see is Mary's unworthiness. His censorious language isn't inappropriate to her callous worldly minimization of Henry's and Maria's conduct, nor to his own vocation; but what is not inappropriate may yet seem crudely mechanical. In Edmund's tone and diction what I hear, in fact, is Jane Austen's deliberate blunting of her *own* sense of language: ' "No reluctance, no horror, no feminine —shall I say? no modest loathings!—This is what the world does." As for Edmund's own part in the experience, ' "the charm is broken. . . . Perhaps it is best for me—since it leaves me so little to regret. Not so, however. Gladly would I submit to all the increased pain of losing her, rather than have to think of her as I do . . . all this together most grievously convinced me that I had never understood her before, and that, as far as related to mind, it had been the creature of my own imagination, not Miss Crawford, that I had been too apt to dwell on for many months past." ' (ch. 47). This isn't the vocabulary of serious moral drama. Having been led astray by the imagined charm of the world, Edmund returns, enlightened but depressed, to the fold. Returns rather self-righteously too: where is even the kind and degree of self-criticism appropriate to a religious tract?

The convincing action of Edmund's disillusionment hasn't then amounted to anything worth the name of education. Yet Jane Austen's refusals in *Mansfield Park* are quiet ones: mature tact avoids the melodrama and the other loud falsities and strains of *Sense and Sensibility*. But her insistence that we admire and love her sickly heroine isn't really the better for being quietly, rather than emphatically, ruthless. And it is disturbing to realize that it is chiefly herself against whom the quiet ruthlessness is directed, in rebuke of what

Professor Trilling, in another connection, finely calls 'the exigent energies of her actual self.'

When we emerge into *Pride and Prejudice* from the constricted world of *Sense and Sensibility*, we encounter the character of Elizabeth Bennet with a feeling of enormous release. Freedom, wit, high spirits, physical energy, open affections, the capacity to charm and the frank interest in charming—Jane Austen has given her heroine all these without stint and without a hint of cautious pessimism, in the frank intention to win our love and approval and the full knowledge that she will succeed. And she rewards her heroine's courageous independence handsomely, in a joyous liberation from Elinor's obsessive prudence. Jane Austen was never again to achieve—or perhaps to need—this exhilaration, which is undoubtedly the most important characteristic of *Pride and Prejudice*. But there is another aspect of freedom in this novel which links it with the far less exuberant *Emma*. In liberating herself from caution, Jane Austen has by no means suppressed or distorted her interest in sense. Elizabeth Bennet is something of a rebel against pretension and pomposity and pride, but when she learns to love Darcy, she sees his strength of principle and soundness of judgement, even his stiff reserve, not as limitations to her freedom, but as means to her own self-fulfilment. In marrying sense, she gives up neither her ego, her wit nor her playfulness; she can laugh lovingly at Darcy's mannerisms without hurting him or in the slightest degree expressing disrespect for him. In that union of opposites that love makes possible, Elizabeth's satiric playfulness—the one talent and habit she notably shares with Jane Austen—is deepened and made fruitful by love.

Yet these meanings—that Darcy represents sense and that Elizabeth's learning experience amounts to falling in love with sense —aren't at all fully achieved or finely worked. The creative energy was entirely given to making the favourite delightful, and the word 'favourite' is an index both to the novel's charm and to its limitations. The character of Darcy, and the dramatic action of the learning experience and of the whole novel, are only sketches, and often there is a real lack of unity. But a sketch is not a blank, and a lack of unity isn't the same thing as wilful disunity. Darcy's theatrically arrogant, even insolent rudeness at the beginning suits his theatrically dazzling wealth and good looks; but if it isn't, to say the least, very finely adjusted with his sense, one doesn't feel this as false and strained. Jane Austen wanted her favourite to marry 'well' in both senses of the word—'glamorously' and 'wisely'—an ambitious and generous but not self-contradictory undertaking. Yet the fact of course remains that we don't 'hear' Darcy very well; his identity isn't firmly realized.

The learning experience too is an ambitious and generous sketch. At the end of *Mansfield Park* Edmund has learned substantially nothing about himself; halfway through *Pride and Prejudice* Elizabeth seems to have learned everything: 'I have courted prepossession and ignorance, and driven reason away . . . Till this moment, I never knew myself.' (ch. 36). The language rings out clearly in the theatre, and one hears Jane Austen's youthful ambition pretty clearly too; but this is a rather hollow set-piece of self-knowledge. And the physical and psychological action in which Elizabeth learns to love Darcy is full of awkward contrivances. After the coincidental meeting at Pemberley, both Elizabeth and Jane Austen seem to be nervously trying to think of just the right words:

> Such a change in a man of so much pride, excited not only astonishment but gratitude—for to love, ardent love, it must be attributed; and as such its impression on her was of a sort to be encouraged, as by no means unpleasing, though it could not be exactly defined. She respected, she esteemed, she was grateful to him, she felt a real interest in his welfare; and she only wanted to know how far she wished that welfare to depend upon herself, and how far it would be for the happiness of both that she should employ the power, which her fancy told her she still possessed, of bringing on the renewal of his addresses.
>
> (ch. 44)

When she does know this, the language firmly establishes Darcy as the man of sense, but seems perfunctory:

> It was an union that must have been to the advantage of both; by her ease and liveliness, his mind might have been softened, his manners improved, and from his judgment, information, and knowledge of the world, she must have received benefit of greater importance.
>
> (ch. 50)

From this point on all the positive moves toward resolution are theatrical: Darcy's secret exertions about Lydia, Lady Catherine's insolence, Mr. Collins's letter, Mrs. Bennet's rudeness—we accept it all and enjoy it all, but we are learning nothing, nor is Elizabeth.

71

The one non-theatrical scene is, interestingly enough, a threat to the happy ending: Elizabeth's painful attempt to convince her father of her love for Darcy. The scene is beautifully conceived and in part well executed, and here the theme of falling in love with sense gets its most poignant expression. But Jane Austen hurries through a summary of the learning process:

> at length, by repeated assurances that Mr. Darcy was really the object of her choice, by explaining the gradual change which her estimation of him had undergone, relating her absolute certainty that his affection was not the work of a day, but had stood the test of many months suspense, and enumerating with energy all his good qualities, she did conquer her father's incredulity, and reconcile him to the match.
>
> (ch. 55)

It is likely that the completely matured art of *Emma* would in any case have mastered the problems of language and action that Jane Austen's generous awkwardness fumbled in *Pride and Prejudice*, but as it happened her genius in inventing the ironical view of Emma, and the radical simplification of the learning experience, simply by-passed these problems. Elizabeth learns to love a man whom she has detested on first acquaintance, doesn't know very well and rarely sees; Emma learns to love a man she has always known and respected, who has in fact always been the most important man in her life and virtually the only important man. She sees him almost daily and almost always with pronounced pleasure; when seeing him isn't pleasant (after their quarrel about Harriet and after Box Hill) it is because she cannot bear to be on bad terms with him, and she takes unusual pains to remedy the situation. And these quarrels and reconciliations make up by far her deepest and indeed most 'passionate' experiences; in them her behaviour is most natural and alive. As a result Jane Austen isn't put to the trouble of inventing any subtle language for gradual change of one kind of feeling into its direct opposite, nor of inventing plausible ways to bring Emma and Knightley together. The ironic perspective further simplifies matters. In *Pride and Prejudice* the highly recognizable shape of the basic fable telegraphs the ending, but in *Emma* we simply *know* what will happen.

All this is more strikingly true in the learning process. Elizabeth, in thinking about Darcy's letter, must conduct a complicated rational inquiry in which she compares in considerable detail the two contradictory reports of Darcy's actions concerning Wickham and her sister; and she must also collect a lot of evidence before she can learn to understand how Darcy's basically principled, generous nature happens to express itself in such misleading ways. Learning that her own admirable love of wit and character-analysis has led her astray is particularly hard, because her mistakes are almost unavoidable: Wickham is an exceptionally open, attractive, likeable and generally well-liked young man who happens to be a liar, and whose lies deceive almost everybody else too; Darcy's behaviour likewise offends nearly everybody; anybody would find him an extremely puzzling man. We too are to some extent misled in all this; the shape of the fable makes us ready and eager to believe the opposite of these 'first impressions' but offers no further help.

Emma's mistakes on the other hand are of startling simplicity, and so is what she learns about herself. Knightley's language isn't too strong: ' "Better be without sense, than misapply it as you do." ' (ch. 8). And with Harriet Emma abuses not only her reason but her own prejudices about rank and gentility. 'Clever' as she unmistakably is, all of her intellectual peers see things that she can't see, nor do they fail to tell her about them: John Knightley tells her that Mr. Elton is in fact courting her and his brother has earlier told her that Elton will never marry injudiciously; Knightley also tells her that there is a special private understanding between Jane Fairfax and Frank Churchill, and Frank himself is so sure that *she* knows this that he almost seeks the release of unburdening himself with a full confession. Her scandalmongering with Frank and her rudeness to Miss Bates are offences against exactly the kind of good manners and good principles she genuinely possesses; and she discovers her mistakes in equally simple ways. It takes no detailed examination of conflicting evidence to discover that Mr. Elton is courting her. After Knightley's reproof of her behaviour toward Miss Bates, she defends herself only for a moment, since she understands perfectly what was wrong with what she did.The discovery why it was 'so much worse that Harriet should be in love with Mr. Knightley, than with Frank Churchill' 'darted through her, with the speed of an arrow.' Serious reflection is to be sure needed to 'understand, thoroughly understand her own heart' (ch. 47); but what needs understanding is *how long* Knightley had been 'so dear to her' and since the answer is 'always,' it comes pretty quickly. We have seen the truths Emma learns dramatically enacted on every page of the novel.

About herself Emma learns nothing as subtle, perhaps, as Elizabeth's analytic understanding of her own nature. But she learns something far more basic, and more exciting: she learns an *act*, the act of sustained self-criticism. What that self-criticism in this instance reveals to her—her wilful blindness—may be forgotten, but we know that self-criticism is in a fair way to becoming a habit. For she marries Knightley.

It is conceivable that these simplicities, which I have been presenting as the signs of Jane Austen's genius, may seem to some readers signs that *Emma* isn't about anything very important. I am of course taking the apparent paradox for granted: one of the world's most complex and finely worked novels owes these qualities in part to the radical simplicity of its design. To speak at length about that complexity would be a great pleasure if I had more space. Professor Mudrick, however, has argued in his eccentric view of *Emma* that there has been no real change at all, much less a significant one, and that Knightley is in for a hard time as the future victim of Emma's domination. And I cannot ignore the question whether in making Emma marry Knightley, whose sense is unquestionable but whose glamour is minimal, Jane Austen isn't making the kind of refusal that I have objected to in *Sense and Sensibility* and *Mansfield Park*. What distinguishes this marriage from that of Marianne and Brandon, or that of Edmund and Fanny?

To these objections the right answer is simple and compendious: the energy and vitality of both Emma and Knightley. About Emma's energetic self-love, her intelligence and style, her assiduous if inadequate attempts at self-knowledge, and about the reasons why all these make us feel 'kind to her,' Professor Trilling has written with brilliant and unanswerable insight, with subtlety and without sophistry. Emma's personal force commands attention; the mistakes of such a person are irresistibly interesting, and the arrant simplicity of the mistakes brings interest to the point of fascination. And Emma has exactly the kind of depth of personality that suits her kind of force, the kind that shows itself most vividly in her capacity to feel shame, as she does so movingly in those 'extraordinary' tears after Box Hill. Learning will never give her the sort of womanly tenderness that Professor Mudrick rightly finds wanting in her, nor is she likely to lose her interest in dominating other people, particularly women; but the novel neither claims explicitly that she will change in these ways, nor generates the kind of atmosphere that would imply it. As for the quality of her love for Knightley one wants to be careful not to make the best the enemy of the good, in love as in every other human concern; one wants also to be as careful as Jane Austen has been in her language about what Emma feels. Knightley is 'dear to her'; he has 'influence, such influence'; 'there had never been a time when... his regard for her had not been infinitely the most dear'; nor are these carefully just words undercut by other equally careful words that emphasize her will: 'Mr. Knightley must marry no one but herself'; 'her happiness depended on being *first* with Mr. Knightley, first in interest and affection.' (ch. 47). Nothing is forced here; Jane Austen knows her heroine.

The notion that Knightley will be dominated by this wilful woman amounts to refusal to see and hear his masculine energy, force and vitality. The clarity with which he represents sense might induce some readers with bad ears to find him stolidly rather than energetically masculine, but readers with bad ears will have a lot of other troubles with *Emma*. Knightley's strong English is one of the book's clearest successes. The splendid vehemence of his final remark in the argument about Frank—' "He is a person I never think of from one month's end to another" ' (ch. 18)—is doubly useful as an example, since the masculinity here is not only energetic but jealous. But perhaps the most brilliant instance is a scene in which we do in fact only *hear* Knightley, through the open window of the Bates's apartments: we hear him offering to do errands for the Bates, refusing to do any for the Coles who have their own servants, almost deciding to join the little party when he hears that Emma is there, deciding not to when he hears that Frank is there too, engaging in some strong satire to entertain and mock the people who are listening, then riding away without saying good-bye in the middle of one of Miss Bates' thanksgivings. His energetic activity in the open air is brilliantly contrasted with the strained atmosphere indoors. And Mrs. Weston's remarks sum up his way of dealing with the closed society which he so successfully inhabits, and dominates: ' "I do not think Mr. Knightley would be much disturbed by Miss Bates. Little things do not irritate him. She might talk on; and if he wanted to say any thing himself, he would only talk louder, and drown her voice." '(ch. 27).

As for readers who fret about Emma's marrying her father-image, better be without Freud than misapply it as they do. Knightley has scolded Emma for years and will continue to do so, but there is an unmistakably alive sexual tension in these dialogues between the masculine directness of sense and the graceful ingenuities of the feminine will. Marianne and Edmund, once chastened, present no 'otherness' to their partners; their quasi-incestuous love fits the definition that Stephen Dedalus quotes from Aquinas in the library scene in *Ulysses*: 'an avarice of the emotions . . . the love so given to one near in blood is covetously withheld from some stranger who, it may be, hungers for it.' It is Jane Austen's avarice that is revealed here, of course. But she grew out of this bad habit and I can't think of a more vivid registration of masculine and feminine voices in a sexually based conflict than the end of the argument about Frank Churchill:

> 'My dear Emma, your own good sense could not endure such a puppy when it came to the point.'
> 'I will say no more about him,' cried Emma, 'you turn everything to evil. We are both prejudiced; you against, I for him; and we have no chance of agreeing till he is really here.'
> 'Prejudiced! I am not prejudiced.'
> 'But I am very much, and without being at all ashamed of it. My love for Mr. and Mrs. Weston gives me a decided prejudice in his favour.'
> 'He is a person I never think of from one month's end to another.'
>
> (ch. 18)

For Jane Austen herself the ironic perspective on her heroine and the simplicity of her learning experience opened up an opportunity for an energy of language that goes far beyond the masteries of exactitude and subtlety that we associate most readily with her name: the language of *Emma* manifests the kind of creativity that we associate with the name of Shakespeare. I have spoken of the passage in which Emma thinks about Mr. Elton's proposal as a learning process of significant simplicity, compared with Elizabeth's thinking about Darcy's letter. But the registration of Emma's mind in action (in Chapter 16), as she deals with the incontrovertible facts of the case, has an intensity, a complexity, a vocal power that makes it the comic equivalent, in both method and value, of Macbeth's 'If it were done when 'tis done.'

> The hair was curled, and the maid sent away, and Emma sat down to think and be miserable.—It was a wretched business, indeed!—Such an overthrow of everything she had been wishing for!—Such a development of every thing most unwelcome!—Such a blow for Harriet!—That was the worst of all. Every part of it brought pain and

humiliation, of some sort or other; but, compared with the evil to Harriet, all was light; and she would gladly have submitted to feel yet more mistaken—more in error—more disgraced by mis-judgment, than she actually was, could the effects of her blunders have been confined to herself.

'If I had not persuaded Harriet into liking the man, I could have born anything. He might have doubled his presumption to me—But poor Harriet!'

How she could have been so deceived!—He protested that he had never thought seriously of Harriet—never! She looked back as well as she could; but it was all confusion. She had taken up the idea, she supposed, and made everything bend to it. His manners, however, must have been unmarked, wavering, dubious, or she could not have been so misled.

The picture!—How eager he had been about the picture!—and the charade!—and an hundred other circumstances;—how clearly they had seemed to point at Harriet. To be sure, the charade, with its 'ready wit' —but then, the 'soft eyes'—in fact it suited neither; it was a jumble without taste or truth. Who could have seen through such thick-headed nonsense?

Certainly she had often, especially of late, thought his manners to herself unnecessarily gallant; but it had passed as his way, as a mere error of judgment, of knowledge, of taste, as one proof among others that he had not always lived in the best society, that with all the gentleness of his address, true elegance was sometimes wanting; but, till this very day, she had never, for an instant, suspected it to mean anything but grateful respect to her as Harriet's friend.

To Mr. John Knightley was she indebted for her first idea on the subject, for the first start of its possibility. There was no denying that those brothers had penetration. She remembered what Mr. Knightley had once said to her about Mr. Elton, the caution he had given, the conviction he had professed that Mr. Elton would never marry indiscreetly; and blushed to think how much truer a knowledge of his character had been there shewn than any she had reached herself. It was dreadfully mortifying; but Mr. Elton was proving himself, in many respects, the very reverse of what she had meant and believed him; proud, assuming, conceited; very full of his own claims, and little concerned about the feelings of others. . . .

Perhaps it was not fair to expect him to feel how very much he was her inferior in talent, and all the elegancies of mind. The very want of such equality might prevent his perception of it. . . . But he had fancied her in love with him; that evidently must have been his dependence; and after raving a little about the seeming incongruity of gentle manners and a conceited head, Emma was obliged in common honesty to stop and admit that her own behaviour to him had been so complaisant and obliging, so full of courtesy and attention, as (supposing her real motive unperceived) might warrant a man of ordinary observation and delicacy, like Mr. Elton, in fancying himself a very decided favourite. If *she* had so misinterpreted his feelings, she had little right to wonder that *he*, with self-interest to blind him, should have mistaken her's.

The first error and the worst lay at her door. It was foolish, it was wrong to take so active a part in bringing any two people together. It was adventuring too far, assuming too much, making light of what ought to be serious, a trick of what ought to be simple. She was quite concerned and ashamed, and resolved to do such things no more.

'Here have I,' said she, 'actually talked poor Harriet into being very much attached to this man. She might never have thought of him but for me; and certainly never would have thought of him with hope, if I had not assured her of his attachment, for she is as modest and humble as I used to think him. Oh! that I had been satisfied with persuading her not to accept young Martin. There I was quite right. That was well done of me; but there I should have stopped, and left the rest to time and chance. I was introducing her into good company, and giving her the opportunity of pleasing some one worth having; I ought not to have attempted more. But now, poor girl, her peace is cut up for some time. I have been but half a friend to her; and if she were *not* to feel this disappointment so very much, I am sure I have not an idea of anybody else who would be at all desirable for her;—William Coxe—Oh! no, I could not endure William Coxe—expert young lawyer.'

She stopt to blush and laugh at her own relapse, and then resumed a more serious, more dispiriting cogitation upon what had been, and might be, and must be. The distressing explanation she had to make to Harriet, and all that poor Harriet would be suffering, with the awkwardness of future meetings, the difficulties of continuing or discontinuing the acquaintance, of subduing feelings, concealing resentment, and avoiding éclat, were enough to occupy her in most unmirthful reflections some time longer, and she went to bed at last with nothing settled but the conviction of her having blundered most dreadfully.

After the rapid details of the first sentence, which enact Emma's impatience, her 'misery' begins in a tone of slightly exaggerated sighing; the faintly theatrical exclamations flow too easily and cost too little. The thought of Harriet's pain brings some plain-speaking:

'That was worst of all.' But this doesn't last, and we listen with high irony to the fulsome resolutions that follow: 'and she would gladly have submitted to feel yet more mistaken—more in error—more disgraced by mis-judgement, than she actually was, could the effects of her blunders have been confined to herself.' Not an entirely meaningful resolution: Emma's mistakes were total, a fact that she cannot help 'knowing' though she can be very adroit at not facing it head-on. The writing is so exact that we can hear her actually hiding the facts from herself by the 'courageously realistic' language with which she is emphatically acknowledging them: 'Mistaken ... error ... disgraced ... blunders': only the highest verbal genius could get us to hear the 'acting' that is going on in this language. Not that our hearing this means that we regard Emma as incapable of honesty: no easy mockery is taking place.

The third paragraph begins the rational inquiry into how it all happened, to which the answer is of course very simple, as Emma already knows. But in the faintly bored inflections of 'She had taken up the idea, she supposed, and made everything bend to it' we hear how self-protective Emma's gingerly progress into the cold-water of self-criticism is going to be; the boredom also registers the *familiarity* of the experience—Emma is repeating a form of self-criticism learned by rote. And this becomes plain when she turns the really *active* emotion of anger against Elton himself: 'His manners, however, must have been unmarked, wavering, dubious, or she could not have been so misled.' The three adjectives begin the process of working herself up into a rage which culminates in the brilliantly comic pitch of vocal intensity at the end of the next paragraph: 'Who could have seen through such thick-headed nonsense?' The diction—as in 'jumble' or 'thick-headed nonsense'—is far outside the decorum that Emma holds herself to in social conversation: the effect is at once to bring us into the most vividly immediate contact with her thinking and to guarantee the energetic vitality of her personality.

This explosion clears the air for the new pretence of serious investigation: 'Certainly she had often, of late, thought his manners to herself unnecessarily gallant.' This beautifully contrived blend of honesty and dishonesty—for Emma is really claiming to have had insight, to have seen through the nonsense—shows that there is a long way to go before anything can be faced squarely. The twists and turns of Ema's mind, as she advances toward knowledge and then finds a way to resist its impact, are of a breath-taking inventiveness; every sentence is worth attention. 'Perhaps it was not fair to expect him to feel how very much he was her inferior in talent, and all the elegancies of mind. The very want of such equality might prevent his perception of it': here the self-congratulating ingenuity of the argument proves, by its poised 'cleverness', that Mr. Elton's scorn of Harriet has actually caused some disturbance. 'She was quite concerned and ashamed, and resolved to do such things no more': the indirect discourse encourages our scepticism and we note that these are not quite the accents of 'common honesty' nor of Emma's most energetic feelings. The blush and the laugh, of course, bring her energy into full play; and the diction that follows is extremely carefully chosen for its unusual weight and thickness: the 'more serious, more dispiriting cogitation' and the 'most unmirthful reflections' guarantee the depth of Emma's mind, and the fact that the truth about herself has reached that depth, although of course her renewed high spirits after a night's sleep testify to some new evasions as well as to her valuable energy.

This superb writing is certainly the sort of thing Professor Trilling had in mind when he noted that one of the reasons why we feel kind toward Emma is that 'the narrative technique of the novel brings us very close to [Emma] and makes us aware of each misstep she will make.' If my view of *Emma* differs from his, it is because this 'narrative technique' is for him only the first, most obvious thing to point to, whereas for me the Shakespearian flexibility and power with which Emma's mind is registered is so overwhelmingly the most important reason why we are drawn to her that it makes the question whether we feel kind to her all but irrelevant. Just as it is really irrelevant to ask whether we 'admire' the character whose mind we know in such an illusion of actuality in 'If it were done'.

*Persuasion* can hardly be anything but a conscious rethinking of *Sense and Sensibility*, and one is deeply moved by this revelation of Jane Austen's own learning experience and change of heart. Yet nothing is more beautiful in *Persuasion* than the lack of argumentative pressure, the relaxed unassertive ease with which Jane Austen comes out against caution, and for risk-taking. And the achieved radiance, and rightness, of the love affair is part of the same tone and atmosphere. The grace of Wentworth's now daringly energetic masculinity, the elegance of Anne's now completely tender femininity—these ideally romantic perfections are also completely life-size and alive, and there is an unmistakably powerful sexual attraction between these beautiful and lovable people. The right feelings are now simply *there*, with no recriminations, insistences or ironies. When Anne says that Lady Russell's advice was wrong but that she was not wrong to have followed it, Jane Austen seems to have understood herself completely, and to have accepted her own career as a writer. I would say the same of even something as pointed as this: 'She tried to be calm, and leave things to take their course; and tried to dwell much on this argument of rational dependence—"Surely, if there be constant attachment on each side, our hearts must understand each other ere long. We are not boy and girl, to be captiously irritable, misled by every moment's inadvertence, and wantonly playing with our own happiness." ' (ch. 22). Here is exactly the sense that Elinor ought to have had and that Jane Austen couldn't then give her. Yet in fact the next sentence realizes ruefully how easily 'inadvertencies and misconstructions of the most mischievous kind' can occur even to these two constant hearts and rational minds. This is the rarest kind of generosity—generosity towards one's own past mistakes.

One passes lightly over the undeniable imperfections of this beautiful novel. It is true, but it seems unimportant, that Anne's learning and change, which has already taken place before the action begins, is narrated with no attempt at dramatization; and that the real action of the novel, including Wentworth's learning and change, is managed awkwardly in several instances. But the awkwardness isn't the kind we saw in *Pride and Prejudice;* one is conscious rather of a certain loss in physical energy. The unparalleled plausibilities of the comings and going in *Emma,* and the fullness and certainty with which they are integrated into the dramatic action—these were achievements not only of mature skill but of sheer stamina. And stamina is something that a novelist, as well as a dancer, only gradually develops; and it can disappear very suddenly. The implausibilities of *Pride and Prejudice* are impetuous; in *Persuasion* they often seem tired. But sometimes a more interesting explanation offers itself. William Elliot's appearance in the inn at Lyme is simply unnecessary: why not accomplish the whole business at Bath, including Wentworth's awareness of Elliot's interest in Anne which helps revive his own? I see here a failure of attention, even interest, which the loss of stamina made it impossible to conceal.

Jane Austen's own learning experience and change have brought her to the point where she takes learning and change pretty much for granted. Her interests have moved on, though one could also say that they have moved back. In the transfiguration of 'sensibility' that we see in Anne Elliot's character and feelings, Jane Austen is repaying debts to Marianne Dashwood in abundance. It is not only that 'second attachments' are finally proved to be impossible. It is that Jane Austen has found her own path to an interest in subtle and sensitive feeling states. In her early work, the stupid codification of the cult of sensibility had alienated her, though her wilful insistence on sense had done its part too. Now, with Anne's sense so easily and so convincingly taken for granted, there is time for her feelings; and it is into the representation of these that the remaining creative energy chiefly went, and with wonderful success. The description of Anne's feelings when Wentworth rescues her from the annoyance of the little Musgrove boy's childish wilfulness, her feelings when she realizes that Wentworth still loves her—these wonderfully successful ventures into an entirely new vocabulary make me want to take back all I said about failure of creative energy.

# V

# CHARACTER AND CARICATURE
# IN JANE AUSTEN

## D. W. Harding

It seems abundantly clear that in reading Jane Austen's novels we
are not intended to take all the figures in the same way. Some are
offered as full and natural portraits of imaginable people; others,
while certainly referring to types of people we might easily have
come across, are yet presented with such exaggeration and simplification that our response to them is expected to be rather different.
When Mr. Collins has annoyed Mrs. Bennet by supposing that one of
her daughters has helped with the cooking

> He begged pardon for having displeased her. In a softened tone she
> declared herself not at all offended; but he continued to apologize for
> about a quarter of an hour.
>
> (ch. 13)

If we were to object that this surely is rather unlikely—two or three
minutes perhaps but hardly a quarter of an hour—it would be a mis-
reading; we should be missing the fact that this is a convention of
joking exaggeration. We accept the same convention when we read
in *Sense and Sensibility* of Charlotte's meaningless laughter. They
arrived at her home and spent the rest of the morning

> in dawdling through the greenhouse, where the loss of her favourite
> plants, unwarily exposed, and nipped by the lingering frost, raised the
> laughter of Charlotte,—and in visiting her poultry-yard, where, in the
> disappointed hopes of her dairymaid, by hens forsaking their nests, or

83

being stolen by a fox, or in the rapid decease of a promising young brood, she found fresh sources of merriment.

(ch. 42)

In Charlotte, the identifying peculiarity is not only exaggerated but recurrent (as so often in Dickens); silly merriment sums up the aspect of her that Jane Austen wants us to attend to, and its repetition takes the place of any extended exploration of her personality.

Of other figures it is the preliminary description which tells us what treatment to expect. Contrast *Emma* and *Persuasion* in their opening paragraphs. The first attunes us to the full and serious study of a character. The second indicates at once, and largely through its tone, that a trait of personality is being as sharply and mockingly emphasized as the nose or eyebrows of a politician in a cartoon. The initial account of Sir Walter Elliot's vanity about his rank and personal appearance concludes

He considered the blessing of beauty as inferior only to the blessing of a baronetcy; and the Sir Walter Elliot who united these gifts was the constant object of his warmest respect and devotion.

(ch. 1)

Not only the exaggeration, but the tone of ironic mockery in describing a defect of personality announces the intention of caricature.

The natural portraiture which contrasts with this sort of treatment is of course a relative matter. All character portrayal is selective, involving the accentuation of some features; and it produces, inevitably, an effect more condensed and more tidily organized than the impression we gain of a real companion in the undramatic and haphazard contacts of everyday life. But this selective emphasis remains consistent with the author's intention of offering a credible portrait. Elizabeth Bennet's angelic sister Jane is certainly meant to be taken seriously as a character even though her wish to think well of everybody is strongly heightened and made into a joke, as for instance when she hears from Elizabeth of the bad feeling between Darcy and Wickham. Greatly troubled she cast about for some way of clearing them:

'They have both,' said she, 'been deceived, I dare say, in some way or other of which we can form no idea. Interested people have perhaps misrepresented each to the other. It is, in short, impossible for us to conjecture the causes or circumstances which may have alienated them without actual blame on either side.'

84

And Elizabeth replies ironically

'Very true, indeed;—and now, my dear Jane, what have you got to say in behalf of the interested people who have probably been concerned in the business?—Do clear them too, or we shall be obliged to think ill of somebody.'

(ch. 17)

We can go further and notice that sometimes a characteristic may be carried to implausible excess without any intention of caricature. Fanny Price's meek piety is so overdone as to verge on unacceptable priggishness, but I see this as a misjudgement in the handling of a portrait, not a way of creating caricature. What matters is a tacit understanding between author and reader as to which technique of presentation is being adopted.

It hardly needs saying that transitional forms may occur on the borderline between character and caricature, and there is occasionally a mixture of the two techniques in one figure, a possibility that must be examined later. Broadly, however, the difference of treatment is plain enough. It can be exemplified by the contrast between, say, Mr. Collins and Wickham in *Pride and Prejudice*, between Mrs. Jennings and Lucy Steele in *Sense and Sensibility*, between Mrs. Elton and Harriet Smith in *Emma*, between Mrs. Norris and Mrs. Grant in *Mansfield Park*, or between Sir Walter Elliot and Mr. Elliot in *Persuasion*. These are all fairly subordinate figures. If instead we compare the heroes or heroines with the caricatures, for instance Elizabeth Bennet with Mr. Collins or Mr. Knightley with Miss Bates, the difference of handling amounts to a sharp antithesis. The question then arises how such very diverse treatments of the figures can be successfully combined in the one work. Certainly in painting it must be rather rare for caricature and full portraiture to be brought together in one group. And the further possibility occurs that besides creating problems the combination of modes may also present an opportunity for effects that could otherwise not be achieved.

We can best approach these questions by taking a further look at the methods by which Jane Austen tacitly conveys to us that a figure is going to be treated as caricature. At the beginning of *Mansfield Park*, after one or two ironic comments, suggestive but not conclusive, on Mrs. Norris's anger and spirit of activity, an unmistakable indication that she is to be a caricature appears in the long speech with which she interrupts Sir Thomas to reply to all the hesitations, whether stated or not, which he may feel about taking Fanny Price into his home. Her arguments are sensible enough, the phrasing not silly, but the speech is so disproportionate in length and dogmatic certainty to Sir Thomas's attempt at cautious consideration that we recognize at once the volubility of the opinionated woman who goes over other people like a steam roller. The long speech, in which she expects and receives no help from social give and take, creates the impression that she is being exhibited and exposed. The stage is set for ridicule. And a little later comes the revelation that she has no intention of having the child in her own house, preceded by an explicit statement, rather in the style of the seventeenth century 'character', of one of the traits which is to be ridiculed throughout the novel:

> As far as walking, talking, and contriving reached, she was thoroughly benevolent, and nobody knew better how to dictate liberality to others: but her love of money was equal to her love of directing, and she knew quite as well how to save her own as to spend that of her friends.
>
> (ch. 1)

The contrast between ostensible generosity and mean intentions could easily have formed part of a natural portrait. That Mrs. Norris is instead seen so promptly to be caricature depends not only on the improbability of her claims to selfless benevolence and the transparently spurious reason she finds for her refusal (the overbearing tone contrasting with the sentiment) but also on the self-exposure resulting from the uninterrupted speeches. It is a method of satire that develops naturally from the letter form of some of the early work; Lady Susan's self-exposure, for example, is complete in her first two letters.

It is not simply length of speech that indicates the intention of satire. Fully portrayed characters may have long speeches, even overlong and prosy like some of Elinor's and Marianne's during the latter's convalescence, but they are none the less offered as part of a true conversational interchange. When caricature is intended the listeners no longer attempt the equal give and take of conversation. On Mrs. Elton's first visit to Hartfield, her speeches comparing Hartfield to Maple Grove, her patronizing references to Mrs. Weston, and all her impudent familiarities, receive the briefest replies from Emma, replies that serve mainly to keep the speaker at arm's length, with the effect of leaving her to make a conversational exhibition of herself rather than conversing. And as the novel goes on the isolation of a speaker for purposes of caricature is carried further. In Miss Bates's speech on her arrival for the ball at the Crown the replies of other people are entirely omitted:

> 'So very obliging of you! No rain at all. Nothing to signify. I do not care for myself. Quite thick shoes. And Jane declares—Well!' (as soon as she was within the door), 'well! This is brilliant indeed! This is admirable! Excellently contrived, upon my word. Nothing wanting. Could not have imagined it. So well lighted up! Jane, Jane, look! did you ever see anything—Oh! Mr. Weston, you must really have had Aladdin's lamp. Good Mrs. Stokes would not know her own room again. I saw her as I came in; she was standing in the entrance. "Oh! Mrs. Stokes", said I—but I had not time for more.' She was now met by Mrs. Weston. 'Very well, I thank you ma'am. I hope you are quite well. Very happy to hear it. So afraid you might have a headache! seeing you pass by so often, and knowing how much trouble you must have. Delighted to hear it indeed!—Ah! dear Mrs. Elton, so obliged to you for the carriage; excellent time; Jane and I quite ready. Did not keep the horses a moment. Most comfortable carriage . . .'
>
> (ch. 38)

And so it goes on and on, with only slight indications here and there that a word from the listeners has been got in edgeways. The extreme form of the technique is represented by the frankly fore-shortened and non-realistic notation of talk that goes on while Mrs. Elton gathers strawberries. Though I think this includes other speakers than Mrs. Elton, yet she so dominates the scene that the quality of caricature affects her primarily:

> Mrs. Elton in all her apparatus of happiness, her large bonnet and her basket, was very ready to lead the way in gathering, accepting, or talking. Strawberries, and only strawberries, could now be thought or spoken of. 'The best fruit in England—everybody's favourite—always wholesome. These the finest beds and finest sorts. Delightful to gather for one's self—the only way of really enjoying them. Morning decidedly the best time—never tired—every sort good—hautboy infinitely superior —no comparison—the others hardly eatable—hautboys very scarce— Chili preferred—white wood finest flavour of all—price of strawberries in London—abundance about Bristol—Maple Grove—cultivation— beds when to be renewed—gardeners thinking exactly different—no general rule—gardeners never to be put out of their way—delicious fruit—only too rich to be eaten much of—inferior to cherries—currants more refreshing—only objection to gathering strawberries the stooping

87

—glaring sun—tired to death—could bear it no longer—must go and sit in the shade.'

Such, for half an hour, was the conversation; interrupted only once by Mrs. Weston, who came out, in her solicitude after her son-in-law, to inquire if he were come . . .

(ch. 42)

The effect of thus cutting away the social background is to make a figure literally egregious. It is what Jane Austen does, with less reliance on conversation, in first bringing Robert Ferrars on to the scene and establishing him as a caricature of a coxcomb. Elinor and Marianne who have no idea who he is simply wait their turn to be attended to at the jewellers while he perpetrates a display of puppyism in choosing his toothpick case:

At last the affair was decided. The ivory, the gold, and the pearls, all received their appointment, and the gentleman having named the last day on which his existence could be continued without the possession of the toothpick case, drew on his gloves with leisurely care, and bestowing another glance on the Miss Dashwoods, but such a one as seemed rather to demand than to express admiration, walked off with an happy air of real conceit and affected indifference.

(ch. 33)

It constitutes a performance in front of the sisters, as well as in front of us, without the mitigation of any personal contact, leaving him a ridiculous object rather than a person entitled to the consideration of equals. The point is made explicit later in the novel when, after one of his more fatuous speeches,

Elinor agreed to it all, for she did not think he deserved the compliment of rational opposition. (ch. 36).

The early presentation of the caricatures differs totally from that of a figure like Harriet Smith, who is presented, certainly, as shy and naïve and at first out of place when she visits Hartfield, and is exposed to our laughter at later points in the novel, but is still offered as a character. Her speeches are always part of a true conversational interchange, and her absurdities (such as treasuring up the mementoes of Mr. Elton) arise out of her particularized and developing experience in the story and are not merely repeated demonstrations of a trait defined once and for all.

With the tacit understanding established that a figure is caricature the reader is prepared for certain differences in its handling. As a general rule attention is then concentrated on a few features or a small segment of the personality to the neglect of much that would make the figure a full human being, and the understanding is that the reader will accept this convention and not inquire closely into the areas of behaviour and personality that the author chooses to avoid. In this respect caricature is one of many conventions in entertainment and communication. It can be compared in its artificiality with the funny anecdote; the listener who, at the improbable climax of a joke, is so unco-operative as to inquire 'Well, and what happened *then*?' or 'What did he say to *that*?' has failed to play his part in the convention which frames off the incident from any real context. Obviously, too, the caricature is a form of the stereotype, which also isolates and exaggerates a few features (the gay, gesticulating, amorous Frenchman, the correct and inhibited Englishman with tightly rolled umbrella, or the spinster in old-fashioned clothes, devoted to her cat). The stereotype serves limited purposes of communication and comment, it may convey elements of true generalization, but it works only because of an implicit agreement to ignore the greater part of any real personality in which the exaggerated features are embedded. Similarly, caricature in fiction will work so long as the reader accepts the bargain and so long as no important action which would be impossible to a more complete personality is made to hinge on the exaggerated feature.

It is of course a further mark of the caricatures that they are in some degree ridiculous, proper targets for laughter even if we condemn them too. The laughter implies that in some sense we see them as not seriously mattering. But that is true only if we discriminate between the reader's view and the view taken by figures in the fiction. For example, while Elizabeth Bennet sees Mr. Collins with contemptuous amusement our view of him as a caricature and her view of him as—within the fictional world—a real person are not noticeably different. When, however, he proposes, and Mrs. Bennet's urgent pressure turns the proposal into a genuine threat, then we have to recognize that although he remains a joke for us he has become no joke for Elizabeth. Nor is he a joke for her when Charlotte Lucas marries him. The handling of him as a caricature is a convention between author and readers; the other fictional figures are not party to it. Lady Catherine in the shrubbery, forbidding Elizabeth to become engaged to Darcy, touches the heights of caricature for us—'Heaven and earth!—of what are you thinking?

Are the shades of Pemberley to be thus polluted?' But for Elizabeth she is a threat, a very real person; Elizabeth for her own part can confidently judge her to be absurd, but at the same time her power, especially over Darcy, is not easily gauged:

> She knew not the exact degree of his affection for his aunt, or his dependence on her judgement, but it was natural to suppose that he thought much higher of her ladyship than *she* could do.

(ch. 57)

When we think of Mrs. Norris and Fanny Price it is inescapable that the figure which *we* are invited to ridicule can certainly be no laughing matter to the heroine. Caricature constitutes communication on a different level between the author and the readers. It assures us that although the heroine may be distressed and in a material sense endangered by the caricatured figure the danger and trouble will always remain external, the threat will not be to the values which make her the heroine. The fully portrayed characters, on the other hand, have a much more intimate relevance to her. Henry Crawford's wooing of Fanny, and the pressures exerted in his favour by Sir Thomas and Edmund, are serious not only to her but to us: his success would change the whole pattern of values to which we have committed ourselves in sympathizing with the heroine and her love of Edmund. The same is true of Mr. Elliot's wooing of Anne.

Of the likeable caricatures—Admiral Croft, Mr. Woodhouse, for example—much the same can be said. Attention is focused on rather a few traits which, it is implied, are all we need know about the figure; each reappearance displays the same traits, with little or no development; and the range of situation and action provided for the caricature is restricted in such a way as to bring no more than a small segment of the personality into view. Moreover, the pleasant caricature, like the unpleasant, meets with a quasi-clinical attitude from the full characters. Just as Mr. Woodhouse is humoured and managed by his daughter, so is Admiral Croft by his wife. As they drive home in their gig the Admiral remarks

> 'I wish Frederick would spread a little more canvas, and bring us home one of these young ladies to Kellynch. Then, there would always be company for them.—And very nice young ladies they both are; I hardly know one from the other.'
>
> 'Very good humoured, unaffected girls, indeed', said Mrs. Croft, in a tone of calmer praise, such as made Anne suspect that her keener powers might not consider either of them as quite worthy of her

brother; 'and a very respectable family. One could not be connected with better people.—My dear admiral, that post!—we shall certainly take that post.'

But by coolly giving the reins a better direction herself, they happily passed the danger; and by once afterwards judiciously putting out her hand, they neither fell into a rut, nor ran foul of a dung-cart; and Anne, with some amusement at their style of driving, which she imagined no bad representation of the general guidance of their affairs, found herself safely deposited by them at the cottage.

(ch. 10)

At this point the technique of caricature threatens to fail if we allow ourselves to reflect that Admiral Croft must have performed distinguished and competent services at sea without his wife's directions; as the seaman ashore he is a fair target for goodnatured fun, but too general a statement about his wife's guidance threatens momentarily to break down the insulation between his present role and his naval career, with the result that Anne's reflection sounds a shade patronizing.

The slight danger at this point brings home the skill and tact with which Jane Austen usually avoids any such impression. It is, of course, just this clinical attitude and the conviction of being entitled to manage someone else that she exposes to condemnation in Emma's treatment of Harriet Smith. We can sympathize with Emma when she brings Harriet to a decision over the choice of ribbons and the destination of the parcel, but our view of Harriet is not restricted to this level; and because she is portrayed over a much wider range of feeling and behaviour—because she is a character—it is an offence on Emma's part to manipulate and manage her affections for her. But Emma's humouring of Mr. Woodhouse, though it reduces him to the status of a child, is made acceptable by the style of caricature in which he is presented—and presented to the very end, when the apprehension he feels at a raid on Mrs Weston's poultry overcomes his apparently unconquerable reluctance to have Emma marry.

To see rather more clearly how a character and a caricature are differentiated it is instructive to watch the developing presentation of the two Steele sisters after their simultaneous entry into the novel. At first they are both potential caricatures while they flatter Lady Middleton by their improbable delight and excessive patience with her intolerably spoiled children. But while the treatment of the elder Miss Steele continues along the line of caricature, simplified and exaggerated, Lucy is made more complex; her greater intelligence and subtlety are quickly demonstrated when she hints that she perfectly appreciates Elinor's juster estimate of the children and wants to reconcile her own behaviour with it:

> 'I have a notion,' said Lucy, 'you think the little Middletons rather too much indulged; perhaps they may be the outside of enough; but it is so natural in Lady Middleton; and for my part, I love to see children full of life and spirits; I cannot bear them if they are quiet and tame.'
>
> (ch. 21)

Soon afterwards when her elder sister has displayed her vulgarity in her discussion of 'smart beaux', which Lucy translates into 'genteel young men', Lucy is again detached from her by being given a little more awareness of Elinor's outlook—

> 'Lord! Anne,' cried her sister, 'you can talk of nothing but beaux;—you will make Miss Dashwood believe you think of nothing else.'
>
> (ch. 21)

There soon follows the private talk in which Lucy—under colour of confiding in another woman whose discretion she trusts—warns Elinor off Edward Ferrars by revealing her own secret engagement to him. In the further talks they have she is shown to be insincere and cunning, but the disclosure of these traits is associated so closely with the particular facts of her relations with Edward and Elinor that she begins to be a unique person in a unique situation and not, like her elder sister, a sketched outline with salient features that could belong to hundreds of vulgar and opportunist women.

It is not only a fictional figure's own behaviour and remarks that decide whether we see him as caricature or character; the behaviour he elicits from the fully drawn characters also counts. Miss Steele, the elder sister, gets very little response from Elinor. The most notable is Elinor's shock on discovering that Miss Steele's account of a conversation between Lucy Steele and Edward Ferrars is based on eavesdropping, and then Elinor's reply is little beyond the copy-book propriety that she is too often provided with. In contrast, Lucy Steele's quality as a full character is conveyed partly through the sharply felt and sometimes unexpected reactions she provokes in Elinor. In their tête-à-tête, while they work on the filigree basket for Lady Middleton's spoilt Annamaria, Lucy affirms her conviction of Edward Ferrars's continuing attachment and Elinor, knowing that she herself has become the object of his love and that Lucy suspects it, replies

> 'If the strength of your reciprocal attachment had failed, as between many people and under many circumstances it naturally would during a four years' engagement, your situation would have been pitiable indeed.'

Lucy here looked up; but Elinor was careful in guarding her countenance from every expression that could give her words a suspicious tendency.

(ch. 24)

A little later Lucy expatiates on her certainty that if Edward had shown the least sign of wavering in his attachment she could not have failed to detect it.

> 'All this,' thought Elinor, 'is very pretty; but it can impose upon neither of us.'

So the covert duel goes on, Lucy steadily and solemnly affirming her tender attachment to Edward and her certainty of his to her; and the effect of her protestations is that

> Elinor sat down to the card table with the melancholy persuasion that Edward was not only without affection for the person who was to be his wife; but that he had not even the chance of being tolerably happy in marriage, which sincere affection on *her* side would have given, for self-interest alone could induce a woman to keep a man to an engagement, of which she seemed so thoroughly aware that he was weary.

(ch. 24)

Elinor's detached distrust and this cynical conclusion give an extra dimension to the preceding dialogue and add depth to the figure of Lucy.

The elder Miss Steele by contrast remains a fairly conventional cardboard figure. Soon after she has served her purpose by blurting out the news of Lucy's secret engagement and producing uproar among the Ferrars's she is eased off the scene. Her last appearance is in Kensington Gardens where she serves to bring news of Lucy's determination to retain her hold on Edward, and after a little joyful anticipation of being teased about the doctor she departs with the assurance that she and Lucy are very ready to accept any invitations that may come their way.

> '...and if anything should happen to take you and your sister away, and Mrs. Jennings should want company, I am sure we should be very

glad to come and stay with her for as long a time as she likes. I suppose Lady Middleton won't ask us any more this bout. Good-bye; I am sorry Miss Marianne was not here. Remember me kindly to her. La! if you have not got your spotted muslin on! I wonder you was not afraid of its being torn.'

(ch. 38)

We see her no more and almost at the end of the book merely hear of Mrs. Jennings's good nature in giving her five guineas to get her back to Exeter when Lucy has borrowed all her money and left her stranded.

The puppet has been put back into its box. And towards the ending of the novels this happens to most of the exaggerated figures. As the 'real people' are drawn more closely together the caricatures are removed to a greater distance and come in only as echoes. It is a device that contributes crucially to the tone of the ending; the serious sentiment which is fundamental in Jane Austen's structure of values might be too much of a contrast, or might even be cloying, if it were offered neat and concentrated at the end. Echoes from the caricatures aerate and lighten it. Mrs. Jennings's letter most dexterously and briefly recapitulates her own good nature and her vulgar and almost mechanical willingness to tease girls about their lovers, together with Miss Steele's cadging of hospitality and craving to be thought still in the running for marriage:

'...Lucy, it seems, borrowed all her money before she went off to be married, on purpose, we suppose, to make a show with, and poor Nancy had not seven shillings in the world; so I was very glad to give her five guineas to take her down to Exeter, where she thinks of staying three or four weeks with Mrs. Burgess, in hopes, as I tell her, to fall in with the doctor again.'

(ch. 49)

The final paragraph of *Emma* exemplifies the same device:

'The wedding was very much like other weddings, where the parties have no taste for finery or parade; and Mrs. Elton, from the particulars detailed by her husband, thought it all extremely shabby, and very inferior to her own. 'Very little white satin, very few lace veils; a most pitiful business! Selina would stare when she heard of it.' But, in spite of these deficiences, the wishes, the hopes, the confidence, the predictions of the small band of true friends who witnessed the ceremony, were fully answered in the perfect happiness of the union.'

(ch. 55)

Mrs. Elton's comments, with the preceding reference to the avoidance of finery and parade, bring back to mind her dinner visit at Hartfield and her comment to Jane Fairfax on Mr. Woodhouse's politeness:

'... I fancy I am rather a favourite; he took notice of my gown. How do you like it?—Selina's choice—handsome, I think, but I do not know whether it is not over-trimmed; I have the greatest dislike to the idea of being over-trimmed;—quite a horror of finery. I must put on a few ornaments *now*, because it is expected of me. A bride, you know, must appear like a bride, but my natural taste is all for simplicity; a simple style of dress is so infinitely preferable to finery. But I am quite in the minority, I believe; few people seem to value simplicity of dress—show and finery are everything. I have some notion of putting such a trimming as this to my white and silver poplin. Do you think it will look well?'

(ch. 35)

And there is the similar passage before the ball at the Crown—'How do you like my gown? How do you like my trimming? —How has Wright done my hair?' ... 'I see very few pearls in the room except mine.' All of this is recapitulated in the last brief echo.

The necessity for fading out or modifying the caricatures towards the end of the novel is one aspect of a general problem: how can contacts between characters and caricatures be managed without creating an unacceptable incongruity? At times the incongruity is too evident and the transition between the two sorts of treatment seems clumsy. To my mind an instance occurs in *Pride and Prejudice* when the Bennets, distressed by Lydia's elopement and probable ruin, sit down to dinner, and Mary, indefatigable in stale moral reflections, remarks to Elizabeth:

'This is a most unfortunate affair, and will probably be much talked of. But we must stem the tide of malice, and pour into the wounded bosoms of each other the balm of sisterly consolation.'
Then perceiving in Elizabeth no inclination of replying, she added, 'Unhappy as the event must be for Lydia, we may draw from it this useful lesson: that loss of virtue in a female is irretrievable, that one false step involves her in endless ruin, that her reputation is no less brittle than it is beautiful, and that she cannot be too much guarded in her behaviour towards the undeserving of the other sex.'
Elizabeth lifted up her eyes in amazement, but was too much

95

oppressed to make any reply. Mary, however, continued to console herself with such kind of moral extractions from the evil before them.

(ch. 47)

Here the passage of caricature comes in rather abruptly, and Elizabeth's reaction provides a less smooth junction between the two techniques than Jane Austen usually manages. The need to associate Elizabeth and Jane with the largely caricatural figures of the rest of the family creates a problem which she usually solves by keeping the two elder sisters quiet while the caricatures exhibit, as she does when Elizabeth and Jane, on their way home from London, are met by Lydia and Catherine who have ordered a meal for them at an inn and entertain them with a noisy account of their folly. Jane and Elizabeth, though present, are in the audience, almost as much spectators as we are, and largely keeping their thoughts to themselves.

*Pride and Prejudice*, however, stands a little apart from the other novels in a certain stageyness of technique which suggests the influence of the theatre (as Mary Lascelles hints). The dialogue is often crisply theatrical in quality. Jane assures Elizabeth, without any success, that she no longer loves Bingley or supposes him to love her, and there follows what could well be stage dialogue:

> 'You are very cruel,' said her sister; 'you will not let me smile, and are provoking me to it every moment.'
> 'How hard it is in some cases to be believed!'
> 'And how impossible in others!'
> 'But why should you wish to persuade me that I feel more than I acknowledge?'
> 'That is a question which I hardly know how to answer. We all love to instruct, though we can teach only what is not worth knowing. Forgive me; and if you persist in indifference, do not make *me* your confidante.'

(ch. 54)

And when Mr. Bennet has been called on to compel Elizabeth to marry Mr. Collins his speech works up to a theatrical climax:

> 'Come here, child,' cried her father, as she appeared. 'I have sent for you on an affair of importance. I understand that Mr. Collins has made you an offer of marriage. Is it true?' Elizabeth replied that it was. 'Very well. And this offer of marriage you have refused?'
> 'I have, sir.'

'Very well. We now come to the point. Your mother insists upon your accepting it.—Is it not so, Mrs. Bennet?'

'Yes, or I will never see her again.'

'An unhappy alternative is before you, Elizabeth. From this day you must be a stranger to one of your parents. Your mother will never see you again if you do *not* marry Mr. Collins, and I will never see you again if you *do*.'

Laughter from the auditorium would carry the scene forward, but there is something of a drop in the continuity passage which actually follows:

Elizabeth could not but smile at such a conclusion of such a beginning; but Mrs. Bennet, who had persuaded herself that her husband regarded the affair as she wished, was excessively disappointed.

(ch. 20)

Several other scenes, conducted mainly in dialogue, have the quality of set pieces: Mr. Collins's proposal, Mr. Darcy's first proposal, Lady Catherine and Elizabeth confronting each other in the little wilderness. In scenes like this there is a suggestion of stage dialogue which contrasts with the greater naturalness of conversation and indirectly reported speech in Mr. Darcy's second proposal or in Elizabeth's interview with her father after Darcy has asked his consent. In these latter scenes the technique of the novel is in control. But the influence of the eighteenth century theatre in some parts of the novel is consistent with the very strongly marked caricature of some figures and a rather sharp transition from them to the seriously portrayed characters.

Where the technique of the novelist is dominant, as it is for the greater part of the later novels, the contacts between characters and caricatures are handled more smoothly. In *Emma* Jane Fairfax presents a considerable problem owing to her being in effective contact for the greater part of the story almost exclusively with Miss Bates and Mrs. Elton, both caricatures. The solution is to minimize her contribution, to use her mainly as a foil, and to have her merits described rather than displayed. Thus when Mrs. Elton at the ball pays her 'a good many compliments on her dress and look' we know nothing of her reply except that they were 'compliments very quietly and properly taken.' When we do hear some sustained interchange between them about securing a position for Jane as a governess a

97

sort of dislocation occurs in the conversation. Jane herself, in her horror of being a governess, becomes the one who holds forth in exaggerated terms. Mrs. Elton insists that they must begin at once to seek a post for her, and Jane replies:

> 'Excuse me, ma'am, but this is by no means my intention; I make no inquiry myself, and should be sorry to have any made by my friends. When I am quite determined as to the time, I am not at all afraid of being long unemployed. There are places in town, offices, where inquiry would soon produce something—offices for the sale, not quite of human flesh, but of human intellect.'
> 'Oh! my dear, human flesh! You quite shock me; if you mean a fling at the slave-trade, I assure you Mr. Suckling was always rather a friend to the abolition.'
> 'I did not mean—I was not thinking of the slave-trade,' replied Jane; 'governess-trade, I assure you, was all that I had in view; widely different, certainly, as to the guilt of those who carry it on; but as to the greater misery of the victims, I do not know where it lies . . .'
>
> (ch. 35)

The dialogue here is unusual in making the character almost outdo the caricature in exaggerated emphasis.

Towards the end of *Emma* Jane Austen brings together her caricature, Mrs. Elton, and her two characters, Jane Fairfax and Emma, in the scene in which Emma tries to convey her good wishes on Jane's engagement and Jane tries to indicate her appreciation but both are frustrated by Mrs. Elton's obtrusive hints that she and Jane alone are in the secret of the engagement. The caricature is given her head for most of the scene and then Jane Austen takes Emma and Jane out on to the stairs and there the two characters have the brief but effective interchange that puts them in touch with each other and assures us that the distance and misunderstanding between them have been overcome.

It would be going much too far to imply that characters and caricatures are never brought into full contact, with both sides actively contributing. The scenes between Elizabeth and Lady Catherine, at Rosings and again at Longbourne, testify that they can be. But it seems rare to have an equal contribution from both figures when one is a portrait and the other a caricature. The more usual contact is represented by Miss Bates talking through the window to Mr. Knightley, or Anne Elliot walking up the street in Bath with Admiral Croft and hearing his account of Louisa's engagement to

Captain Benwick. The character in such interchanges generally says much less and occupies a superior position (superior in terms of the values implied by the novel) to some extent humouring the other.

At other points the interaction between the two modes of presentation secures special effects of communication between author and readers. Thus the handling of Mrs. Norris assures us from the start how awful she is, but Sir Thomas, handled as a character, is supposed to be taken in by her, not unaware of her peculiarities but believing her to be guided by fundamentally sound principles and good intentions. Caricature brings out to us what to him is hidden, and consequently makes a limiting comment on the ponderous rationality which for him takes the place of insight. In this respect, one can argue, the technique of caricature allows Jane Austen to express what a person of her acute insight must always feel—astonishment at the way the most outrageously deformed personalities are allowed an effective part in society, because society attends seriously to lip service and rationalization. It is against the blindness and injustice of such a society that Fanny Price is finally vindicated. Rather more subtly Jane Austen insists on the reality of the monstrous Mr. Collins in two ways: first by showing the real pressure that Mrs. Bennet exerts to make Elizabeth marry him; and secondly, and more thoughtfully, by allowing him to secure Charlotte, a real person, and letting Elizabeth gradually realize, once over the first shock of horror, that her friend was after all making a tolerable life for herself in the second-best world that most people except heroines have to inhabit.

In general the convincing interaction of caricatures with characters is not brought about through any denial of the element of caricature There are only a few figures about which we could feel some doubt as to which technique of presentation is being employed, whether the traits of a real character are being heightened to the point of implausibility or whether what is offered is to be understood as caricature. About Mr. Bennet there may be some such uncertainty. But Marianne Dashwood is the clearest and most interesting example of the mixed treatment. Her early romanticism is presented in such a way that although she is beyond doubt a character, some of whose experiences we are expected to enter into very deeply, there are moments of exaggeration that would be unacceptably implausible unless we tacitly realized that we and the author were mutually engaged in the convention of joking. When at last it dawns on

Marianne that Mrs. Jennings is teasing her about being loved by Colonel Brandon 'she considered it as an unfeeling reflection on the colonel's advanced years', he being thirty-five. When her mother, aged forty, protests a little Marianne goes on

> 'but he is old enough to be *my* father; and if he were ever animated enough to be in love, must have long outlived every sensation of the kind. It is too ridiculous! When is a man to be safe from such wit, if age and infirmity will not protect him?'

Challenged by Elinor for evidence of his infirmity she replies that he complained of rheumatism. Under further pressure she admits that a woman of twenty-seven, since she could 'never hope to feel or inspire affection again' might be induced to marry him and act as a nurse in exchange for a home. Elinor replies

> 'I must object to your dooming Colonel Brandon and his wife to the constant confinement of a sick chamber, merely because he chanced to complain yesterday (a very cold damp day) of a slight rheumatic feel in one of his shoulders.'
>
> 'But he talked of flannel waistcoats,' said Marianne; 'and with me a flannel waistcoat is invariably connected with aches, cramps, rheumatisms, and every species of ailment that can afflict the old and feeble.'
>
> 'Had he been only in a violent fever, you would not have despised him half so much. Confess, Marianne, is not there something interesting to you in the flushed cheek, hollow eye, and quick pulse of a fever?'
>
> (ch. 8)

All this interchange, diverting as much of it is (and with significant dramatic irony in the final remark, since Marianne comes to experience the reality of a fever), tacitly invites us to share a joke. It would otherwise be highly implausible; a girl of Marianne's intelligence, reading, and sensitivity couldn't really be quite so silly. Her discussion of the picturesque with Edward Ferrars and her concern that Elinor's lover should be so insensitive is in the same idiom of caricature. In reply to Marianne's enthusiasm for the scenery round their home Edward confesses

> 'I like a fine prospect, but not on picturesque principles. I do not like crooked, twisted, blasted trees. I admire them much more if they are tall, straight and flourishing. I do not like ruined, tattered cottages. I

am not fond of nettles, or thistles, or heath blossoms. I have more
pleasure in a snug farm-house than a watch-tower—and a troop of tidy,
happy villagers please me better than the finest banditti in the world.'
Marianne looked with amazement at Edward, with compassion at
her sister.

(ch. 18)

And when Edward asks whether at seventeen she still holds her
opinion that no one can be in love more than once in his life she
answers

'Undoubtedly. At my time of life opinions are tolerably fixed. It is not
likely that I should now see or hear anything to change them.'

(ch. 17)

And consider the way a sleepless night is referred to. Emma Woodhouse, a character, has experienced the intense agitation of finding
that Mr. Knightley loves her:

As long as Mr. Knightley remained with them, Emma's fever continued; but when he was gone, she began to be a little tranquillized
and subdued—and in the course of a sleepless night, which was the tax
for such an evening, she found one or two very serious points to consider . . .

(ch. 50)

By contrast, when Willoughby has left them,

Marianne would have thought herself very inexcusable had she been
able to sleep at all the first night after parting from Willoughby. She
would have been ashamed to look her family in the face the next
morning, had she not risen from her bed in more need of repose than
when she lay down in it. But the feelings which made such composure
a disgrace, left her in no danger of incurring it. She was awake the whole
night, and she wept the greatest part of it. She got up with an head-
ache, was unable to talk, and unwilling to take any nourishment;
giving pain every moment to her mother and sisters, and forbidding all
attempt at consolation from either. Her sensibility was potent enough!

(ch. 16)

Passages like these leave no doubt that the treatment of Marianne in
the early chapters of *Sense and Sensibility* carries over the technique
of caricature from the juvenilia written for the entertainment of the
Austen family. That technique has of course to be abandoned when
Marianne's outlook alters so dramatically after her illness, and the
change from one mode of presentation to the other adds a little to

the difficulty we should in any case feel in accepting the transformation of Marianne herself and entering wholeheartedly into her new fortunes with Colonel Brandon.

We can see a rather similar uncertainty in the handling of Catherine Morland who, although the heroine and undoubtedly meant to have our sympathy, is still treated at many points as a caricature. Her Gothic imaginings in the Abbey are an example. Northanger Abbey was, after all, a very early work which Jane Austen revised towards the end of her life at about the same time as she wrote *Persuasion,* and this makes it understandable that Catherine should be on the borderline between caricature and character. Jane Austen succeeds in making her a portrait, even though a portrait of an immature girl with highly emphasized naïvetés. But the technique of presentation remains very mixed in spite of revision and presents a sharp contrast to the technical certainty of *Persuasion.* It is not surprising that Jane Austen hesitated over issuing *Northanger Abbey,* which came out only after her death. She told her niece that *Persuasion* was ready for publication but said of *Northanger Abbey* 'Miss Catherine is put upon the shelve for the present'. It is partly due to the strong elements of caricature in both figures that the development of outlook in Catherine and Marianne, though so important to the themes of the two novels, is infinitely less impressive than the development in Elizabeth Bennet and Darcy, let alone Emma Woodhouse, all of whom are handled consistently as characters.

Caricature is maintained by concentrating on the outer layers of social behaviour and selecting narrowly even from them. In the same way that national stereotypes partly dissolve when we come to know a foreigner as a real person, so fictional caricatures may be given fuller human relevance as the outer layers are penetrated and less grotesque features of personality are indicated. It is not only Marianne but we too who have to enlarge our view of Mrs. Jennings to give a juster estimate of her good nature. We are taken beyond the Lady Bertram of needlework and pug when she is shocked into genuine feeling at the sight of her son Tom desperately ill. But it is in Miss Bates that Jane Austen exploits most delicately the technique of going behind the ridiculous features of the caricature. What she does, more than once, is unexpectedly to give Miss Bates the moral advantage in a social situation, with the effect of taking down a peg those—including us—who have felt comfortably superior to her This happens on the occasion when Frank Churchill makes his blunder by revealing that Mr. Perry had intended to set up his carriage. Miss Bates shoulders responsibility for the leakage of the story, which Mrs. Perry had told Mrs. Bates in confidence:

> 'She had no objection to her telling us, of course, but it was not to go beyond: and, from that day to this, I never mentioned it to a soul that I know of. At the same time, I will not positively answer for my having never dropt a hint, because I know I do sometimes pop out a thing before I am aware. I am a talker, you know; I am rather a talker; and now and then I have let a thing escape me which I should not. I am not like Jane; I wish I were. I will answer for it *she* never betrayed the least thing in the world.'
>
> (ch. 41)

Frank Churchill and Jane know, as we know later, that he got the story through their clandestine correspondence. Miss Bates, honestly admitting her weakness, which this time is not to blame, leaves us feeling a little small. A similar effect is secured when Emma calls on the Bates's and is admitted too promptly; she sees Jane hurry into her bedroom to escape her

> and, before the door had shut them out, she heard Miss Bates saying, 'Well, my dear, I shall *say* you are laid down upon the bed, and I am sure you are ill enough.'

We are prepared to hear Miss Bates's white lie when she returns and to see Emma in the superior position of knowing that it is a lie. Instead Miss Bates says

> 'You will excuse her not coming to you—she is not able—she is gone into her own room—I want her to lie down upon the bed. "My dear," said I, "I shall say you are laid down upon the bed:" but, however, she is not; she is walking about the room.'
>
> (ch. 44)

Again, the figure of fun has rather turned the tables on us.

That episode comes immediately after Emma's much more serious lapse in permitting herself a hurtful jibe at Miss Bates during the Box Hill Party. Like us, she has let herself be trapped into regarding Miss Bates simply as a figure of fun, something to caricature, and now in her wounded feelings we are reminded that Miss Bates is after all a person. Because she has been treated in the spirit of caricature it is not easy for her serious reaction to be conveyed in her ordinary mode of speech; it is given in what amounts to an aside to Mr. Knightley. And it is through its effect on him, one of the full characters, that the reality of her hurt is reinforced. His later reproaches and their sobering effect on Emma bring out the seriousness of the episode. It is taken as the occasion for a short but pregnant discussion of the problem of ridicule. He emphasizes Miss Bates's good points:

> 'Oh!' cried Emma, 'I know there is not a better creature in the world: but you must allow, that what is good and what is ridiculous are most unfortunately blended in her.' 'They are blended,' said he, 'I acknowledge; and, were she prosperous, I could allow much for the occasional prevalence of the ridiculous over the good. Were she a woman of fortune, I would leave every harmless absurdity to take its chance, I would not quarrel with you for any liberties of manner. Were she your equal in situation—but, Emma, consider how far this is from being the case. She is poor; she has sunk from the comforts she was born to; and, if she live to old age, must probably sink more. Her situation should secure your compassion. It was badly done, indeed!—You, whom she had known from an infant, whom she had seen grow up from a period when her notice was an honour, to have you now, in thoughtless spirits, and the pride of the moment, laugh at her, humble her—and before her niece, too—and before others, many of whom (certainly *some*,) would be entirely guided by *your* treatment of her.— . . .'

He supposed her angry with him, but

> He had misinterpreted the feelings which had kept her face averted, and her tongue motionless. They were combined only of anger against herself, mortification, and deep concern . . . Never had she felt so agitated, mortified, grieved, at any circumstance in her life. She was most forcibly struck. The truth of his representation there was no denying. She felt it at her heart. How could she have been so brutal, so cruel to Miss Bates!

(ch. 43)

Although in part her distress is at losing Mr. Knightley's good opinion, it still comes mainly from what she sees she has done to Miss Bates; and this represents an intense irruption of human relevance in a figure we had been invited to think of as far out caricature. It brings up the whole problem of ridicule, which it is easy to believe may have been a real one for Jane Austen. The *Letters* give evidence enough of an eye for the ridiculous and a witty tongue. But she also had her religious upbringing and serious Christian principles, and the third of the surviving Prayers she wrote includes the passage

> Incline us oh God! to think humbly of ourselves, to be severe only in the examination of our own conduct, to consider our fellow-creatures with kindness, and to judge of all they say and do with that charity which we would desire from them ourselves.

This is the sort of prayer Emma might have uttered after her behaviour to Miss Bates. The device of giving these occasional glimpses of something behind the surface she caricatures is an aspect of the serious moral framework within which Jane Austen wrote; it is a means of reminding herself and us of the limited validity of ridicule.

# VI

# JANE AUSTEN AND THE
# MORALISTS

## *Gilbert Ryle*

---

### I

JANE AUSTEN is often described as just a miniature-painter. Her blessed 'little bit (two inches wide) of ivory' has too often set the tone of criticism. I mean to show that she was more than this. Whether we like it or not, she was also a moralist. In a thin sense of the word, of course, every novelist is a moralist who shows us the ways or *mores* of his characters and their society. But Jane Austen was a moralist in a thick sense, that she wrote what and as she wrote partly from a deep interest in some perfectly general, even theoretical questions about human nature and human conduct. To say this is not, however, to say that she was a moralizer. There is indeed some moralizing in *Sense and Sensibility* and she does descend to covert preaching in *Mansfield Park*. Here I do discern, with regret, the tones of voice of the anxious aunt, and even occasionally of the prig But for the most part, I am glad to say, she explores and does not shepherd.

I am not going to try to make out that Jane Austen was a philosopher or even a philosopher *manquée*. But I am going to argue that she was interested from the south side in some quite general or theoretical problems about human nature and conduct in which philosophers proper were and are interested from the north side.

To begin with, we should consider the titles of three of her novels, namely '*Sense and Sensibility*', '*Pride and Prejudice*' and '*Persuasion*'. It is not for nothing that these titles are composed of abstract nouns. *Sense and Sensibility* really is about the relations between Sense and Sensibility or, as we might put it, between Head and Heart, Thought and Feeling, Judgement and Emotion, or Sensibleness and Sensitiveness. *Pride and Prejudice* really is about pride and about the misjudgements that stem from baseless pride, excessive pride, deficient pride, pride in trivial objects, and so on. *Persuasion* really is or rather does set out to be about persuadability, unpersuadability and over-persuadability.

To go into detail. In *Sense and Sensibility* it is not only Elinor, Marianne and Mrs. Dashwood who exemplify equilibrium or else inequilibrium between judiciousness and feeling. Nearly all the characters in the novel do so, in their different ways and their different degrees. John Dashwood has his filial and fraternal feelings, but they are shallow ones. They do not overcome his and his wife's calculating selfishness. Sir John Middleton is genuinely and briskly kind, but with a cordiality too general to be really thoughtful. What he does for one person he does with equal zest for another, without considering their differences of need, desert or predilection. He would be in his element in a Butlin's Holiday Camp. Mrs. Jennings, whose character changes during the novel, is a thoroughly vulgar woman who yet has, in matters of importance, a sterling heart and not too bad a head. Lucy Steele professes deep feelings, but they are sham ones, while her eye for the main chance is clear and unwavering. Like her future mother-in-law she has too little heart and too much sense of a heartless sort.

Marianne and Elinor are alike in that their feelings are deep and genuine. The difference is that Marianne lets her joy, anxiety or grief so overwhelm her that she behaves like a person crazed. Elinor keeps her head. She continues to behave as she knows she should behave. She is deeply grieved or worried, but she does not throw to the winds all considerations of duty, prudence, decorum or good taste. She is sensitive *and* sensible, in our sense of the latter adjective. I think that Elinor too often and Marianne sometimes collapse into two-dimensional samples of abstract types; Elinor's conversation occasionally degenerates into lecture or even homily. This very fact bears out my view that Jane Austen regularly had one eye, and here an eye and a half, on a theoretical issue. The issue here was this: must Head and Heart be antagonists? Must a person who is deeply grieved or deeply joyous be crazy with grief or joy? To which Jane Austen's answer, the correct answer, is 'No, the best Heart and the best Head are combined in the best person'. But Elinor sometimes collapses into a Head rather loosely buttoned on to a Heart, and then she ceases to be a person at all.

Jane Austen brings out the precise kinds of the sensibility exhibited by Elinor and Marianne by her wine-taster's technique of matching them not only against one another, but also against nearly all the other characters in their little world. The contrast between Lucy Steele and both Elinor and Marianne is the contrast between sham and real sensibility or emotion; the contrast between Willoughby and, say, Edward is the contrast between the genuine but shallow feelings of the one and the genuine and deep feelings of the other. Lady Middleton's feelings are few and are concentrated entirely on her own children. Her husband's feelings are spread abroad quite undiscriminatingly. He just wants everyone to be jolly.

I want briefly to enlarge on this special wine-taster's technique of comparative character-delineation. Jane Austen's great predecessor, Theophrastus, had described just one person at a time, the Garrulous Man by himself, say, or the Mean Man by himself. So the Garrulity or the Meanness are not picked out by any contrasts or affinities with contiguous qualities. Our view of the Garrulous Man is not clarified by his being matched against the Conversationally Fertile Man on the one side, or against the Conversationally Arid Man on the other. The Meanness of the Mean Man is not brought into relief by being put into adjacency with the meritorious Austerity of a Socrates or the allowable Close Bargaining of a dealer. By contrast, Jane Austen's technique is the method of the vintner. She pin-points the exact quality of character in which she is interested, and the exact degree of that quality, by matching it against the same quality in different degrees, against simulations of that quality, against deficiences of it, and against qualities which though different, are brothers or cousins of that selected quality. The ecstatic emotionality of her Marianne is made to stand out against the sham, the shallow, the inarticulate and the controlled feelings of Lucy Steele, Willoughby, Edward and Elinor. To discriminate the individual taste of any one character is to discriminate by comparison the individual taste of every other character. That is to say, in a given novel Jane Austen's characters are not merely blankly different, as Cheltenham is blankly different from Helvellyn. They are different inside the same genus, as Cheltenham is different from Bath or Middlesbrough, or as Helvellyn is different from Skiddaw or Boar's Hill.

Thus in *Pride and Prejudice* almost every character exhibits too much or too little pride, pride of a bad or silly sort or pride of a good sort, sham pride or genuine pride and so forth. Elizabeth Bennet combines a dangerous cocksureness in her assessments of people with a proper sense of her own worth. Jane is quite uncocksure. She is too diffident. She does not resent being put upon or even realize that she is being put upon. There is no proper pride, and so no fight in her. Their mother is so stupid and vulgar that she has no sense of dignity at all, only silly vanities about her dishes and her daughters' conquests. Mr. Bennet has genuine pride. He does despise the despicable. But it is inert, unexecutive pride. He voices his just contempt in witty words, but he does nothing to prevent or repair what he contemns. It is the pride of a mere don, though a good don. Bingley has no special pride, and so, though a nice man, spinelessly lets himself be managed by others where he should not. His sisters are proud in the sense of being vain and snobbish.

Darcy is, to start with, haughty and snobbish, a true nephew of Lady Catherine de Burgh. His early love for Elizabeth is vitiated by condescension. He reforms into a man with pride of the right sort. He is proud to be able to help Elizabeth and her socially embarrassing family. He now knows what is due from him as well as what is due to him. Mr. Collins is the incarnation of vacuous complacency. He glories in what are mere reflections from the rank of his titled patroness and from his own status as a clergyman. He is a soap-bubble with nothing at all inside him and only bulging refractions from other things on his rotund surface.

The same pattern obtains in *Persuasion*. Not only Anne Elliot but her father, sisters, friends and acquaintances are described in terms of their kinds and degrees of persuadability and unpersuadability. Anne had suffered from having dutifully taken the bad advice of the over-cautious Lady Russell. Her father and sister Elizabeth can be persuaded to live within their means only by the solicitor's shrewd appeals to quite unworthy considerations. Her sister Mary is so full of self-pity that she can be prevailed on only by dexterous coaxings. Lydia Musgrove is too headstrong to listen to advice, so she cracks her skull. Her sister Henrietta is so over-persuadable that she is a mere weathercock. Mr. Elliot, after his suspect youth, is apparently eminently rational. But it turns out that he is amenable to reason only so long as reason is on the side of self-interest. This particular theme-notion of persuadability was, in my opinion, too boring to repay Jane Austen's selection of it, and I believe that she herself found that her story tended to break away from its rather flimsy ethical frame. Certainly, when Anne and Wentworth at last come together again, their talk does duly turn on the justification of Anne's original yielding to Lady Russell's persuasion and on the unfairness of Wentworth's resentment of her so yielding. But we, and I think Jane Austen herself, are happy to hear the last of this particular theme. We are greatly interested in Anne, but not because she had been dutifully docile as a girl. We think only fairly well of Lydia Musgrove, but her deafness to counsels of prudence is not what makes our esteem so tepid. Some of the solidest characters in the novel, namely the naval characters, are not described in terms of their persuadability or unpersuadability at all, and we are not sorry.

I hope I have made out something of a case for the view that the abstract nouns in the titles 'Sense and Sensibility', 'Pride and Prejudice' and 'Persuasion' really do indicate the controlling themes of the novels; that Jane Austen wrote Sense and Sensibility partly, at least, from an interest in the quite general or theoretical question whether deep feeling is compatible with being reasonable; that she wrote Pride and Prejudice from an interest in the quite general question what sorts and degrees of pride do, and what sorts and degrees of pride do not go with right thinking and right acting; and that she wrote Persuasion from an interest—I think a waning interest and one which I do not share—in the general question when should people and when should they not let themselves be persuaded by what sorts of counsels.

I shall now become bolder. I shall now say what corresponding theme-notions constitute the frames of Emma and Mansfield Park, though no abstract nouns occur in their titles.

If cacophony had not forbidden, Emma could and I think would have been entitled 'Influence and Interference'. Or it might have been called more generically 'Solicitude'. Jane Austen's question here was: What makes it sometimes legitimate or even obligatory for one person deliberately to try to modify the course of another person's life, while sometimes such attempts are wrong? Where is the line between Meddling and Helping? Or, more generally, between proper and improper solicitude and unsolicitude about the destinies and welfares of others? Why was Emma wrong to try to arrange Harriet's life, when Mr. Knightley was right to try to improve Emma's mind and character? Jane Austen's answer is the right answer. Emma was treating Harriet as a puppet to be worked by hidden strings. Mr. Knightley advised and scolded Emma to her face. Emma knew what Mr. Knightley required of her and hoped for her. Harriet was not to know what Emma was scheming on her behalf. Mr. Knightley dealt with Emma as a potentially responsible and rational being. Emma dealt with Harriet as a doll. Proper solicitude is open and not secret. Furthermore, proper solicitude is actuated by genuine good will. Improper solicitude is actuated by love of power, jealousy, conceit, sentimentality and so on.

To corroborate this interpretation we should notice, what we now expect, that the novel's other characters also are systematically described in terms of their different kinds or degrees of concernment or unconcernment with the lives of others. Emma's father is a fusser, who wants to impose his own hypochondriacal regimen on others. But his intentions are kindly and his objectives are not concealed. He is a silly old darling, but he is not a schemer. He tries in vain to influence his friends' meals and his grandchildren's holiday resorts. He is over-solicitous and solicitous about trivialities, but he does not meddle, save, nearly, once, and then John Knightley properly loses his temper with him. Mrs. Elton is silly and vulgar. Her fault is that of officiousness. She tries to force her services on other people. She is a nuisance, but there is nothing underhand about her; rather the reverse, she advertises too much the unwanted benefits that she tries to impose on her victims. John Knightley is somewhat refreshingly unconcerned with other people's affairs outside his own family circle. He is honest, forthright and perceptive, but, unlike his wife, her father and her sister Emma, he does not interest himself in things that are not his business. He is not brutal or callous, and only twice or three times is he even testy; but other people's affairs are not naturally interesting to him. Gossip bores him and social gatherings seem to him a weary waste of time. Mr. Elton differs from John Knightley in just this respect, that Mr. Elton affects solicitude without really feeling it, while John Knightley is frankly unsolicitous. By contrast, Miss Bates is an incessant, though entirely kindly natterer about other people's affairs. She cares very much about everybody's welfare, though her concern is, through no fault of her own, confined to talk. She is debarred from doing anything for anyone save her old mother, but all her little thoughts and all her little utterances are enthusiastically benevolent ones. She is the twittering voice of universal good will. Mr. Knightley is like her in good will, but unlike her in that his is executive and efficient good will. He says little; he just helps. He does what needs to be done for people, but he does not do it behind their backs, nor does he shout about it to the world. Finally, Frank Churchill is matched against Mr. Knightley in that while he too does things which make small or big differences to other people's lives, he often does surreptitous things. He does not hurry to come to meet his new step-mother; and when he does come it is because his crypto-fiancée has just returned to the village. He flirts with Emma, but does not let her know that he is only playing a game, and playing a game as a camouflage. He forces a piano on his fiancée without letting her know to whom she is indebted. He is not wicked, but he is not above-board, so many of his actions affecting others belong to the class of interference, and not of legitimate intervention. He is ready to make use of people without their knowledge or consent, in order to get himself out of difficulties. He is like Emma in being a bit of a schemer, but he is unlike her in that she tried to shape the whole life of Harriet; he tricked people only for momentary purposes. He did not want to make big or lasting differences to anybody's life, save his own and his fiancée's; but he was reckless of the danger of making such a difference without intending it. He meddled by covert gambling, she meddled by covert plotting. It is no accident that he was the adopted son of a domineering and wealthy old lady and her intimidated husband. In effect they had trained him not to be forthright. This theme-notion of *Emma*, that of *Influence and Interference*, is explicitly brought out in the conversation in which the heroine and hero first open their hearts to each other. These two abstract nouns both occur there, as they occur sporadically elsewhere in the novel.

Now for *Mansfield Park*, Jane Austen's profoundest, but also her most didactic novel. Its theme-notion is the connection, to use her own ugly phrase, between fraternal and conjugal ties. Here nearly all the characters are systematically described in terms of the affection which they feel, or do not feel, or which they only pretend to feel for their own flesh and blood. Their capacities or incapacities to make good husbands or wives are a direct function of their lovingness or unlovingness inside their own families. Fanny's devotedness to her brother William, her cousins, aunt and uncle gets its reward in happy marriage; while her coldheartedness at home results in marital disaster for Maria.

Jane Austen duly describes not only the major but also many of the minor characters in terms of their excellences and defects as brothers, aunts, daughters, cousins and parents. Sir Thomas Bertram is genuinely fond of his wife, children and niece. But he is too stiff and pompous to be intimate with them. He is affectionate at a distance. So his children do not love him and he does not understand them. Lady Bertram is drowsily fond of her family but is so bovine and inert that she seldom does anything or says anything to affect anybody. Her sister, Mrs. Norris, is an officious and mischief-making aunt and an unforgiving sister. Her eloquent professions of love for the Bertrams are a mere cover for self-importance. With such parents and such an aunt, Tom, Maria and her sister grow up selfish and cold-hearted. Maria marries for the wrong reasons and destroys her marriage for worse ones.

The real hero of the story is Fanny's brother, William. He is gay, affectionate, vigorous, straight and brave, and he makes Fanny happy. It is their brother-sister love which is the paradigm against which to assess all the others. Fanny's love for her cousin Edmund had begun as a child's love for a deputy-William.

Henry and Mary Crawford have accomplishments, vitality, wit, artistic tastes and charm. But they speak undutifully in public about the unsatisfactory uncle who had brought them up; they resent the unexpected return of Sir Thomas Bertram from Antigua to the bosom of his own family, simply because it puts a stop to their theatricals; and even between brother and sister the relations are cordial rather than intimate. Unlike William, Henry never writes a proper letter to his sister. Nor does he mind setting the Bertram sisters at loggerheads by flirting with both at once. He has little personal or vicarious family feeling. Critics have lamented that Henry Crawford does not marry Fanny. But this would have ruined the point. He has indeed everything that she or we could wish her husband to have—everything save two. He lacks high principles, and he lacks filial and fraternal lovingness. He is without those very qualities which make William the ideal brother. Henry could never be what Edmund was, a deputy-William. Though by no means without a heart, he was too shallow-hearted for him and Fanny ever to be the centres and circumferences of one another's lives.

*Northanger Abbey* is the one novel of the six which does not have an abstract ethical theme for its backbone. I think that when Jane Austen began to write this novel, it had been her sole intention to burlesque such novels as *The Mysteries of Udolpho* by depicting a nice but gullible teenager looking at the actual world through, so to speak, the celluloid film of Gothic romances. But even here Jane Austen's ethical interest came quite soon to make its contribution. For we soon begin to find that Catherine, though a gullible ninny about how the actual world runs, is quite ungullible about what is right and wrong, decorous and indecorous. Her standards of conduct, unlike her criteria of actuality, are those of a candid, scrupulous and well-brought up girl, not those of the unschooled, novel-struck girl that she also is. Jane Austen began *Northanger Abbey* just poking fun at factual gullibility; but she soon became much more interested in moral ungullibility. Jane Austen the moralist quickly outgrew Jane Austen the burlesquer.

## II

Jane Austen did, then, consider quite general or theoretical questions. These questions were all moral questions; though only in *Mansfield Park* and *Sense and Sensibility* did she cross over the boundary into moralizing. I am now going to be more specific and say what sorts of moral ideas were most congenial to her. I will try to bring out together both what I mean by this question and what its answer is.

In the eighteenth century, and in other centuries too, moralists tended to belong to one of two camps. There was what I shall call, with conscious crudity, the Calvinist camp, and there was what I shall call the Aristotelian camp. A moralist of the Calvinist type thinks, like a criminal lawyer, of human beings as either Saved or Damned, either Elect or Reject, either children of Virtue or children of Vice, either heading for Heaven or heading for Hell, either White or Black, either Innocent or Guilty, either Saints or Sinners. The Calvinists' moral psychology is correspondingly bi-polar. People are dragged upwards by Soul or Spirit or Reason or Conscience; but they are dragged down by Body or Flesh or Passion or Pleasure or Desire or Inclination. A man is an unhappy combination of a white angelic part and a black satanic part. At the best, the angelic part has the satanic part cowed and starved and subjugated now, and can hope to be released altogether from it in the future. Man's life here is either a life of Sin or else it is a life of self-extrication from Sin. We find people being depicted in such terms in plenty of places. The seducer in *The Vicar of Wakefield* is Wickedness incarnate. So he has no other ordinary qualities. Fanny Burney's bad characters are pure stage-villains. Occasionally Johnson in *The Rambler* depicts persons who are all Black; and since they possess no Tuesday morning attributes, we cannot remember a thing about them afterwards. They are black cardboard and nothing more. The less frequent angelic or saintly characters are equally unalive, flat and forgettable.

In contrast with this, the Aristotelian pattern of ethical ideas represents people as differing from one another in degree and not in kind, and differing from one another in respect not just of a single generic Sunday attribute, Goodness, say, or else Wickedness, but in respect of a whole spectrum of specific week-day attributes. *A* is a bit more irritable and ambitious than *B*, but less indolent and less sentimental. *C* is meaner and quicker-witted than *D*, and *D* is greedier and more athletic than *C*. And so on. A person is not black or white, but iridescent with all the colours of the rainbow; and he is not a flat plane, but a highly irregular solid. He is not blankly Good or Bad, blankly angelic or fiendish; he is better than most in one respect, about level with the average in another respect, and a bit, perhaps a big bit, deficient in a third respect. In fact he is like the people we really know, in a way in which we do not know and could not know any people who are just Bad or else just Good.

Jane Austen's moral ideas are, with certain exceptions, ideas of the Aristotelian and not the Calvinist pattern. Much though she had learned from Johnson, this she had not learned from him. When Johnson is being ethically solemn, he draws people in black and white. So they never come to life, any more than the North Pole and the South Pole display any scenic features. Jane Austen's people are, nearly always, alive all over, all through and all round, displaying admirably or amusingly or deplorably proportioned mixtures of all the colours that there are, save pure White and pure Black. If a Calvinist critic were to ask us whether Mr. Collins was Hell-bound or Heaven-bent, we could not answer. The question does not apply. Mr. Collins belongs to neither pole; he belongs to a very particular parish in the English Midlands. He is a stupid, complacent and inflated ass, but a Sinner? No. A Saint? No. He is just a ridiculous figure, that is, a figure for which the Calvinist ethical psychology does not cater. The questions Was Emma Good? Was she Bad? are equally unanswerable and equally uninteresting. Obviously she should have been smacked more often when young; obviously, too, eternal Hell-fire is not required for her.

Let me now bring out my reservations. Jane Austen does, with obvious reluctance and literary embarrassment, use the criminal lawyer's Black-White process three or four times. Willoughby in *Sense and Sensibility* begins by being or at least seems to be, behind his attractive exterior, black-hearted. It turns out that he is only a bit grey at heart and not black. The latter shade is reserved for his fiancée, whom therefore we do not meet. In *Pride and Prejudice* Wickham and Lydia do become regulation Sinners, as do Mr. Elliot and Mrs. Clay in *Persuasion*. Fortunately London exists, that desperate but comfortingly remote metropolis; so Jane Austen smartly bundles off her shadowy representatives of vice to that convenient sink. It is in London that Henry Crawford and Maria enjoy or endure their guilty association. Thus Jane Austen is exempted by the width of the Home Counties from having to try to portray in her pastel-shades the ebony complexion of urban sin. Human saints and angels gave her no such literary anxieties. She just forgot that there were officially supposed to exist such arctic paragons, a piece of forgetfulness for which we are not inclined to reprove her.

As early as in *Northanger Abbey* Jane Austen explicitly relinquishes the Black-White, Sinner-Saint dichotomy. Catherine Morland, brought to her senses, reflects:

Charming as were all Mrs. Radcliffe's works ... it was not in them, perhaps, that human nature, at least in the midland counties of England, was to be looked for. Of the Alps and Pyrenees, with their pine-forests and their vices, they might give a faithful delineation; and Italy, Switzerland and the South of France might be as fruitful in horrors as they were there represented. Catherine dared not doubt beyond her own country, and even of that, if hard pressed, would have yielded the northern and western extremities. But in the central part of England there was surely some security of existence even of a wife nót beloved; in the laws of the land, and the manners of the age. Murder was not tolerated; servants were not slaves, and neither poison nor sleeping potions were to be procured, like rhubarb, from every druggist. Among the Alps and Pyrenees perhaps, there were no mixed characters. There, such as were not as spotless as an angel, might have the dispositions of a fiend. But in England it was not so; among the English, she believed, in their hearts and habits there was a general though unequal mixture of good and bad. Upon this conviction she would not be surprised if even in Henry and Eleanor Tilney some slight imperfection might hereafter appear; . . .

(ch. 25)

In *Persuasion* Jane Austen gives us what she would have been surprised to hear was a good rendering of Aristotle's doctrine of the Mean.

Anne wondered whether it ever occurred to him [Wentworth] to question the justness of his own previous opinion as to the universal felicity and advantages of firmness of character; and whether it might not strike him that like all other qualities of mind it should have its proportions and limits.

(ch. 12)

Not only was Jane Austen's ethic, if that is not too academic a word, Aristotelian in type, as opposed to Calvinistic. It was also secular as opposed to religious. I am sure that she was personally not merely the dutiful daughter of a clergyman, but was genuinely pious. Yet hardly a whisper of piety enters into even the most serious and most anguished meditations of her heroines. They never pray and they never give thanks on their knees. Three of her heroes go into the Church, and Edmund has to defend his vocation against the cynicisms of the Crawfords. But not a hint is given that he regards his clerical duty as that of saving souls. Routine church-going on Sunday with the rest of the family gets a passing mention three or four times, and Fanny is once stated to be religious. But that is all. I am not suggesting that Jane Austen's girls are atheists, agnostics or Deists. I am only saying that when Jane Austen writes about them, she draws the curtain between her Sunday thoughts, whatever they were, and her creative imagination. Her heroines face their moral difficulties and solve their moral problems without recourse to religious faith or theological doctrines. Nor does it ever occur to them to seek the counsels of a clergyman.

Lastly, her ethical vocabulary and idioms are quite strongly laced with aesthetic terms. We hear of 'Moral taste', 'Moral and literary tastes', 'Beauty of mind', 'the beauty of truth and sincerity', 'delicacy of principle', 'the Sublime of Pleasures'. Moreover there is a prevailing correlation between sense of duty, sense of propriety and aesthetic taste. Most of her people who lack any one of these three, lack the other two as well. Mrs. Jennings is the only one of Jane Austen's vulgarians who is allowed, none the less, to have a lively and just moral sense. Catherine Morland, whose sense of what is right and decorous is unfailing, is too much of an ignoramus yet to have acquired aesthetic sensibility, but the two Tilneys have all three tastes or senses. The Crawfords are her only people who combine musical, literary and dramatic sensitivity with moral laxity; Henry Crawford reads Shakespeare movingly, and yet is a bit of a cad. Elinor Dashwood, Anne Elliot and Fanny Price have good taste in all three dimensions. Emma Woodhouse is shaky in all three dimensions and all for the same reason, that she is not effectively self-critical.

## III

So Jane Austen's moral system was a secular, Aristotelian ethic-cum-aesthetic. But to say all this is to say that her moral *Weltanschauung* was akin to that of Lord Shaftesbury. Shaftesbury too had, a century before, assimilated moral sense to artistic sense, aesthetic taste to moral taste. A Grecian by study and predilection, he had followed Aristotle in preference to Plato, the Stoics or the Epicureans. A Deist rather than a Christian, he had based his religion, such as it was, on his ethics and aesthetics, rather than these on his religion. So I now put forward the historical hypothesis that Jane Austen's specific moral ideas derived, directly or indirectly, knowingly or unknowingly, from Shaftesbury. Certainly she never mentions him by name; but nor is any moralist mentioned by name, even in those contexts in which her girl-characters are described as studying the writings of moralists. Anne Elliot does advise the melancholy Captain Benwick to read, *inter alios*, 'our best moralists'; Fanny Price tutors her young sister, Susan, in history and morals; that teen-aged bluestocking, Mary Bennet, makes long extracts from the writings of moralists, and regales her company with their most striking platitudes. But the word 'moralist' would cover Goldsmith or Pope as well as Hutcheson or Hume, Johnson or Addison as well as Shaftesbury or Butler. We cannot argue just from the fact that Jane Austen speaks of moralists to the conclusion that she has any accredited moral philosophers in mind.

My reasons for thinking that Shaftesbury was the direct or indirect source of Jane Austen's moral furniture are these: (1) I have the impression, not based on research or wide reading, that throughout the eighteenth and early nineteenth centuries the natural, habitual and orthodox ethic was, with various modifications and mitigations, that Black-White, Saint-Sinner ethic that I have crudely dubbed 'Calvinistic'. Hutcheson, Butler and Hume, who were considerably influenced by Shaftesbury, all dissociate themselves from the Angel-Fiend psychology, as if this was prevalent. The essays, whether in *The Spectator*, *The Idler* or *The Rambler*, though I have only dipped into them, seem to me to use the Black-White process when very serious moral matters are discussed; but, perhaps partly for this reason, they tend not to treat very often such sermon-topics. The light touch necessary for an essay could not without awkwardness be applied to Salvation or Damnation. Fielding, who did know his Shaftesbury, was too jolly to bother much with satanic or angelic characters. There are many Hogarthian caricatures in his novels, but they are there to be laughed at. They are not Awful Warnings. That is, I have the impression that the secular and aesthetic Aristotelianism of Shaftesbury had not acquired a very wide vogue. It was not in the air breathed by the generality of novelists, poets and essayists. Perhaps there were latitudinarian sermons, other than Bishop Butler's, in which concessions were made to Shaftesbury and Hutcheson. I do not know. But I fancy that these ideas were current chiefly inside small, sophisticated circles in which 'Deist' was not a term of abuse and in which one could refer without explanation or apology to Locke and Descartes, Hobbes and Aristotle, Epicurus and Spinoza. So, if I am right in my assimilation of Jane Austen's moral ideas to those of Shaftesbury, then I think that she did not absorb these ideas merely from the literary, ecclesiastical and conversational atmosphere around her. I do not, on the other hand, insist that she got them by studying the writings of Shaftesbury himself, though if I was told that she got them either from Shaftesbury himself or from his donnish Scotch disciple, Hutcheson, I should without hesitation say 'Then she got them from Shaftesbury'. Of Hutcheson's epistemological professionalization of Shaftesbury there is not an echo in Jane Austen. She talks of 'Moral Sense' without considering the academic question whether or not it is literally a Sixth Sense. Nor do I find any echoes in her from Butler or from Hume, who in their turn echo little or nothing of the aestheticism of Shaftesbury. (2) Another thing that persuades me that Jane Austen was influenced fairly directly by Shaftesbury himself, besides the general secular and aesthetic Aristotelianism which she shares with him, is the vocabulary in which she talks about people. Her stock of general terms in which she describes their minds and characters, their faults and excellences is, *en bloc*, Shaftesbury's. Almost never does she use either the bi-polar ethical vocabulary or the corresponding bi-polar psychological vocabulary of the Black-White ethic. The flat, generic antitheses of Virtue and Vice, Reason and Passion, Thought and Desire, Soul and Body, Spirit and Flesh, Conscience and Inclination, Duty and Pleasure, hardly occur in her novels. Instead we get an ample, variegated and many-dimensional vocabulary. Her descriptions of people mention their tempers, habits, dispositions, moods, inclinations, impulses, sentiments, feelings, affections, thoughts, reflections, opinions, principles, prejudices, imaginations and fancies. Her people have or lack moral sense, sense of duty, good sense, taste, good-breeding, self-command, spirits and good humour; they do or do not regulate their imaginations and discipline their tempers. Her people have or lack knowledge of their own hearts or their own dispositions; they are or are not properly acquainted with themselves; they do or do not practise self-examination and soliloquy. None of these general terms or idioms is, by itself, so far as I know, peculiar to Shaftesbury and herself. It is the amplitude of the stock of them, and the constant interplays of them which smack strongly of Shaftesbury. It had been Shaftesbury's business, so to speak, to Anglicize the copious and elastic discriminations of which Aristotle had been the discoverer. In Jane Austen Shaftesbury's Anglicization is consummated without his floridity.

Given the stilted bi-polar vocabulary of, say, 'Reason and Passion' or 'Spirit and Flesh', then it is easy and tempting to reserve the top-drawer for one and the bottom-drawer for the other. But given the copious, specific and plastic vocabulary of Aristotle or Shaftesbury, it then becomes a hopeless as well as a repellent task to split it up into, say, fifteen top-drawer terms and seventeen bottom-drawer terms, into a platoon of sheep-terms for angelic and a platoon of goat-terms for satanic powers, impulses and propensities. To the employer of a hundred crayons the dichotomy 'Chalk or Charcoal' has no appeal. For example, John Knightley's occasional testiness was obviously not a Virtue. But nor was it a Vice. At worst it was a slight weakness, and in his particular domestic situation it was even a venial and rather likeable condiment. Where the icing-sugar is too thick, a splash of lemon-juice is a welcome corrective. We would not wish to be surrounded by John Knightleys. But we would not wish to be without them altogether. (3) There is one word which Shaftesbury and Jane Austen do frequently use in the same apparently idiosyncratic way, and that a way which is alien to us and I think, subject to correction, alien to most of the other eighteenth and early nineteenth century writers. This is the word 'Mind', often used without the definite or indefinite article, to stand not just for intellect or intelligence, but for the whole complex unity of a conscious, thinking, feeling and acting person. I am not here referring to the philosophico-theological use of 'Mind' for, roughly speaking, the Deist's or Pantheist's God. We do find this use occurring now and then in Shaftesbury, as in Pope.

Shaftesbury and Jane Austen both speak of the Beauty of Mind or the Beauty of a Mind, where they are talking about ordinary people; and when Shaftesbury speaks of the Graces and Perfections of Minds, of the Harmony of a Mind, of the Symmetry and Order of a Mind and of the Freedom of Mind he is talking in his jointly aesthetic and ethical manner just of laudable human beings. Jane Austen employs a lot of analogous phrases: 'Inferior in talent and all the elegancies of mind', 'delicacy of mind', 'liberty of mind or limb' (all from *Emma*); '[he] has a thinking mind', '. . . in temper and mind', 'Marianne's mind could not be controlled', 'her want of delicacy, rectitude and integrity of mind' (all from *Sense and Sensibility*). In 'one of those extraordinary bursts of mind' (*Persuasion*, ch. 7) the word 'mind' perhaps means 'intelligence' or just 'memory'. Now I think that Shaftesbury used this term 'Mind' as his preferred rendering of Aristotle's 'psyche', for which the normal rendering by 'Soul' would, I guess, have had for him too Christian or too parsonical a ring. He does once or twice use the disjunction 'mind or soul'. Jane Austen is even charier than Shaftesbury of employing the word 'soul'; and she, I surmise, just takes over the Shaftesburian use of 'Mind', very likely without feeling, what I think most philosophers would have felt, that this use was an irregular and strained one. If the Shaftesburian uses of the word 'Mind' did not subsequently become current in literature, sermons or conversation, or even, as I am sure they did not, in the philosophical writings of Butler and Hume, then the fact that Jane Austen often makes the same and similar uses of it would be fairly strong evidence that she drew directly on Shaftesbury. But whether this is the case or not is a matter of philological history, in which field I am not even an amateur. I am primarily arguing for the general, if vague, conclusion that Jane Austen was, whether she knew it or not, a Shaftesburian. It is a dispensable sub-hypothesis that she had studied the rather tedious and high-flown writings of Shaftesbury himself. Shaftesbury had opened a window through which a relatively few people in the eighteenth century inhaled some air with Aristotelian oxygen in it. Jane Austen had sniffed this oxygen. It may be that she did not know who had opened the window. But I shall put an edge on the issue by surmising, incidentally, that she did know.

# VII

# TRADITION AND MISS AUSTEN
## J. I. M. Stewart

IN *Aspects of the Novel* E. M. Forster invites us 'to visualize the English novelists not as floating down that stream which bears all its sons away unless they are careful, but as seated together in a room, a circular room, a sort of British Museum reading-room—all writing their novels simultaneously'. There is another place in Forster—I think *The Longest Journey*—which also has a scene in the British Museum reading-room; some of the readers get whispering together, and have to be sent an admonitory note by the superintendent. But what if it was the English novelists who got whispering? What should we overhear? Or—to make the question manageable—what might we hear them say about each other's standing in that tradition to which criticism declares them to belong?

There is here a large field for conjecture, particularly if we continue to disregard that stream 'which bears all its sons away' and so accord our whisperers the ability to look after as well as before. What, for example, would Miss Austen say about *Women in Love* or *The Plumed Serpent*? As we ask this question a deep and surely significant darkness descends upon us. We may dimly discern that Miss Austen would not find D. H. Lawrence's descent from her either plausible if asserted or agreeable if proved, but further than this it would be injudicious to go. Universal literature is very various and very vast; and it is all, whether we like it or not, afloat on the river of time. The synoptic view, Forster's reading-room view, is almost impossible of attainment.

Nevertheless the attempt can be made. It is even arguable that it ought to be made; that the distinguishing—in prose fiction, for example—of principles and standards wrought into being by pioneers, sustained and fortified by successors, invariably distinguishable upon scrutiny in all relevant work worthy to be summoned within the sphere of criticism: it is arguable that here is the activity to which we, in our turn, are summoned by imaginative literature. This kind of approach, if confidently and pertinaciously conducted, comes to render a great effect of centrality, authority, fastidious discrimination, and high seriousness. It also saves a great deal of time, since the class-list has virtually been established for us before we begin to read the scripts.

I use this academic metaphor I hope felicitously. A rigidly hierarchical view of any literary kind—a strong consciousness not only of the First Class but of the best, the only considerable, man to have taken the School since So-and-So, now a Fellow of All Souls—this is something accordant with the life of academies. Move away into the world of letters and you get something different. Authority is less immediately apparent, for in place of the wise old Chief Examiner with his infallible alphas and gammas there are only the actual writers, regularly contradicting each other and frequently contradicting themselves. There is something unruly about them; they won't keep in line; they are apt to say quite the wrong thing about the order of precedence one has established for them in one's lecture or book.

Something of this state of affairs can perhaps be grasped by returning to the British Museum and listening in. Let us make the attempt. For our purpose, as it happens, we needn't make anything up, except in a fashion the most harmless and obvious.

There they are, then: the writers of English fiction in the great tradition. Miss Austen requires a word of apology; she is rather a shadowy figure, since the proper book about her has not yet been published; but there is no doubt about the authenticity of her ticket. You see what she has ranged on the little shelf in front of her. There are Fanny Burney's novels, but not many others (she has been told not to waste her time with Fielding and that crowd). There are a few plays. The one she has pushed under her writing paper is called *Lovers' Vows;* Mrs. Inchbald has translated it from the German of Kotzebue, and I am sorry to tell you that it is the most shocking rubbish. We also notice, however, the whole of *The Rambler,* together with various other specimens of moral prose; *Marmion*; a couple of recent lives of the poet Cowper; but nothing very much in what could be called a philosophical or historical way.

Now notice the portly gentleman nearby. He is Mr. James—Mr. Henry James Jnr.—and you will observe that he is reading a novel called *Sons and Lovers*. Here, he murmurs to Miss Austen (they have been introduced, so it is entirely proper)—here is decidedly a nearer view of commoner things. This third novel by Mr. Lawrence (she will not have met him; it would be an unsuitable relation; but he is the young man a couple of places away—the one with the bright mud-coloured hair growing so oddly forward from the crown of his head)—this third novel of the good little Mr. Lawrence fairly smells of the real, and it is a pity that it is virtually innocent of any controlling idea. Mr. James has, as it happens, been reading a number of these new novelists recently: Mr. Gilbert Cannan, for example, and Mr. Compton Mackenzie and Mr. Hugh Walpole. Viewed along with these, he has to confess, Mr. Lawrence hangs somewhat in the dusty rear.

But now Mr. James has fallen silent. He is not really going on with *Sons and Lovers*; 'I have trifled with the exordia', he will soon be explaining to Edith Wharton when she seeks information on the extent of his acquaintance with Lawrence's work. Instead, he is thinking about Miss Austen (who has nerved herself to make notes on *Lovers' Vows*: Baron Wildenhaim will be just right for the Hon. John Yates). She too, he reflects, gets close to the real in her own way. But who could pretend that she doesn't leave much more untold than told about the aspects and manners even of the confined circle in which her muse revolves? Something about the artlessness of bird song: that would be the image to go for had her quality to be determined.

And now, across the reading-room, James's glance falls on Joseph Conrad. The poor fellow is hard at work, James tells himself, upon something really of the strangest: steeping his matter in perfect eventual obscuration, to a grand effect of some general and diffused lapse of authenticity. But James is in error here; Conrad isn't working; he is talking to H. G. Wells (something he ought not to be doing, since Wells is a total outsider, so far as our tradition is concerned) and is working himself up into one of the irritable frenzies to which he is liable. This is because he has caught sight of Miss Austen, and can't understand why she is in this gallery at all. 'What is all this about Jane Austen?' he demands of Wells. 'What is there *in* her? What is it all about?' We never learn Wells's reply. The superintendent has sent one of his notes.

The superintendent might equally be sending one of his notes to young Mr. Lawrence. For Lawrence is occupying his time in a manner improper in the reading-room; he is simply scribbling a private letter. His correspondent is a Mrs. Jackson, who has written a novel under her maiden name of Catherine Carswell and posted him the manuscript. He tells her that she has a simply *beastly* style, stiff-kneed and stupid. As for the stuff of her novel, that's abominably muddled. But—mysteriously enough—'nearly all of it is *marvellously* good'. And in a postscript it is pronounced to be 'like Jane Austen at a deeper level'. The ultimate heir to the great tradition, we must feel, here produces a splendid throwaway line.

If Lawrence's glance travels to Conrad on our occasion, it probably doesn't dwell there. He has no great admiration for Conrad, who is a Writer among the Ruins, and always giving in before he starts. Why should we snivel in a wet hanky like Lord Jim? George Eliot is another matter: a solid, useful woman, from whom one can learn how to construct substantial novels of English provincial life. The thing is to take two couples and develop their relationships. All beginners should have a go at George Eliot.

As it happens, George Eliot has just come into the reading-room. Normally she is a London Library woman; she feels that she owes that institution something since it decided, hard upon its foundation, to admit her fiction, and her fiction alone, to its shelves. Now, she may be said to occasion a considerable stir of interest. Henry James's eye moves from her to Miss Austen and back. There is at least a relation, he is thinking. But of a subtleness! Of the most baffling! Is it not true that in George Eliot the sun sinks forever to the west, and the shadows are long, and the afternoon wanes, and the trees vaguely rustle, and the colour of the sky is much inclined to yellow—whereas in Jane Austen we sit quite resigned in an arrested spring? Is Miss Austen, in all the extraordinary grace of her facility, all her light felicity; is Miss Austen before whom we find ourselves so incurious as to her process or the experience that fed it; is Miss Austen who is—ah, that is it!—a brown thrush telling his story from the garden bough: is this pioneer among the 'nameable sisterhood' in all the unconsciousness of her art really a progenitor of the formidable lady who has just entered the reading-room—the least inconsiderable of all English novelists, but so prone to proceed from the abstract to the concrete, to evolve her figures and characters less from observation than from her moral consciousness?

We must leave James. He is rather inclined to go on and on—and besides, as you will have seen, he has this tiresome trick of saying quite the wrong thing. Nor can George Eliot, as it turns out, detain us for very long. It is said that of all our eminent writers, whether here present or not, it is perhaps she who esteems Miss Austen most. 'It is not for nothing,' Dr. Leavis writes, 'that George Eliot admired her work profoundly, and wrote one of the earliest appreciations of it to be published.' But this appreciation appears really to have been written by G. H. Lewes, and we find that Miss Austen's novels seem to have existed for George Eliot largely for agreeable reading aloud. 'The evening passed by pleasantly reading *Emma*' is what the six volumes of her correspondence yield in the way of critical appreciation. We take pleasure in this as evidence that moments of relaxation came to her, since she is almost wholly without that lightness of air which—intermittently, at least—distinguishes most practising artists, and which so often alienates the investigating classes in their adventurings among them. But I suspect George Eliot to have felt Miss Austen to be rather a lightweight writer—one far from commanding those heavy batteries which could compel the London Library to capitulate to prose fiction as an intellectually respectable literary form.

As we leave the reading-room we are bound to feel, I think, that it is without having received, from these other novelists who are so at sixes and sevens, any strong impression of Miss Austen as the acknowledged founder of a line. The eminent writers just don't seem to see her that way. Is there any other eminent writer who has anything illuminating to say about her? Let me propose Rudyard Kipling. Kipling wrote a short story called 'The Janeites'. If the very title makes us shudder, so much the better, for it means we are beginning to learn whose property Miss Austen is.

> Jane lies in Winchester—blessed be her shade!
> Praise the Lord for making her, and her for all she made!
> And while the stones of Winchester, or Milsom Street, remain,
> Glory, love, and honour unto England's Jane!

This comes at the start of the story. At the end there is another poem in which we learn that Jane dies, goes to Paradise, is conducted upstairs by Sir Walter Scott, and met by a kind of reception committee composed of Fielding, Smollett, Cervantes and Shakespeare. She is offered anything in Heaven's gift, asks for love, and is straightway accorded the hand—the ghostly hand—of Captain Wentworth out of *Persuasion*. This is not, you see, the Miss Austen who belongs to Miss Lascelles and Mrs. Leavis, Dr. Chapman and Professor Trilling. And in the story itself she is shown, on the contrary, as belonging to the members of an English battery in Flanders during the First World War; they keep a grip of themselves, gentle and simple, by elaborating a convention of ceaseless allusive reference to her novels; these see them through until the battery is destroyed and most of them are killed. 'There's no one to touch Jane when you're in a tight place,' one of the survivors says.

But, you may say, the minds of men in day-long fear of death or horrible mutilation are not to be relied upon in literary matters. Very well—consider what may be our own more humdrum case. We prove to have caught a chill in the British Museum, a putrid fever has followed, it has even been feared that the lungs (like poor Mary Crawford's mind) may be tainted. How much we look forward to being on the mend, so that the six novels may be brought in to hasten our recovery! And here we are one with the whole host of common readers. No novels can touch Miss Austen's when it comes to straight solace and refreshment. They must have been read and read again in convalescence more than any other books in English with the exception of those bundled together as the Holy Bible. This is a very great achievement; and no theory of the nature of art or of the function of imaginative literature that is restive before it can be other than of an arid and ungenial order. If we are minded to establish a kind of Top Ten from the most delightful books in the language, all six of these novels have a claim. It is a staggering triumph on Miss Austen's, on Jane's, part. How is it to be explained?

The simplest answer comes from her detractors—or from those of them who assert, in effect, that the books represent a perfectly achieved invalid cookery. People don't often die in them, or not in an untimely manner—or if they do they will at least be among the unimportant and unattractive characters, like that unpromising son over whom Mrs. Musgrove is so foolish as to perpetuate her large fat sighings. Again, indigence never causes anybody to fail of a meal today, or even to fear of failing of one tomorrow. The discernible universe is totally lacking in urgent political, social or economic problems of any sort, and the most tremendous event in the history of modern Europe is represented by a couple of needle-books, 'made by some emigrant', with which Mrs. Dashwood favours the Miss Steeles. Indeed, no sort of general ideas exist, so we have no occasion to reflect on how inadequate our own particular brains are for per-pending them. Far from the abodes of noise, disorder, and impro-priety, we enjoy the society of sensible, gentlemanlike men and rational, unaffected women, whose tempers are mild but whose principles are steady, and even among whose most distant acquaint-ance irreligious or immoral habits—even Sunday travelling—are reassuringly rare. Nobody need really do any work—except military and naval officers, after a fashion; rather low connections in business or the law in London; and servants and the labouring poor. There is moderate and healthful activity, all the same. We go out shooting; we interview stewards and bailiffs; we sketch, embroider, perform on the pianoforte, attend balls, and go on expeditions and picnics. This last pursuit is perhaps a little rackety; various social disasters can occur; and Mr. Knightley is doubtless his own judicious self when he declares that 'the simplicity of gentlemen and ladies . . . is best observed by meals within doors'. In short, we are offered a universe in which it is entirely laudable to centre our wishes, like Edward Ferrars, 'in domestic comfort and the quiet of private life'.

Many people have, of course, made fun of Miss Austen by com-piling such catalogues. Other detractors, more subtle, point out how much she remains an amateur writer, and how much of our pleasure in her is sophisticated and even perverse. We relish a certain quaint-ness about the whole exhibition, a delicious absurdity when the author steps an inch beyond her range. Think of the accident on the Cobb at Lyme Regis, with Captain Wentworth 'staggering against the wall for his support', and all the rest of it. It is superbly and undesignedly funny. As Sir Herbert Read has remarked, Miss Austen often exhibits 'a simplicity or naïvety of phrasing which is perhaps the secret of the attraction which her style undoubtedly has for a large number of people'.

There is something in all this; it goes with the 'period' feel ministered to in those superior editions of the novels embellished with delicate contemporary illustrations of Regency costume and furniture. Yet we are not taken very far in accounting for even the superficial attractiveness of the books by reviewing merely those aspects of them that are as pleasantly undemanding as a cup of

Ovaltine at bedtime. Their effect, after all, is of something quite different; it is very much of that best of invalid beverages, a dry champagne. There is a world of gaiety and vivacity in every glass. It is like having the stuff in your room on draught; you command an inexhaustible flow of social comedy at the turn of a tap.

So far as their 'charm' goes, indeed, the novels are largely accounted for as soon as we mark the dexterity with which a high talent for burlesque, irony, satire and humour is secured constant employment within a world drastically purged of almost everything alarming and mysterious in the human situation. That this abstractive labour is performed with the most perfect art appears to me most undeniable—although not readily to be analyzed—in the field of sexual relations. Professor Garrod declares that Miss Austen 'describes everything in the youth of women which does not matter', and he appears to regard her refusal to take account of the fact that nice girls do eventually get bundled into bed as a kind of deliberate bluestocking insult to the male principle. One can only say here that perhaps it ought to be so, but it isn't. We know very well that we are not being introduced to her young men entirely in the round. But they are aware of what they are about, and they seldom evince that sort of radical failure in masculinity which afflicts, for example, some of the heroes of Henry James. That the girls are aware of what they are about too—knowing because Miss Austen knows—is demonstrable (for a start) in the story of Marianne Dashwood. In short, nothing in Miss Austen's manner of ignoring what she ignores falsifies what she exhibits.

There is again a great deal of art—or of art co-operating with temperament—about the manner in which the whole exhibition, so purged of all major disagreeables as it is, avoids a disabling overplus of that 'sunshine and unselfishness' of which Lord David Cecil speaks in defining the appeal of the books. Miss Austen's settled dislikes have their function: of children, for example, and the aristocracy, and the elements. (The climate is nearly always abominable. Rain, wind and mud threaten the health of young ladies in winter, and in summer they have to contend with 'the unmitigated glare of day'. Even indoors it can be uncomfortable in hot weather, particularly if one lacks a sitting-room with a northern exposure, or has to put up with one facing west in the afternoon.) And so too with the local astringencies and direct statements of disapprobation. Suddenly ceasing to prick, the irony pierces—as if the ironist had dropped her embroidery needle and in her hand were a rapier. Or the weapon is dropped entirely and we are told the brutal truth. Mr. Woodhouse's 'talents could not have recommended him at any time'. Mrs. Bennet is 'a woman of mean understanding, little information, and uncertain temper'. Lady Bertram—for long seemingly no more usefully to be censured than her pug—becomes for a moment quite simply one who 'never thought of being useful to anybody'.

We have now arrived some way—not all the way—in accounting for the status of the six novels simply as bedside books. Their creator is the mistress of a quaintly confined world, inviolate to ideas and admitting only the most distant reverberations of the passions, and she brings to it a transforming *vis comica* which can create Mr. Woodhouse and Mr. Collins and Mrs. Norris and Lady Catherine de Bourgh. Is this the whole story? It certainly is not. And what we have chiefly missed out is the heroines—the attractiveness of whom by our bedside is immediate enough. But the heroines take us further. It is along with these young women that we can best explore Miss Austen's claim to trespass beyond the bounds of light literature, and herself to illustrate that larger potentiality of prose fiction which is asserted, rather oddly, in the fifth chapter of *Northanger Abbey*.

We come here to the question of that 'intense moral preoccupation' without which, Dr. Leavis has said, Miss Austen would not have been a great novelist. It is not an easy question. The moral climate within which she grew up, and which she appears in large part to have accepted without dubiety, was not in itself, I feel, much to the advantage of her development as an artist—or, for that matter, as a Christian. It is a narrow and prudential morality, much tainted by material interest. And it percolates into the novels in ways apt to elicit that perverse kind of enjoyment upon which I have already remarked. Thus early in *Sense and Sensibility* we are told of Willoughby that 'in slighting too easily the forms of worldly propriety, he displayed a want of caution which Elinor could not approve'. If ever so fleetingly, we must be either chilled or diverted by this, and neither reaction is intended by the writer. (Elinor recovers in our regard when we learn that, since Marianne's sensibility made it impossible for her to say what she did not feel, however trivial the occasion, there fell upon that severe moralist her elder sister 'the whole task of telling lies when politeness required it'.) Or consider in *Emma* the occasion upon which Frank Churchill (who has his own reasons) judges the Crown Inn a capital place for a dance, and makes light of Emma's objection that a socially homogeneous gathering could not be contrived. He cannot see that 'there would be the smallest difficulty in everybody's returning into their proper place the next morning'. Emma, deprecating his lack of 'pride', reflects that 'his indifference to a confusion of rank bordered too much on inelegance of mind'. Again we are either amused or—like Sir Harold Nicolson—disapproving. And it won't quite do to tell us that the passage is dramatic and personative, a reflection of the injudicious sense of consequence indulged by Miss Emma Woodhouse of Hartfield. We suspect from much else in the books that what Sir Harold calls 'the meaningless subtleties of social status' are not treated by Miss Austen herself with the fine disdain that you and I can manage.

It is when graver issues come up, particularly those of sexual morality, that we are most perplexed. Elizabeth Bennet sees her sister Lydia very clearly; she knows just where 'wild volatility', 'assurance', and 'disdain of all restraint' are likely to lead; but it is of the damage to 'our importance, our respectability' that she first thinks. Yet it is *Mansfield Park* that is really puzzling, and what seems the probable reason is significant enough. According to Professor Trilling, this novel represents 'an unusual state of the author's mind'. But does it not rather represent the temporary exacerbation of an itch to turn formal moralist which in fact constitutes, from first to last, the main threat to the integrity of her art?

> 'But was there nothing in her conversation that struck you, Fanny, as not quite right?'
> 'Oh, yes! she ought not to have spoken of her uncle as she did. I was quite astonished.'
>
> (ch. 7)

Edmund Bertram and Fanny Price lose no time in getting into this sort of stride; their final effort, when the Crawfords have disgraced themselves, recalls that dismal form of Puritan literature in which two or more justified persons largely discourse to one another on the failings of their reprobate neighbours. Nevertheless *Mansfield Park* remains a rich and sensitive novel. This is because it does not come into being quite as Dr. Leavis and Professor Trilling assume it to have come into being—or as Miss Austen herself, for that matter, may have assumed.

It is clear that, often enough, she started off with a certain admixture of what I must venture to call bad intentions: the embodying of moral propositions in prose fiction. These propositions were quite commonplace. She was not a particularly well-educated woman —only a woman of high genius, living in a restricted society composed for the most part of intellectually and socially timid people. She was, in consequence, prone to overestimate the promise of ideas that seemed simple and edifying. Even words command her; *Sense and Sensibility* leans heavily on 'exertion', and throughout *Emma* 'rational' comes to toll like a bell. *Mansfield Park* was to be about 'ordination', with bits on 'education' thrown in; and it can only be described as a non-starter in either field. There is, indeed, one set discussion of ordination; it is a failure as being the product of a mind unable to conceive, or at least express, the problem of religious vocation; it represents Edmund and Fanny as wholly priggish (which, to be fair, they are not), and Miss Crawford as ill-bred (which she is not, either). No writer even of mere talent—Mrs. Humphry Ward, say, rather than George Eliot—persevering with this project from the standpoint of 'an intense moral interest' in what appears to be Dr. Leavis's sense, could leave it so totally unexamined in the end. But even in *Mansfield Park*, fortunately, Miss Austen's better artistic intuition gains, on the whole, the upper hand.

Dr. Leavis, if I understand his emphasis rightly, sees Miss Austen as regularly starting from 'certain problems that life compels on her as personal ones'. She then 'impersonalizes her moral tensions'— which means (I take it) writes her novels. It is an orthodox Freudian view of art. Professor Trilling sees *Mansfield Park* as starting in the same way: from 'a crisis in the author's spiritual life'. I think myself that there is substance in this, although it is perhaps rather grandly expressed. Miss Austen seems to me to have been—at this time, and so far as her conscious mind went—more than usually caught up in the common rectitudinous attitudes of her society. However this may be, Professor Trilling sees clearly enough the actual points of hazard in the novel: no work of genius has ever spoken so insistently for cautiousness and constraint; its impulse is not to forgive but to condemn; the shade of Pamela hangs over Fanny Price's career; Fanny in her physical debility hitches on to a tradition affirming the peculiar sanctity of the sick, the weak, and the dying—a tradition that stretches from Richardson's Clarissa Harlowe to Henry James's Milly Theale. All this is true. But when he comes to the theatricals undertaken in Sir Thomas Bertram's absence, Professor Trilling has to remind us that 'the American philosopher George Mead' has written learnedly on the 'assumption of roles' as an important element of Romanticism; and he tells us in the same paragraph that 'Jane Austen puts the question of literature at the moral centre of her novel'. Miss Austen, he says, knows that, 'for the sake of its moral life', her novel 'must violate its own beauty by incorporating some of the irreducible prosy actuality of the world'. And Sir Thomas—to return to *Lovers' Vows*—'instinctively resists the diversification of the self that is implied by the assumption of roles'. He does this because 'his own self is an integer'.

We are here surely beckoned into regions remote from any activity of mind that Miss Austen can conceivably have had traffic with. Yet Professor Trilling goes on to what appears to me a wholly just perception. What we respond to in Jane Austen is her primacy and brilliance in placing personality at the centre of the moral life. Finally, Professor Trilling goes a little further. Just this, he implies, is going to be common enough in subsequent fiction. *Mansfield Park* has a special interest. It exhibits Jane Austen imposing upon the personality the sanctions of principle, and in this finding a path to that wholeness of self which is peace.

'Principle, active principle, had been wanting.' The word stands to *Mansfield Park* as 'exertion' does to *Sense and Sensibility* and 'rational' to *Emma*, but it fails to take us very far towards understanding the Misses Bertram on the one hand or their cousin Fanny on the other. Nor does it much advance us in an understanding of Miss Austen's creative process. The truth is surely that *Mansfield Park*—what is alive in it—was not born of meditations on the virtues of principle indulged in during quiet walks in the shrubbery. It was born with the coming to birth of its people, and particularly of its heroine, Fanny Price. The true moral intensities, or lackings in intensity, in the novel are those that distil themselves as its personalities, at one depth or another, are revealed as they are explored. And it is, perhaps, only thus—only by a humble waiting before the gates of his own imagination—that the artist can achieve what Johnson calls 'a faithful Miniature of human Transactions'. This first law of representative fiction was known to Miss Austen; was known, at least, to the Jane who went to Paradise. There was, one has to admit, another Jane. Her note is governessy, and her influence occasionally baleful. For example, she seems to have constrained the Jane bound for Paradise rather to throw up the sponge in the final chapter of *Mansfield Park*.

If I am a painter and set up my canvas before a natural scene I may fairly accurately be described as making love to it as I paint. As I model into its recesses—like Lily Briscoe, say, in *To the Lighthouse* —it is that sort of communion that is going on. The fascination of the scene lies in its otherness; I am not striving to carry my own identity into it; its own identity is there already, so that my act of possession is all exploration; and I shall get no further in my task than the particular degree of my empathic power admits. Miss Austen's characters, particularly her heroines, are the product of such a mechanism operating with delicacy and certainty. They have not been put together out of this and that; by a paradox of the imagination they have existed in their own right from the moment of their creator's glimpsing them; failures in art apart, they are contemplated objects of a complete purity. When it comes to morals, they prove to be, on the whole, persons better than ourselves (it is with such that art of any dignity tends to concern itself, as Aristotle noticed), but they are in no sense what the poet Shelley liked to mix up nice girls with the notion of: beautiful idealisms of moral excellence.

Hence, it seems to me, the reserve with which we ought to receive an interpretation of *Mansfield Park* like Professor Trilling's or the more generalized assumption of Dr. Leavis. Miss Austen doesn't start out from a critique of society, or from a Freudian resolution so to exploit 'art' as to make her own perplexities widely interesting and palatable. It isn't even her own ability to be morally perceptive that is of prime importance to her. It is to understand and convey the play of moral feelings, and of other feelings, within the defined area of fiction that she has made her own.

# VIII

## JANE AUSTEN AND 'THE QUIET THING' — A STUDY OF *MANSFIELD PARK*

### *Tony Tanner*

---

MANY GREAT novels concern themselves with characters whose place in society is not fixed or assured. Foundlings, orphans, outsiders, people moving from one country to another, people moving from one class to another, those who have to create the shape of their lives as they go along, or those who find themselves involved in movements or changes over which they have only partial control—such people are common frequenters of the novel. Whether we think of Tom Jones, or Julien Sorel (in *Le Rouge et le Noir*), or Becky Sharp (in *Vanity Fair*), or Jude Fawley (in *Jude the Obscure*), or Isabel Archer (in *The Portrait of a Lady*), or Paul Morel (in *Sons and Lovers*), or even of Saul Bellow's Augie March, these are all characters who at the start of the novel are not defined or fulfilled by their status or locality or position. They cannot and do not take their place in society for granted, and they end up—whether happily or otherwise—with a different social identity. In the course of such novels there has been choice and change. The characters might have their virtue ultimately rewarded, like Tom Jones; or their ambitions thwarted, like Jude; or they may be imprisoned by the hateful consequences of their own errors, like Isabel Archer. In every case we can generally say that we are watching the initially undefined and uncommitted self having to take on definition through what happens to it in society. The self may be able to choose what happens, it may simply permit it, or it may have to suffer it: its quest for definition may entail true discovery of the self, and it may finally precipitate destruction of the self. But whatever else happens to these characters, they have moved. They are not where they were; they are not what they were. And so it is with Fanny Price, the heroine of *Mansfield Park*.

Fanny starts her life in a very lower-middle-class family in Portsmouth: we last see her effectively accepted as the mistress of Mansfield Park. Initially an object of charity, she ends up cherished as the indispensable mainstay of the Mansfield family. With her marriage and full social and familial recognition, her self is successfully and rightfully defined. And yet Fanny Price exhibits few of the qualities we usually associate with the traditional hero or heroine. We expect them to have vigour and vitality: Fanny is weak and sickly. We look to them for a certain venturesomeness or audacity, a bravery, a resilience, even a recklessness: but Fanny is timid, silent, unassertive, shrinking and excessively vulnerable. Above all, perhaps, we expect heroes and heroines to be active, rising to opposition, resisting coercion, asserting their own energy: but Fanny is almost totally passive. Indeed, one of the strange aspects of this singular book is that regarded externally, it is the story of a girl who triumphs by doing nothing. She sits, she waits, she endures; and when she is finally promoted, through marriage, into an unexpectedly high social position, it seems to be a reward, not so much for her vitality, as for her extraordinary immobility. This is odd enough; yet there is another unusual and even less sympathetic aspect to this heroine. She is never, ever, wrong. Jane Austen, usually so ironic about her heroines, in this instance vindicates Fanny Price without qualification. We are used to seeing heroes and heroines confused, fallible, error-prone. But Fanny always thinks, feels, speaks, and behaves exactly as she ought. Every other character in the book, without exception, falls into error—some fall irredeemably. But not Fanny. She does not put a foot wrong. Indeed, she hardly risks any steps at all; and there is an intimate and significant connection between her virtue and her immobility. The result of these unusual traits has been to make her a very unpopular heroine. Even sympathetic readers have often found her something of a prig, and severer strictures have not been lacking. Kingsley Amis calls her 'a monster of complacency and pride.' It is not as though Jane Austen could not create attractive heroines: Elizabeth Bennet and Emma Woodhouse are among the most beloved figures in English fiction. But nobody falls in love with Fanny Price. What, then, was Jane Austen doing in this book?

The question is worth asking because if Fanny Price is her least popular heroine, it is arguable that *Mansfield Park* is her most profound novel (indeed, to my mind, it is one of the most profound novels of the nineteenth century). And what such a poor sort of heroine is doing in such a great book is a matter worth examining with some care.

To grasp the full meaning of the various characters and incidents, it is important to understand the world of the novel and be alert to the significant differences between life in Portsmouth, life in London, and life at Mansfield Park. To this end it might be worth offering a very brief summary of what England was like in the years 1811–13, the very eve of Waterloo, when Jane Austen was writing the novel. In general we can see that it was a period of great stability just about to give way to a time of unimagined changes. At that time most of the population (some thirteen million) were involved in rural and agricultural work: yet within another twenty years, the majority of Englishmen became urban dwellers involved with industry, and the great railway age had begun. Throughout the early years of the century the cities were growing at a great rate; the network of canals was completed, the main roads were being remade. Regency London, in particular, boomed and became, among other things, a great centre of fashion. On the other hand England in 1813 was still predominantly a land of country towns and villages, a land of rural routines which were scarcely touched by the seven campaigns of the Peninsular War against Napoleon. Since the question of attitude towards traditional rural life is important in Jane Austen, it is worth drawing on a quotation from William Cobbett which reveals the emergence of a new, and wrong, type of landowner. Cobbett often stressed

the difference between a resident *native* gentry, attached to the soil, known to every farmer and labourer from their childhood, frequently mixing with them in those pursuits where all artificial distinctions are lost, practising hospitality without ceremony, from habit and not on calculation; and a gentry only now-and-then resident at all, having no relish for country delights, foreign in their manners, distant and haughty in their behaviour, looking to the soil only for its rents, viewing it as a mere object of speculation, unacquainted with its cultivators, despising them and their pursuits, and relying, for influence, not upon the good will of the vicinage, but upon the dread of their power.

Jane Austen, the daughter of a Tory parson, valued the old rural way of life, and she too was well aware of a new attitude abroad in the land—speculative, acquisitive, calculating, and irreverent. In *Mansfield Park* quite a lot can be told about people from their differing attitudes to rural life.

But if her age was still predominantly one of rural quiet, it was also the age of the French Revolution, the War of American Independence, the start of the Industrial Revolution, and the first generation of the Romantic poets: and Jane Austen was certainly not unaware of what was going on in the world around her. She had two brothers in the Royal Navy; family connections with Warren Hastings; and a cousin whose husband was guillotined in the Terror. And although her favourite prose writer was Dr. Johnson, she clearly knew the work of writers like Goethe, Wordsworth, Scott, Byron, Southey, Godwin and other, very definitely nineteenth-century, authors. If Jane Austen does seem to have lived a life of placid rural seclusion in north Hampshire she was at the same time very aware of a whole range of new energies and impulses, new ideas and powers, which were changing or about to change England —and indeed the whole western world—with a violence, a suddenness, and a heedlessness, which would soon make Jane Austen's world seem as remote as the Elizabethan Age. It is well to remember that a few years later when Thomas Arnold saw his first train tearing through the Rugby countryside he said: 'Feudality is gone forever'. So close was it possible then to feel to the immemorial, static feudal way of life: so quickly was that way of life to vanish as the modern world laboured to be born. Jane Austen, then, was living in a diminishing enclave of traditional rural stability just prior to a period of convulsive, uncontrollable change; and *Mansfield Park* is, among other things, a novel about rest and restlessness, stability and change—the moving and the immovable.

Seen against this general background what, then, is the larger significance of the three major areas or 'worlds' in the novel—Mansfield Park, London, and Portsmouth? Mansfield Park (based on Cottesbrooke) is set in the county of Northampton and is effectively a stronghold of the old rural Tory values. Growing up inside this world and exposed to the shortcomings of its inhabitants, Fanny does not really comprehend the symbolic value of Mansfield Park until she returns to visit her birthplace in Portsmouth. The contrast throws the differing values of each world into clear relief. The house in Portsmouth is 'the abode of noise, disorder, and impropriety.

Nobody was in their right place, nothing was done as it ought to be.'
Her father is a dirty, boorish drinker; her mother, an incompetent,
ill-judging slattern. The children are brought up wrongly in as much
as they are not brought up at all. Here there is no real affection, no
true delicacy of feeling, no harmony or coherence of behaviour. As
Fanny's brother William says so suggestively—'The house is always
in confusion.' It is not a place of vice, but a place of chaos. Nothing
has been done to shape and restrain life into any decency or decorum.
Human impulses here are not perverted; but they are unregulated.
In this house of confusion, Fanny 'could think of nothing but Mansfield, its beloved inmates, its happy ways. Everything where she
now was was in full contrast to it. The elegance, propriety, regularity,
harmony—and perhaps, above all, the peace and tranquillity of Mansfield, were brought to her remembrance every hour of the day, by
the prevalence of everything opposite to them *here*.' (ch. 39). Fanny
is idealizing Mansfield (Mrs. Norris, for instance, is nastier than
anyone in the Portsmouth house); but that is only to say that she is
discovering the true symbolic value of all it stands for. It becomes
a house of order, in which there is very little noise and no unnecessary movement—'no sounds of contention, no raised voice, no abrupt
bursts, no tread of violence.'

It is important that it is while she is staying at Portsmouth that
the question of which is her true 'home' occurs to Fanny. 'When she
had been coming to Portsmouth, she had loved to call it her home,
had been fond of saying that she was going home; the word had
been very dear to her; and so it still was, but it must be applied to
Mansfield. *That* was now the home. Portsmouth was Portsmouth;
Mansfield was home.' (ch. 45). This is important, because when the
uncommitted self finally chooses its 'home', it is in effect identifying
itself with a certain way of life and a role within it. Throughout
*The Portrait of a Lady*, for example, Isabel Archer is inspecting
houses to see whether she can find one she is willing to call 'home'.
Her final choice of Osmond's sterile little palace of art is a major
error: Fanny's transfer of her allegiances from her actual birthplace
to her place of upbringing is evidence of her capacity for true judgement. She has found her real, spiritual, 'home'. Very early in the
novel, when there is some chance of Fanny going to live with Mrs.
Norris, the insensitive Lady Bertram says to her: 'It can make very
little difference to you, whether you are in one house or the other.'
But when houses come to represent edifices of values, as they do in

this novel, it makes all the difference in the world. It is entirely right that when Fanny finally returns to Mansfield Park, soon to become one of its most important guardians, Jane Austen invests the landscape with a verdant, symbolic promise. 'It was three months, full three months, since her quitting it; and the change was from winter to summer. Her eye fell every where on lawns and plantations of the freshest green; and the trees, though not full clothed, were in that delightful state, when farther beauty is known to be at hand, and when, while much is actually given to the sight, more yet remains for the imagination.' (ch. 46). The prospects in the landscape reflect the prospects in Fanny's life.

Mansfield, as a place, as an institution, can take raw material from Portsmouth and refine it—as it does with Fanny, as it effectively does with her brother William (by securing him a career in the Navy), as it promises to do with her sister Susan. Indeed, these new recruitments are essential to the maintaining of the 'house' because so many of its actual blood descendants go to the bad and betray their trust. Jane Austen is conceivably making a class point here: without going outside to the unformed world of Portsmouth for fresh potential, the world of Mansfield Park may wither from within. But London, the world of liberty, amusement and fashion, has no redeeming virtues. It is there that Maria falls into the ways which will lead to her adulterous corruption and ultimate disgrace and banishment. It is there that Julia involves herself with the worthless Mr. Yates. It is there that Tom wastes his substance and, as a result, nearly loses his life. Above all, it is London that has made and formed the attractive Crawfords who very nearly bring total ruin to the world of Mansfield Park. For if Mansfield, at its best, perfects people, London, at its worst, perverts them.

It is, significantly, during the absence of Sir Thomas, the patriarchal guardian of Mansfield, that Mary and Henry Crawford arrive; thus suggesting that the absence of the responsible law-giver of Mansfield Park makes its rural ethos vulnerable to the disruptive forces of a newer, urban, world. From the start the Crawfords are identified with London. As soon as they arrive, Mrs. Grant is worried lest they get bored, because they are 'mostly used to London'. They are indeed all for amusements, and translated into the rural world of Mansfield their irresponsible taste for distractions becomes a potentially dangerous force. Thus Henry Crawford distracts Julia, seduces Maria, and tries to ensnare Fanny; while Mary toys with

Tom and all but seduces Edmund from his high-mindedness and his clerical calling. Thus between them they tamper with all the young people who are responsible for the continuance of Mansfield Park: and, as we shall see, it is only Fanny's stubborn tenacity that prevents their complete usurpation and demolition of that world. The Crawfords are far from villains: indeed Jane Austen had the insight to endow them with many of the most superficially attractive qualities in the book: but they have been spoilt and subtly corrupted by their prolonged immersion in the amoral fashionable London world. (It was, it is worth remembering, the age of Beau Brummel.) Fanny, we read, 'was disposed to think the influence of London very much at war with all respectable attachments'. And so it proves to be in the book. We infer—through the Crawfords—that London is a world of glamour, excitement, activity, amusement and all the attractions of worldly wit and casual relationships: but we also infer that it is a world of endlessly false appearances, a world in which manners substitute for morals, a world given over to cold deception, manipulation, and exploitation.

A minor incident, prophetic of the disruptive threat which the Crawfords pose to the life connected with Mansfield, occurs shortly after their arrival. Mary reveals that she had surprising difficulty in trying to hire a cart for the transportation of her harp (fit accessory for the siren she is—Fanny, typically, cannot play a musical instrument). She expresses her rather contemptuous amazement that because of the harvesting to be done, there was no cart to be had at any price—indeed, that she offended the farmers by expecting to be able to procure one. It is gently pointed out to her how important it is for the farmers to get the harvest in, how impossible it should be that they could spare any carts. Mary answers: 'I shall understand all your ways in time; but coming down with the true London maxim, that everything is to be got with money, I was a little embarrassed at first by the sturdy independence of your country customs.' Much of the novel is implied here. Mary comes from a world governed only by considerations of money: she has no instinct for the traditional rural ways and values. She would interfere with the harvest to satisfy a whim. The point is—will those country customs be sturdy enough to resist her London manners and her London code? The issue is raised another way when Mary's sister, Mrs. Grant, chides her for her worldly standards and her bantering manner: 'You are as bad as your brother, Mary; but we will cure you both. Mansfield shall cure you both—and without any taking in. Stay with us and we will cure you.' Can Mansfield cure what has been spoilt by London: or will the products of London finally undermine all that Mansfield strives to perpetuate? The novel thus reveals a battle between worlds as well as concentrating on the relationships of a few characters. Without any crude allegorizing—indeed, with a minute attention to local detail—Jane Austen has produced a story which touches profoundly on the past and future of England itself. And if, in the novel, she allowed the world of Mansfield to triumph, even though she sensed that the future belonged to London, then that is something we must consider later.

We can now consider the various characters from the point of view of their varying relationships with Mansfield Park. We may group them thus: the guardians, the inheritors, and the interlopers. Fanny we will consider separately. Sir Thomas is of course the chief guardian. He believes in 'duty' and is just, benevolent and responsible. In his absence Mansfield Park falls into confusion: after his return, order is re-imposed. It is he who finally signals Fanny's real reception into the family by ordering a fire to be put in her cold room. But—nearly all his children go wrong and it is made clear that he is not blameless: 'though a truly anxious father, he was not outwardly affectionate, and the reserve of his manner repressed all the flow of their spirits before him.' Worse, he entrusts their upbringing to Mrs. Norris, which must be accounted a major failure of judgement: hence his relief when she finally leaves Mansfield Park—'she seemed a part of himself', that is, she has been like a cancer he has permitted to grow in his own family, in his own mind. Clearing his mind involves cutting her away. It is a mark of his increased self-knowledge that he comes to see where he has been at fault in the education of his children. He has cared about their 'elegance and accomplishments' but has been negligent of any 'moral effect on the mind'. 'He had meant them to be good, but his cares had been directed to the understanding and manners, not the disposition; and of the necessity of self-denial and humility, he feared they had never heard from any lips that could profit them.' Not only is he cold and remote, his domestic instincts are slightly corrupted by mercenary considerations. He allows Maria to marry Mr. Rushworth, though he knows him to be a fool, because he is very rich. Worse, he tries to force Fanny to marry Henry Crawford against her will because it would be such a fine match. It is not that he is a cruel tyrant; but he is lacking in an important quality. As Fanny muses after he has exerted pressure on her to marry Crawford: 'He who had married a daughter to Mr. Rushworth. Romantic delicacy was certainly not to be expected from him.' An adherence to duty is insufficient if it is not tempered by a sense of delicacy. With his repressive, indelicate inflexibility, Sir Thomas nearly brings about the ruin of Mansfield Park, and it is only at the end that he finds himself truly 'sick of ambitious and mercenary connections' and more and more appreciative of 'the sterling good of principle and temper'. Yet he does also represent the values of Mansfield, although it is only Fanny who can properly appreciate this. When the other children complain of the gloom Sir Thomas brings into the house, Fanny says: 'I think he values the very quietness you speak of, and that the repose of his family-circle is all he wants.' In standing for 'quietness' and 'repose', Sir Thomas is upholding two of the major values in the world of the book.

Lady Bertram is a travesty of those values. She is utterly inert, unaware, and entirely incapable of volition, effort, or independent judgement. She is of course an immensely amusing character: but she also reveals the Mansfield values run to seed. In effect, she never thinks, moves, or cares: amiable enough in that she is not malicious, she is, in her insentient indolence, useless as a guardian of Mansfield Park and positively culpable as a parent. And it is her sofa-bound inertia which permits the ascendancy of Mrs. Norris. Lady Bertram does not represent quietness and repose so much as indifference and collapse. Mrs. Norris is one of Jane Austen's most impressive creations and indeed one of the most plausibly odious characters in fiction. Pretending, perhaps believing herself, to be one of the guardians of Mansfield, she most nearly contrives its destruction through her arid selfishness, and her stupid and vicious interferences and meddlings. In her combination of malice and menace she is the nearest thing to real evil in the world of the book. That such a figure should have attained such a position of influence in Mansfield is a damning comment on the current state of guardianship. It is she who arranges Maria's disastrous marriage; it is she who encourages the dangerous theatricals; it is she who is responsible for the superficial and unprincipled education of the Bertram children. And above all it is she who persecutes Fanny with remorseless malevolence and unmotivated hatred—as though she had an instinctive loathing for all guileless sincerity. Mrs. Norris is far too addicted to 'arranging' things—often cruelly, always wrongly; her mean officious ways are so devoid of delicacy and affection that they usually promote discomfort or disaster. If Lady Bertram represents the wrong kind of quietness, Mrs. Norris reveals very much the wrong sort of administration. It is a comment on the internal deterioration of Mansfield Park that it takes so long to expel Mrs. Norris: and she only goes when the healing presence of Fanny finally becomes dominant in the house.

Under such guardians it is hardly surprising that the legitimate inheritors go wrong, since they have not been brought up to respect and maintain their heritage. Tom, the eldest son, dissipates his energy in racing and generally gadding about. His life is not at all 'self-denying' and it takes a nearly fatal illness to bring him to some consciousness of true Mansfield values: 'He had suffered, and he had learnt to think, two advantages that he had never known before. ... He became what he ought to be, useful to his father, steady and quiet, and not living merely for himself.' Maria and Julia suffer from the bad influence of Mrs. Norris: they are 'entirely deficient in the less common acquirements of self-knowledge, generosity, and humility.' With Maria, Mrs. Norris's favourite, the rot goes deepest. Mansfield Park merely signifies repression to her flighty mind, while she makes her foolish marriage for entirely base reasons. As Jane Austen makes clear in one of her most bitterly ironic passages: 'In all the important preparations of the mind she was complete; being prepared for matrimony by an hatred of home, restraint, and tranquillity; by the misery of disappointed affection, and contempt of the man she was to marry. The rest might wait.' (ch. 21). It is worth noting that all the characters who go wrong share a distaste for 'tranquillity'. It is harsh but fitting that Maria should end up in a little hell with Mrs. Norris. Julia elopes with a trivial man but she is perhaps redeemable since 'education had not given her so very hurtful a degree of self-consequence.' Edmund is the most nearly perfect inheritor. He is quite sincere in his desire to be ordained and wishes to devote himself to true Christian activities. He it is, alone in the family, who takes pity on Fanny and helps to educate her properly. He is indeed quite as solemn and committed to piety as Fanny—yet he too is flawed. He is deceived by the surface attractiveness of the Crawfords; he finally succumbs to the theatricals and agrees to take a part; he is blind enough to Mary's faults to imagine himself in love with her. And in Fanny's hour of need, he too deserts her and tries to persuade her to marry Henry Crawford. It is only after much tribulation that he recognizes Fanny as his true mate. But for her, *all* the inheritors would have gone astray.

The interlopers are in many ways the most interesting characters in the book and in depicting them Jane Austen reveals her great insight. For in making them attractive and investing them with many engaging qualities she shows how subtle their threat is, how intimately it is bound up with characteristics which we all like and respond to. (More than one critic has suggested that Mary Crawford, with her quick wit, her vitality and resilience, is much more like Jane Austen herself than is the shrinking Fanny.) We must examine the Crawfords's qualities carefully and see where they shade off into faults. From the start 'the manners of both were lively and pleasant', and they soon become the indispensable centre of all the gay goings-on at Mansfield Park during Sir Thomas's absence. Perhaps the first thing to stress is that they are both associated with movement, the unhindered expenditure of energy. They have the wealth and the vitality to scorn limits and limitations. They dislike 'quiet' and the absence of distraction. Mary reveals much of her temperament when she takes to horse riding, for she is soon going at an exhilarating canter. Indeed, the hint is there that her taste for movement is excessive: 'Miss Crawford's enjoyment of riding was such, that she did not know how to leave off.' As she herself confesses, she only feels 'alive' when she is doing something. Similarly, Henry is a keen hunter, and more generally, 'to anything like a permanence of abode, or limitation of society, Henry Crawford had, unluckily, a great dislike.' In addition they both have 'lively' minds, and are accomplished, witty, amusing talkers. Neither mentally nor physically do they like to be still. They are both 'active and fearless' in a way which, initially, is decidedly attractive. Where then are the faults?

In a general way we can say that their energy has become divorced from any moral guidance or control: they respond to the opportunities of the world but they are deaf to the claims of principle. Mary, for instance, regards marriage as 'a manoeuvring business' and, a true Londoner, thinks that 'a large income is the best recipé for happiness I ever heard of.' More serious is her contempt for the profession of clergyman: she thinks it insignificant socially, and cannot believe that anyone could choose it out of a sincere sense of vocation. Since she is attracted to Edmund she does all she can to tease, mock and seduce him from his high calling. When she finds he is still intent on ordination she is angry and sets out to harden herself against him. Worldly considerations distort her emotional instincts. She is indeed frankly selfish and ambitious: 'It is everybody's duty to do as well for themselves as they can'. She can simulate affection and devotion but, as Fanny sees, she is 'careless as a woman and a friend'. This 'carelessness' finally reveals itself to Edmund after Henry has run away with Maria, since Mary blames them only for their 'folly' and cares nothing for the actual evil. Indeed, she even has suggestions as to how 'appearances' may be preserved. She has no feeling for the underlying realities. As Edmund says 'This is what the world does'. When she makes one final effort to seduce Edmund with an inviting 'saucy playful smile', she is revealed as the purely worldly creature that she is. She is superb in the world of 'appearances', but as a moral essence she does not exist. She is not a conscious villain, more a product of her world. As Fanny can discern, Mary has a mind 'led astray and bewildered, and without any suspicion of being so; darkened, yet fancying itself light.'

Henry is comparably 'careless', 'thoughtless and selfish from prosperity and bad example'. He is not 'in the habit of examining his motives' and he regards other people only as they may provide 'an amusement to his sated mind'. He too is addicted to 'change and moving about': he too has a 'corrupted mind' and mocks those who are concerned about genuine virtue. As Fanny says to herself, 'he can feel nothing as he ought'. What is more interesting is his attitude to Fanny. He starts by coolly deciding to make her love him and then break her heart—just for his own amusement. Then he finds he is seriously attracted to her, drawn perhaps by a quality and depth of sincerity he has never known. He presses her to marry him in a manner which convinces the world of his sincerity. Yet Fanny is always aware of the element of selfishness in his apparently disinterested love. She sees, more subtly, that in fact he is really amusing himself by *playing* at being the honest devoted suitor. He is acting, albeit unconsciously. There is no genuine depth and staying power in his love, as is revealed by his sudden reversion to an old flirtation with Maria out of idle 'curiosity'. His relapse into adultery is a reversion to his true self. I will return to the importance of 'acting' in this novel. Here let us just realize what would have happened to the world of Mansfield Park if Fanny and Edmund had succumbed to Henry and Mary Crawford—with their centreless energy, their taste for movement untrammelled by morals, their world-darkened minds, and their insincere hearts.

It is next to the ebullient Crawfords that we must try and appreciate Fanny's stillness, quietness, weakness, and self-retraction. Her weakness, which is almost a sickness (she has to be lifted on to her horse which, moreover, never canters when she is on it). We must attempt to understand by bearing in mind that, as Lionel Trilling has pointed out, the traditional Christian heroine is often depicted as sickly, enfeebled, even dying—as in *Clarissa* or in *The Wings of the Dove*. It is a way of showing that they are not quite at home in the world, cannot compete with its rampant appetitive energies. In Fanny's case this weakness is also a token of the exhaustion and strain she incurs through her 'heroism of principle'. In her stillness she is not inactive: on the contrary, she is often holding on strenuously to standards and values which others all around her are thoughtlessly abandoning. Typically she welcomes the 'tranquillity' made possible by Mansfield Park at its best. She is content to remain apart, silent, unnoticed, out of the 'festivities'. Whereas Mary is a distinctly forward woman, always in her element in the arena of society, Fanny is marked by 'natural shyness'. Indeed, when all the others complain of the dullness which comes over the house after Sir Thomas returns, she defends it, saying 'There must be a sort of shyness'. To appreciate the full implications of this we should bear in mind a late remark of Jane Austen's: 'What is become of all the shyness in the world?' By which she clearly means not a false modesty but a true unassertive reticence of soul. A selflessness: a quietness.

Fanny's position is at first ambiguous in Mansfield Park. Mary asks 'Is she out, or is she not?' She means, has she officially come out into society, and in the widest sense the answer is that although she is involved in it, she is never wholly a part of it. This is the significance of her little cold room at the far end of the house to which she often retires and where she reads or meditates and communes with herself. It implies that she is not, at first, considered an integral part of the home. In a way there is a little of the artist about her: she speaks for the value of literature, of memory, of fancy; she alone reveals a true appreciation of nature. More important, she is in a way the supreme consciousness of the society she moves in. Like many Jamesian figures she does not fully participate in the world but as a result she sees things more clearly and accurately than those who do. As Edmund says: 'Fanny is the only one who has judged rightly throughout, who has been consistent.' She prefers custom and habit to novelty and innovation, and her resolute immobility, frail and beset though it is, is a last gesture of resistance against the corrosions of unfettered impulse and change. She stands for the difficulty of delicate right thinking in a world of inadequate perception and subtly corrupted instincts. Her toils and her triumphs are all mental and moral. She suffers to be still in a world where pleasure seems to lie in release and movement. If she is vindicated it is only after much pain, for Jane Austen suggests that Fanny has to go through all 'the vicissitudes of the human mind'. But she remains firm. Her immobility, her refusal to be 'moved' are not symptoms of mule-like stubbornness or paralysed fear, but a measure of her integrity, her adherence to her own clear evaluation of how things stand. She speaks for the 'inner light' in a world of falling worldly standards. As she says to Edmund (who instinctively comes to her for advice and approval), 'We have all a better guide in ourselves, if we would attend to it, than any other person can be'. We can see her as a lonely conscience—ignored, despised, bullied, at times besieged by the forces of worldly persuasion, yet finally recognized as the true preserver of the values represented by Mansfield Park. Her real significance is made apparent when Sir Thomas realizes that 'Fanny was indeed the daughter that he wanted.' She is the true inheritor of Mansfield Park.

The characters, of course, reveal their inner qualities by their actions, and it is worth stressing the extraordinary skill with which Jane Austen describes the various incidents so that a meticulous surface accuracy carries at the same time a subtle symbolic power. She was indeed unusually meticulous and went to great pains to get her details correct. She clearly used a calendar to get all the days and dates correct; she took the names of actual contemporary ships, and so on. Yet she can make the details of the comparatively uneventful country life she describes convey deep meanings and reveal crucial aspects of her characters. For example the card game in Chapter 15. The game is called 'Speculation' and during the game the real 'speculators' in that world reveal themselves. Fanny, significantly, 'had never played the game nor seen it played in her life'. Henry tries to involve her in the game, 'to inspirit her play, sharpen her avarice, and harden her heart' but in the game, as in life, Fanny resists his urgings and compulsions. Henry is of course very good at the game and teaches it to other people, much as he so suavely meddles with other people's lives. Mary plays a daring, rash game which has many innuendos indicative of her particular outlook and temperament. After winning a round at 'an exorbitant rate' she says: 'There, I will stake my last like a woman of spirit. No cold prudence for me. I am not born to sit still and do nothing. If I lose the game, it shall not be from not striving for it.' As in all things she prefers action to prudence. 'The game was her's, and only did not pay her for what she had given to secure it.' That deceptively simple sentence goes to the heart of Mary Crawford. She is indeed one of those who wins the stakes and finds that the game was not worth the candle. One can think of her as winning the world at the too high price of losing her soul. Ultimately all her energy is misspent. In such ways does Jane Austen make an ephemeral incident like a card game reflect the hidden dispositions and drives of the participants (compare Henry James's use of the card game at a crucial point in *The Golden Bowl*).

We could similarly explore the symbolic significance of the moment when Fanny finds 'a fire lighted and burning' in her room. Again, we can note how suggestively Jane Austen exploits the matter of Fanny's cross and chain for the ball. The amber cross is from her beloved brother William and she is determined to wear it, just as she wears him, close to her heart. (Typically, this amber cross had a real origin, for Jane Austen herself was fond of the 'gold chains and topaze crosses' which the young Charles Austen had sent to his sisters from the Mediterranean in 1801: her symbolism is firmly grounded in the actual.) The question is, which chain will Fanny wear to carry the cross? Henry slyly forces a fancy chain on her, while Edmund later gives her a tastefully simple one. She is persuaded to wear Henry's (just as they are trying to force her to accept him as a husband), but fortunately it will not go through the cross so she can wear Edmund's with a good conscience. Thus the two tokens of the two people she loves most are linked together round her neck when she leads her first ball: and in that moment the final emotional situation at the end of the book is foreshadowed. But the two most significant episodes we should consider are the journey to Sotherton to discuss the 'improvement' of Mr. Rushworth's country home, and the theatricals.

It was quite common at the time to 'improve' estates according to picturesque principles of gardening and architecture, but out of this plausible contemporary practice, Jane Austen has constructed a key episode in the novel. Fanny, typically, would prefer to see Sotherton 'in its old state', but Henry Crawford is an avid 'improver' (as indeed he is always interfering with the *status quo*), and Mr. Rushworth eagerly seeks his help. When they are all at Sotherton they find the house oppressive, and as soon as they come to a door leading to the open 'as by one impulse, one wish for air and liberty, all walked out.' To appreciate what happens subsequently it is important to keep the layout in mind. First there is a walled lawn—nature tamed, ordered, and civilized. But beyond that is a 'wilderness'—here things are less refined, less restrained, darker. Providentially the door into it is unlocked and into the dark wood they all, variously, go. Here it is that Mary tries to undermine Edmund's intention to be a clergyman. (In the course of this conversation they leave 'the great path' and take 'a very serpentine course'—again outer action mimics the life within.) It is here that Fanny desires to sit down and be still, and she does so on a bench which confronts an iron gate which separates the wilderness from the unenclosed spaces of the park beyond. This is one of the most important gestures in the book. Mary, typically, has no taste for stillness. ' "I must move," said she, "resting fatigues me" ' and, leaving Fanny immobile, she entices Edmund back into the wood. Then Henry Crawford and Maria and Mr. Rushworth appear. Maria, always impatient of all restraints and enclosures, wishes to go beyond the gates and into the wider freedom of the park. The gate—perfect image for the rigid restrictions imposed by the conventions of civilized life—is locked. Mr. Rushworth goes to fetch the key. Being engaged to Maria, he is in many ways the lawful person to 'open the gates' (there is perhaps a reference to virginity here, just as the locked garden represents virginity in medieval paintings). But in his absence, Henry engages in some very persuasive and suggestive *double entendre* with Maria. The improver of the estate is also the disturber of conventional life. The whole conversation should be looked at carefully; particularly when Maria complains that the iron gate 'gives me a feeling of restraint and hardship' and Henry answers: 'I think you might with little difficulty pass round the edge of the gate, here, with my assistance; I think it might be done, if you really wished to be more at large, and could allow yourself to think it not prohibited.' Their final adultery—also a bypassing of the 'iron' codes of society—is here prefigured. Fanny warns against the danger, but Maria manages to slip round the gate without any harm from the spikes. Subsequently the spikes of convention will damage her more deeply. Again, Fanny is 'left to her solitude'. And so it goes on. Mr. Rushworth appears, upset to find he has been left behind: Julia turns up breathless and angry: Edmund and Mary continue their 'winding' walk in the woods. Only Fanny is still, silent, alone; not involved in the confused antics of all the others who are variously pursuing their own desires and indulging their impulses. When they do all meet up again, one feels that some irreparable damage has been done. 'By their own accounts they had been all walking after each other, and the junction which had taken place at last seemed, to Fanny's observation, to have been as much too late for re-establishing harmony, as it confessedly had been for determining on any alteration.' Nothing constructive has been achieved, but the seeds of future disharmony have been sown, for the confused, often furtive, criss-crossing moving around in the increasing liberty and concealment of garden, wood, and park, portends the more serious disorder that many of the characters will make of their subsequent lives. Fanny's staying put is a small gesture of moral tenacity while the others dangerously roam.

The theatricals provide the core of the book; and, indeed, they are the occasion of one of the most subtle and searching pieces in English fiction. We know from the *Memoir* by Jane Austen's nephew, James Edward Austen-Leigh, that amateur home theatricals were popular in her family and by no means disapproved of as they are in the book. But in the novel she uses them as a vehicle to explore the profound implications of 'acting' and 'role-playing' for the individual and society. Her brilliant exploitation of the suggestiveness and relevance of 'theatricals' to modern life amply justifies Lionel Trilling's claim that 'it was Jane Austen who first represented the specifically modern personality and the culture in which it had its being.' The theatricals represent the culmination of the irresponsible licence indulged in during Sir Thomas's absence ('They were relieved by it from all restraint'). Of course the idea of home theatricals seems harmless if not positively charming to us. But in terms of the world of the book we must see the attempt to turn Mansfield Park into a theatre as a dangerous act of desecration: it is like transforming a temple of order into a school for scandal.

Interestingly enough, all the characters sense that Sir Thomas would disapprove, but Tom over-rules Edmund's objections by saying 'His house shall not be hurt'. But in a deeper sense Mansfield Park is all but destroyed once 'the inclination to act was awakened'. For Mansfield Park is a place where you must be true to your best self: the theatre is a place where you can explore and experiment with other selves. A person cannot live in both.

It is perhaps helpful to bear in mind the old Platonic objection to acting: Plato thought a person could not be both a good citizen and an actor because just to simulate a base character has a debasing and demoralizing influence on the civilized self. There is a long history of comparable suspicion of the insidious dangers of acting. On the other hand, at least since the Romantic movement, there has been an increasing interest in role-playing, acting, masks and so on; the feeling being that perhaps the self can only come to a full realization of itself through experiments in different roles and by trying on different masks. (Diderot's crucial work, *Rameau's Nephew*, written sometime in the late 1760s, in many ways anticipates this Romantic feeling. It shows a man who has tremendous energy and life-hunger, but somehow no stable centre. He can play every role, simulate every feeling, he is 'a one-man show featuring dancers, male and female, singers of both sexes, a whole orchestra, a complete opera-house, dividing himself into twenty different stage parts' and so on —the very dissolution of the individual through the multiplicity of the people and things he mimics. Like Henry Crawford, the nephew of Rameau sets great store by his claim to be a supremely good 'actor'.) One of the prevailing Romanic convictions is that we are very much more than the conscious mind tells us, that a man is a crowd of almost infinite potentialities (thus Whitman, 'I contain multitudes'). There has been a corresponding desire to try to extend life and consciousness by acting out many different roles. By 'losing yourself in a part', as we revealingly say, you may find another, buried part of yourself: the stage is a great place for dis-covering those hidden inner multitudes that Whitman mentions. Even reading offers important scope for vicarious role-playing. Clearly one danger in all this is that although the self might enjoy an enhanced and enriched life by going from role to role, it may dissipate itself until the inner man loses himself in the actor and the face dissolves into the mask. Certainly, role-playing must make against stability and fixity: if the self is fluid, there is no limit to what it might do, no knowing how it might behave. Instead of life conceived of as a rigid adherence to firm moral standards, it may turn into a series of improvisations suggested by the milieu of the moment.

The theatrical germ is brought to Mansfield Park by Mr. Yates, a foolish visitor from the world of 'fashion and expense': very soon all the younger people desire to act or, as Tom puts it, 'exercise our powers in something new'. Again it should be noted that it is in the absence of Sir Thomas that a whole range of hitherto restrained 'powers' and impulses start to press for expression and indulgence. Lady Bertram of course offers no obstructions; Mrs. Norris positively likes the idea because 'she foresaw in it all the comforts of hurry, bustle, and importance.' Only Edmund disapproves—and, of course, Fanny. They both refuse to 'act'. Fanny's words have a special emphasis. 'I could not act anything if you were to give me the world. No indeed, I cannot act.' (It is interesting to compare Jane Eyre's refusal to join in the charades in *Jane Eyre*.) Henry Crawford is, revealingly, 'considerably the best actor of all'—even Fanny admits his great talents in this sphere. The point is, of course, that these talents stray out of the theatre and into real life: off stage he is 'at treacherous play' with the feelings of Julia and Maria—the latter being only too happy to indulge her illicit passion for Henry under the guise of 'acting'. Mary is also in her element in the theatre, and it is her teasing and tempting which finally undermine Edmund's resolution so that he allows himself to be persuaded to take a part. For when she provocatively asks: 'What gentleman among you am I to have the pleasure of making love to?' Edmund cannot resist the proferred role. This has important implications. Edmund has chosen to be a clergyman by profession: a profession is, in effect, the fixed role that we choose, as responsibly as possible, for life. Edmund at this moment symbolically abandons his profession, his role in life, to play at being a stage clergyman indulging in a love affair (for such is his part). It involves an abdication of his true self in order to indulge a passional impulse. And with his defection to the actors only Fanny is left among the 'players' as a centre of true judgement and responsible clear-sightedness. The rest are no longer their true selves: 'and no man was his own' in Shakespearean terms.

Everything about the theatricals portends disharmony. First of all the would-be actors squabble selfishly over which play to choose because, of course, everyone is solely concerned with seeking a desirable role. Then the house itself is physically disrupted as it is altered to make it more like a real theatre. The actual play, *Lovers' Vows*, though trivial enough, turns on unnatural or dangerous relationships; in particular, Maria playing an abandoned mother and Henry playing her illegitimate son have the opportunity to develop an insidious intimacy. As the rehearsals continue, suppressed and dubious desires start to emerge because of the release permitted by the playing of roles. Only Fanny stays apart. In fact she becomes strangely necessary, receiving their complaints, hearing their lines, acting as prompter, 'judge and critic'. She is, moreover, 'at peace' (except for the agonizing moment when she has to listen to Mary and Edmund rehearse their love scene in her presence). More significantly, only Fanny is truly *aware*. Aware, for instance, of Julia's suffering, and of what Henry and Maria are really up to, and of how Edmund is deceived in Mary. This clarity of consciousness is of paramount importance because it is the only clear-mindedness still remaining at Mansfield Park. Even Edmund 'between his theatrical and his real part ... was equally unobservant'. There is no one left except Fanny to uphold the claims and necessity of lucid moral consciousness. The others are lost in their roles; blind behind their masks. This may occasionally make Fanny appear as a prig; but we must respond to her symbolic value. This is why the last moments of Chapter 18 are so dramatic. Because of the indisposition of Mrs. Grant just before the first full rehearsal, there is a role left vacant. In despair the actors turn to Fanny and try to persuade and bully her into just reading the part. Even Edmund exerts his pressure on her to participate in the play. And indeed, it seems finally that she too must succumb to the actors. Then Sir Thomas suddenly returns, the actors scatter, and the theatre is once more Mansfield Park. The return may seem melodramatic, but what we are to feel is that if Sir Thomas had not come back, then Fanny would have been forced to 'act' and Mansfield Park would have been fully transformed into a theatre. Again, one has to respond to the subtle symbolism of this and see Fanny's consciousness as a single clear light in the darkening house; so that when the actors crowd round her, forcing her to play a part, one must feel that the last light of reliable awareness is about to be snuffed out. It is not extinguished because of the potent authority of Sir Thomas's sheer presence. And because it isn't, because Fanny does hold out, she will be the one who truly saves Mansfield Park when, at the end of the book, the disorder suggested by the theatricals becomes a moral chaos in real life.

One final word about 'acting'. With Sir Thomas's return, all traces of the theatre are erased and the house returns to its former 'sameness and gloom', so that even Edmund finds it distinctly less 'lively' than before. It is a long time before he can see the theatricals as 'that period of general folly'. Mary, as we might expect, recalls them as her finest hour. 'If I had the power of recalling any one week of my existence, it should be that week, that acting week.' And Henry, actor supreme, also rejoices in the memory of that 'acting week'. 'We were all alive. . . . I never was happier.' And that is the profound truth about the Crawfords, brought up on the great stage of London life—they only feel alive when they are acting a role. In themselves, in repose, they are nothing. They are master stylists, with an easy mastery of the whole range of responses: like some other great actors they can mimic all feelings perhaps because deep down they can feel none. They are doomed to be insincere, because they lack the instinct for sincere feelings. In this, in their strange combination of energy and emptiness, they are a very modern pair. Henry's acting ability is again stressed when he is courting Fanny. He picks up a copy of *Henry VIII* (surely Jane Austen's joke, for both Henrys show a decided preference for a plurality of ladies), and by sheer instinct he is able to read *every* part perfectly. 'The King, the Queen, Buckingham, Wolsey, Cromwell, all were given in turn . . . he could always light, at will, on the best scene, the best speeches of each; and whether it were dignity or pride, or tenderness or remorse, or whatever were to be expressed, he could do it with equal beauty.— It was truly dramatic.' Thus Henry Crawford, with his 'great turn for acting' reveals what is, in effect, his curse. For if you can play every part equally well, how can you know who you really are; and if you can simulate all moods and affections how can you know what you really feel? Henry Crawford is a man of whom we say 'he puts his heart into his acting': unfortunately he has also put his acting into his heart. In his courtship of Fanny, Crawford is perhaps trying to play the most difficult role of all—the role of sincerity. But despite genuine efforts, he cannot keep it up, and Fanny, the most determined non-actor, is vindicated. We must feel that it is only because of her resistance and resoluteness that the actors—in every sense—are kept out of Mansfield Park.

In a letter Jane Austen said the subject of this book was 'ordination'; and certainly Edmund's choice of the profession of clergyman is a serious issue—Mary despising it and trying to entice him into the world, Fanny admiring it and giving Edmund all the support she can. But we can see that there are also other very important issues in this book. Some of these can be indicated by juxtaposing certain abstract words, for Jane Austen uses abstractions with the power and certainty and fine discrimination of an eighteenth-century writer. There is a contrast between appearance and reality, the Crawfords' plausible stylishness off-set by Fanny's reticent genuineness. We are also made aware of the conflict between the joys of personality and the rigours of principle. We are shown the need to distinguish between what is 'sweet' and what is 'sound', between what is 'pleasant' and what is 'prudent'. 'Duty' of course is deeply important, but superadded to it there must be 'delicacy'. And, a harder lesson perhaps, we are shown that the delightfulness of 'wit' (and who enjoyed that more than Jane Austen?) is trivial compared with the soberness of wisdom. As she wrote in a letter: 'Wisdom is better than Wit, & in the long run will certainly have the laugh on her side.' In a more general way the book does seem, as some critics have noted, to speak for repression and negation, fixity and enclosure, the timidity of caution and routine opposed to the exhilaration of risk and change. But if we are sympathetic to the symbolic implications of the world of the book we can see that, at its most profound, it is a book about the difficulty of preserving true moral consciousness amid the selfish manoeuvring and jostling of society. Fanny is constantly subjected to persuasion, victimization, coercion and opposition. At the end of Volume One (Chapters 1 to 18 in modern editions) she barely escapes being pressured into acting. At the end of Volume Two (Chapters 19 to 31) we leave her isolated and uncomforted with everyone trying to force her into a much more false situation—marriage with Henry Crawford. As Lionel Trilling has noted, in our age we tend to believe that 'right action can be performed with no pain to the self', but Jane Austen knew that virtue was a hard affair and morality might involve renunciation, sacrifice, and solitary anguish. Again, we tend to admire energy; but, to return to Trilling's point, Jane Austen had a firm grasp of the paradox 'that the self may destroy the self by the very energies that define its being, that the self may be preserved by the negation of its own energies.' In the debilitated but undeviating figure of Fanny Price we should perceive the pain and labour involved in maintaining true values in a corrosive world of dangerous energies and selfish power-play. She suffers in her stillness. For Righteousness' sake. Jane Austen always accepted the fact that life has to be defined and lived within limits: she never canvassed the idea of a flight from society into non-social freedom. But she seems to have become increasingly aware of the pain and misery involved in what D. W. Harding calls 'the impossibility of being cut off from objectionable people'. Many of the characters in Jane Austen's late fictional world remind one of Sartre's notion—'hell is other people'. Looking back at *Pride and Prejudice* in later years, Jane Austen wrote 'the work is rather too light, and bright, and sparkling'. By the time of *Mansfield Park* much of the lightness and brightness has gone out of the world and, although Jane Austen's incomparable comic sense is as alive as ever, she now seems more aware of the real evils and real sufferings inextricably involved in life in society. In addition to this, I think she was aware of the tremendous changes already fermenting in England. Not, indeed, that Jane Austen refers specifically to social change: in this sense her world remains singularly devoid of depth and width of background. But she does seem to catch some crucial alteration of psyche in people which, in little, reflects a radical shift in national behaviour. Thus, I think that her suspicion of impetuous movement, which we have noted in *Mansfield Park*, is her oblique comment on some larger trend. To justify this claim, I suggest that it is worth looking at *Sanditon*, the novel she was working on at the time of her death. Unlike most of her other novels (which usually start with some statement about the social position of a person or family) this fragment opens with a dramatic incident. A couple in a carriage travelling too fast along a rough road on 'Business' are 'overturned'. The commercial spirit is abroad and in its haste it has crashed! By contrast, the family that helps the shaken couple are devotees of a stable rural way of life. Thus, the Heywoods 'never left home'; they have always been 'stationary and healthy'. Like Fanny, they believe in 'Prudence' and 'Habit'. Like her they do not move. The couple who have the accident, however, have changed their old modest comfortable house in a valley for a new one upon a hill which is more glamorous but far less comfortable. A change of abode reflects a change in a way of life; and what the Parkers have done reflects what England was in the process of doing (there are clear indications that the events take place after Waterloo). One of the Heywood girls, Charlotte, goes to stay with the Parkers and what she sees is not unlike what Fanny sees. There is a fashionable rake with sleek manners who, like Henry Crawford, 'lives too much in the World to be settled'. More generally, the ridiculous (and very amusing) turmoil and bustle which Charlotte witnesses at Sanditon prompt her to the thought that here is 'Activity run mad'. Rather like the confusion during the outing to Sotherton, there is a manic disorder at Sanditon which leads the author to comment, ironically but seriously: 'Everybody must now "move in a Circle",—to the prevalence of which rotatory Motion, is perhaps to be attributed the Giddiness & false steps of many.' Such a sentence could well stand as a mordant comment on the new forces which threaten the stable values of Mansfield Park.

But if, as this fragment makes clear, Jane Austen could see that a world of frantic change was about to supplant the world of peaceful fixity she knew, why then does she allow the spirit of Mansfield, in the figure of Fanny, to triumph over the forces of change, as exemplified by the Crawfords? I think one could put it this way. To a world abandoning itself to the dangers of thoughtless restlessness, Jane Austen is holding up an image of the values of thoughtful rest. Aware that the trend was for more and more people to explore the excitements of personality, she wanted to show how much there was to be said for the 'heroism of principle'. It is a stoic book in that it speaks for stillness rather than movement, firmness rather than fluidity, arrest rather than change, endurance rather than adventure. In the figure of Fanny it elevates the mind that 'struggles against itself', as opposed to the ego which indulges its promiscuous potentialities. Fanny is a true heroine because in a turbulent world it is harder to refrain from action than to let energy and impulse run riot. This is a point of Sir Thomas's final insight when he comes to 'acknowledge the advantages of early hardship and discipline, and the consciousness of being born to struggle and endure.' Fanny has that consciousness. Mansfield Park as a place has many faults and is inhabited by some silly and nasty people. Fanny's life there has many pains. But a place may be more valuable than the people living in it; and, moreover, as Anne Elliot says in *Persuasion*, 'one does not love a place the less for having suffered in it.' As a place it symbolically upholds the stoic values of control, stability, endurance. And Jane Austen offers it in this book as an image of quiet resistance at the start of what was to be the most convulsive century of change in the whole of English history.

Finally, to suggest the sort of place *Mansfield Park* occupies in English fiction, I want to suggest a brief comparison with another work which was written about England at a moment of climactic transition almost exactly one hundred years later. I am referring to Ford Madox Ford's *Parade's End*. If Jane Austen's novel can be said to be about eighteenth-century England giving way to the nineteenth century, so Ford's tetralogy is clearly about nineteenth-century England giving way to the twentieth century at the time of the First World War. Like Jane Austen, Ford portrays a world of traditional values being infiltrated and undermined by modern types—unscrupulous, ambitious, cruel, selfish and false. And the central figure, Christopher Tietjens, comes to represent all the old stoic values of rural England. Like Fanny he is abused, vilified, despised. But though he is wounded, exhausted and abandoned, like Fanny he endures. He too displays the 'heroism of principle' in a world of self-aggrandizing opportunism: as he says, 'Principles are like a skeleton map of a country—you know whether you're going east or north.' In his figure Ford, like Jane Austen, vindicates passivity and abstention. And Tietjens, like Fanny, strengthens himself by holding on to an image of old English rural peace and stability—in his case, as exemplified by the figure of George Herbert, the seventeenth-century poet-priest. Here is one of his meditations in time of war, from *A Man Could Stand Up*.

> But what chance had quiet fields, Anglican sainthood, accuracy of thought, heavy-leaved, timbered hedge-rows, slowly creeping plough-lands moving up the slopes? . . . Still the land remains. . . .
> The land remains . . . It remains! . . . At the same moment the dawn was wetly revealing; over there in George Herbert's parish . . . what was it called? . . . What the devil was its name? Oh, Hell! . . . Between Salisbury and Wilton . . . The tiny church . . . But he refused to consider the plough-lands, the heavy groves, the slow highroad above the church that the dawn was at that moment wetly revealing—until he could remember that name. He refused to consider that, probably even today, the land ran to . . . produced the stock of . . . Anglican sainthood. The quiet thing!

Jane Austen is of course a far greater writer. But she too was aware of an England that was passing away. She too knew about the passion which turns to lechery, the activity which becomes destructive, the energy which results in the collapse of a world. And, quite as deeply as Ford, she appreciated the value of 'the quiet thing', and knew, too, the incredible moral strength required to achieve and maintain it. And that, above all, is what *Mansfield Park* is about.

# IX

# JANE AUSTEN'S COMEDY AND THE NINETEENTH CENTURY

*Rachel Trickett*

JANE AUSTEN's high reputation as a novelist was established in the nineteenth century though not in her own lifetime. In his recent edition of *Persuasion* Professor Andrew Wright remarks:

> her life seems to have been far more exemplary than the cult which grew up about her more than two decades after her death, and which has hobbled much genuine appreciation of her work on account of the over-ripe zeal with which it is articulated: these genteel admirers call themselves, or allow themselves to be called 'Janeites' (after a fine story by Kipling), and will call Jane Austen 'Miss Austen' a solecism the hilarity of which would not have been lost on Jane Austen, who as a younger sister was never Miss Austen, but Miss Jane Austen.[1]

The vague chronology and generalized tone of this is misleading about nineteenth-century attitudes to Jane Austen. Not until Lady Ritchie (Anne Thackeray, the novelist) published her article in the *Cornhill Magazine*, August 1871, was there any hint of the adulatory cult Professor Wright deplores. Lady Ritchie chose to present a picture of the novelist which described her private life, emphasized the domesticity of her work, and fixed attention on the woman rather than the writer—an intimate biographical approach encouraged by J. E. Austen-Leigh's *A Memoir of Jane Austen* which appeared in its first unexpanded form in 1870. But the *Memoir* itself was not uncritically received, and at least another two decades were to pass before the 'Janeites' were heard of. Perhaps there was less excuse for that hilarious solecism after the *Memoir*, but Miss Austen was, of course, the familiar courtesy title by which the novelist had been known in all previous notices of her work since Archbishop Whately's in the *Quarterly Review*, January 1821, and it was these notices, far from grossly adulatory themselves, which helped to create the sympathetic atmosphere in which a less critical cult might flourish. Nevertheless, such serious estimates of Jane Austen's work deserve to be better known, both for their own sake, and for what they tell us about the nineteenth century's idea of her art, and how that, in its turn, has affected our own.

George Henry Lewes was the first critic to discuss Jane Austen as an artist in her own right in his article 'The Novels of Jane Austen' in *Blackwood's Magazine*, July 1859. He was able to do so because of the supremacy of the novel as a form in the middle of the century, but he followed the main lines of appreciation that Scott and Whately had already laid down, and he knew T. H. Lister's account of Jane Austen's work in his review of Mrs. Gore's *Women as they Are* in the *Edinburgh Review*, July 1830, and Macaulay's enthusiastic paragraph in his essay on Madame D'Arblay in the same journal thirteen years later.

Scott's review of *Emma* (*Quarterly Review*, October 1815) is well known. His main points rise out of the contrast he draws between the romantic novel of incident and the new kind of fiction which had grown up 'within the last fifteen or twenty years', of which the scene was ordinary life, and for which the author must create subtler characters and display 'depth of knowledge and dexterity of execution'. For these qualities Scott finds that Jane Austen 'stands alone'. The naturalness, the pervasive realism of her work struck him immediately:

> The author's knowledge of the world, and the peculiar tact with which she presents characters that the reader cannot fail to recognize, reminds us something of the merits of the Flemish school of painting. The subjects are not often elegant, and certainly never grand, but they are finished up to nature, and with a precision which delights the reader.[2]

The earlier type of novel was still the prevailing fashion when Scott was writing; he himself had brilliantly adapted and developed it, and had encouraged others to blend its improbabilities with greater realism of setting and sentiment. It was scarcely surprising that the perfection of Jane Austen's naturalism was the first thing to catch his attention. Even less practised readers felt the same. In the

*Opinions of Mansfield Park* and *Emma* which Jane Austen herself jotted down from her own circle, Lady Gordon is recorded as saying:

> In most novels you are amused for the time with a set of Ideal People whom you never think of afterwards or whom you the least expect to meet in common life, whereas in Miss A–s works, & especially in M.P. you actually *live* with them, you fancy yourself one of the family; & the scenes are so exactly descriptive, so perfectly natural, that there is scarcely an Incident or conversation, or a person that you are not inclined to imagine you have at one time or other in your Life been a witness to, born a part in, & been acquainted with.[3]

Mrs. Guiton, on the other hand, thought *Emma* 'too natural to be interesting', and the perils, familiar now to any novelist, of such realism are neatly illustrated by Miss Isabella Herries's reaction, who

> did not like it—objected to my exposing the sex in the character of the Heroine—convinced that I had meant Mrs & Miss Bates for some acquaintance of theirs—People whom I never heard of before.[4]

Richard Whately, later Archbishop of Dublin, writing six years after Scott's review, went further than Scott in analysing Jane Austen's peculiar kind of realism, and defined it as dramatic:

> describing without scruple private conversations and uncommunicated feelings ... and giving a dramatic air to the narrative by introducing frequent conversations; which she conducts with a regard to character hardly exceeded by Shakespeare himself.[5]

He particularly admired her discrimination of character. Like Shakespeare's, her fools are as distinct from each other as her heroes. And Whately was especially pleased by what had shocked Miss Isabella Herries: Jane Austen's unromantic candour confirmed what he had always suspected of women:

> Her heroines are what one knows women must be, though one can never get them to acknowledge it. As liable to 'fall in love first', as anxious to attract the attention of agreeable men, as much taken with a striking manner, or a handsome face, as unequally gifted with constancy and firmness, as liable to have their affection biassed by convenience or fashion, as we, on our part will admit men to be.[6]

The novelist Thomas Henry Lister, in his review of Mrs. Gore's fashionable work in 1830, where he claims that 'in this age of literary quackery' Jane Austen has not received her reward, tries, like Whately, to explain her naturalism in terms of art:

> Ordinary readers have been apt to judge of her as Partridge, in Fielding's novel, judged of Garrick's acting.... She was too natural for them. It semed to them as if there could be very little merit in making characters act and talk so exactly like the people whom they saw around them every day. They did not consider that the highest triumph of art consists in its concealment; and here the art was so little perceptible, that they believed there was none.... Her forte lay not so much in describing events, as in drawing characters; and in this she stands almost alone. She possessed the rare and difficult art of making her readers intimately acquainted with the character of all whom she describes. We feel as if we had lived among them; 'and yet she employs no elaborate description—no metaphysical analysis—no antithetical balance of their good and bad qualities. She scarcely does more than make them act and talk, and we know them directly.[7]

Twenty-nine years after this, Lewes, though he refers directly to Scott, Whately and Macaulay (who had also compared Jane Austen to Shakespeare, but added little to Whatley's critical analysis) draws very heavily on Lister's article, even taking over his phraseology and his neat comparison of public ignorance of art to Partridge's opinion of Garrick's acting. In 1859 he finds nothing new to say of Jane Austen's powers of characterization or her naturalism. He speaks of it familiarly—Elizabeth Bennet is 'one of the few heroines one would seriously like to marry', but he no longer feels called on to justify the genre, and the realism of the style strikes him less freshly. Lewes quotes a passage from *Scenes of Clerical Life* to show that though George Eliot is inferior to Jane Austen in 'the economy of art' she is her equal in 'truthfulness, dramatic ventriloquism and humour', and when he summarizes Jane Austen's achievement in character-study he merely repeats what Whately, Lister and Macaulay had already said:

> instead of *description*, the common and easy resource of novelists, she has the rare and difficult art of *dramatic presentation*; instead of telling us what her characters are, and what they feel, she presents the people, and they reveal themselves. In this she has never perhaps been surpassed, not even by Shakespeare himself.[8]

A hard-pressed journalist may understandably return to a familiar and well-presented case. But Lewes's article, as we shall see, contained several more original critical points; only in the matter of characterization he evidently felt no need to restate in any new way the accepted nineteenth-century view that it is the highest achievement of literary art.

One of our difficulties in responding to these earlier critics is that this is a view we are less convinced of. Bradley's approach to Shakespeare, for example, has gone; in its place we analyse the plays as dramatic poems or symbolic representations. We tend to think of character in literature as a kind of ideogram rather than an imitation of life. And the naturalness, the deceptive simplicity which so astonished Jane Austen's early readers and is still the first impression her books make, is not easily discussed in our critical terms. Today we generally feel that the more complex the surface of a work, the more worthy it is of attention. The early novels of Dickens have suffered because of this, and the later ones have been overpraised because their complicated texture invites us to find obscure inspirations lurking behind that more familiar façade. But we have not yet developed any new methods or terms for examining and defining the creative vigour that expresses itself in terms of character and dialogue. And we are afraid that the old terms may lead us into some critical fatuity—comparisons with Shakespeare, for instance, or worse still, with life, as if we had forgotten that this is fiction not fact.

For this reason some critics have neglected Jane Austen's characterization for the moral vision embodied in her society—a society familiar enough to the nineteenth century, but remote from us and more open to our speculation. Here, too, the naturalness of her technique lays some dangerous snares. A great deal of painstaking ingenuity has been spent in explaining the violence of Sir Thomas Bertram's disapproval of amateur theatricals in the home, and Jane Austen's evident sympathy with it. Grave views of the importance of reality, and the moral danger of assuming a role, an illusory persona, have been attributed to her to account for this peculiarity. The simple fact that Sir Thomas's attitude was commonly held by people of his kind and class until at least the end of the nineteenth century seems too coldly pedantic to the mind bent on interpretation. The novel appears too 'real', too immediate and unlike a museum piece to be treated historically. Thus the sheer effectiveness of Jane Austen's naturalism in an age when it is no longer a familiar idiom can lead to even worse solecisms than a genteel slip in nomenclature.

A serious reading of the nineteenth-century critics makes it worth considering whether they were entirely misguided in supposing successful character creation to be a mark of superior genius, and whether an effect of extreme naturalness may not also be an attribute of the highest art. Writers like Jane Austen, Balzac and Tolstoy, different though they are, should make us wonder whether, in the novel, it may not be true that the nearer the approximation to the experience of life in its ordered, finished, surface sense, rather than its disordered, rudimentary and interior sense, the higher the art. Fiction uses material already shaped by social experience—people and their environment—and organizes it into a construction which conceals its artifice as poetry seldom can, because its content is always related in some precise way—even at the simple level of story—to rational, ordered existence. Hence the art which conceals art is not only more congenial but may even be more proper to the novel as a form than to poetry itself. Of course the organization can be disrupted. In *Tristram Shandy* Sterne exploits its rhetorical problems, but he does not challenge the principle; he obliquely re-affirms it. The confused elements of his narrative keep crystallizing into the recognizable outlines of character: Uncle Toby, Walter, Yorick and the rest are the fixed poles round which the narrator's struggle for order and sequence revolves.

In his recent book on Tolstoy,[9] John Bayley comments on the peculiar way in which his characters appear before us without pre-paration, explanation, or any exposition of their past to account for their present state and actions. This is what early critics of Jane Austen meant, presumably, when they spoke of her dramatic presen-tation, the way in which her people reveal themselves, and Mr. Bayley, like them, compares the art to Shakespeare's. It seems to him a sign of the most assured and comprehensive genius. Jane Austen's characters clearly posses this same self-sufficiency. But in her novels it is one of the factors of comedy, which conceives of characters in terms of the whole scheme of interractions of person and event that the author has devised for them. This does not prevent us from ever thinking of them outside the terms of the story, for the sublety of Jane Austen's art lies in the way she achieves this concentrated organization, and at the same time matches a formal illusion of completeness or unity against a more compre-hensive illusion of reality. There is a continued interplay between the two, the one throwing the other into relief, which is characteristic of great comedy. Or, to put it another way from the angle of our response, the reader's mind is constantly kept busy between admiration and concern.

That Jane Austen's characters were wholly conceived in terms of her story was not at first perceived by her admirers. Scott declared that *Emma* had even less story than the preceding novels, and Susan Ferrier, writing to a friend a year after his review, repeated the criticism: 'I have been reading "Emma" which is excellent; there is no story whatever'.[10] Jane Austen's brother Charles had said that *Mansfield Park* 'wanted incident'.[11] They all meant that the novels lacked plot in the episodic narrative sense, where the climax is reached through a variety of adventures. 'Story' to them had different implications from the older term 'fable' with its suggestion of a series of events contrived to illustrate a prevailing theme. Whately, himself the author of a book on rhetoric, was more alert to Jane Austen's devices of plot. He had noticed that the instruction found in eighteenth-century moral essays was now embodied in the kind of novel she wrote, and perhaps because he came to her work both as a rhetorician and with a very eighteenth-century predilection for theme, he recognized her brilliance of construction. A story to be justifiable to Whately must be a 'fable', and the value of his position appears in the skill with which it enables him to examine the relationship in her work between naturalism and art, between probability or verisimilitude on the one hand, and the unity of action, the comic contrivance of plot on the other. He writes:

> Her fables appear to us to be, in their own way, nearly faultless; they do not consist . . . of a string of unconnected events which have little or no bearing on one plot . . . ; but have all that compactness of plan and unity of action which is generally produced by a sacrifice of probability; yet they have little or nothing that is not probable; the story proceeds without the aid of extraordinary accidents; the events that take place are the necessary or natural consequences of what has preceded; and yet (which is a very rare merit indeed) the final catastrophe is scarcely ever clearly foreseen from the beginning, and very often comes, upon the generality of readers at least, quite unexpected. We know not whether Miss Austen ever had access to the precepts of Aristotle; but there are few, if any writers of fiction who have illustrated them more successfully.[12]

Whatley makes no direct connection between this construction and the art of comedy, however. Nor did Lewes, though coming nearer to it. He sees that Jane Austen's dramatic instinct 'probably made the construction of her stories so admirable' and defines construction as a process of selection which prevents our interest flagging 'because one chapter evolves the next, one character is necessary for the elucidation of another'.[13] He compares her in this 'economy of art' to Sophocles and Molière and prefers her construction to Fielding's, but though twice in the course of the article he associates her with great comic writers—she is better than Fielding and a little lower than Molière—he never quite relates this to the peculiarly comic nature of her art.

To have done so would have revealed how traditional Jane Austen's comedy is. The form of comedy consists of a contrived pattern of inter-relations between character and event devised to obstruct the course which should lead direct to the happy ending. The art of comedy is to display these contrivances so that we are delighted by the way they hold up the denouement, because, though they continually confuse our expectation of the happy ending, they never really disturb it. The medium in which Jane Austen works helps to conceal art, but the structure of her novels displays the extraordinary skill with which she controls our response from within it.

Sometimes she develops a number of small complications, as in *Mansfield Park* where the heroine's dependent position naturally gives rise to a great many nuisances which serve to set off the real obstacle of Edmund's infatuation with Mary Crawford. More often she produces one culminating complication after a series of lesser ones, just before the denouement , like General Tilney's displeasure or Wickham's elopement, both of which in fact precipitate the very conclusion they seem designed to prevent. In *Emma*, the most original and skilfully planned of her novels, she devised a yet more formal structure. The action moves in three parts like the acts of a play, the first two centring on the suitors favoured by Emma for Harriet. The first is a simple comedy of self-deceit, concluding with the final scene in the carriage where Mr. Elton proposes to Emma. The second, dealing with Frank Churchill, is more complicated since Churchill is at first Emma's own interest whom she only surrenders as a suitably romantic match for Harriet when she has grown bored with him. The reversal of this section has no final scene; it moves by gradual transition into the final act where Harriet reveals her own independent and confident choice of a lover—Mr.

Knightley. Each act so far has exposed Emma further to our mirth and her own mortification, but the last, contrived again as if to prevent the happy ending, reveals to Emma her real feelings and to us the true nature of the work, in one of the wittiest and most 'achieving' lines in comedy: 'It shot through her with the speed of an arrow that Mr. Knightley must marry no one but herself.' This same sentence, the pivot of the whole comedy, resolves the subdued suspense which has existed from the start about the identity of Emma's future husband, and the resolution convinces us that we have always known it as effectively as it convinces Emma herself.

*Emma* is unusually constructed with the greater formality, the obvious comic convention, coming at the beginning of the book. The middle section develops more naturally and the denouement, though a perfect example of comic reversal and comic timing, is so well contained within the realistic atmosphere of the preceding part, that it illustrates exactly that interplay of formal unity with the wider effect of reality that we have already noticed. And all this is achieved without any blurring of the outlines of the form, or any sacrifice of the point and clarity of the comic construction.

These devices could be matched in Shakespeare, in Molière, in Congreve and in Fielding; they are among the first principles of comic art. But they are often overlooked in Jane Austen because she is writing in the realistic medium of prose fiction. Her earlier critics were deceived into ignoring them even while they admired her skill; they had not related them to the mode of comedy. There was also another reason why they failed to appreciate her in this wider character—their ambiguous attitude to comedy itself. Until Meredith, the main stress in nineteenth-century criticism was upon humour, a particular mood and temper of comedy, rather than on comedy as a form. Wit, that artifice of thought and language, on which so much of Jane Austen's comedy depends, made little appeal to them.

None of her earlier critics uses the word wit to describe her attitude or her style. Lewes, summarizing her qualities at the end of his article, says that our delight in them arises from 'our relish of humour, and our intellectual pleasure in art for art's sake'. This is a curious early use of a now familiar phrase, and it suggests that the relish or taste an admirer of Jane Austen must have is a peculiarly detached one. As sympathy is generally associated with humour, so is detachment with wit, yet elsewhere in the article, Lewes contrives to give an impression of actual dullness in Jane Austen's style; she has 'neither epigrams nor aphorisms, neither subtle analyses nor eloquent descriptions'. It is extraordinary that he could have missed the almost self-indulgent wit of the early works, the comments she could not resist making, as when the gentleman holding up Marianne and Elinor Dashwood in the jeweller's shop, imprints on them 'the remembrance of a person and face of strong, natural, sterling insignificance'. Lewes had little clear sense of what constituted her humour, either, for in a review of Charlotte Bronte's *Shirley* in the *Edinburgh Review*, January 1850, he put her together with Maria Edgeworth and Susan Ferrier as capable of 'sly humourous touches', but, like all women, unable to match 'the lusty mirth and riotous humour of Shakespeare, Rabelais, Butler, Swift, Fielding, Smollet, or Dickens or Thackeray'.[14] Yet Maria Edgeworth and Susan Ferrier, unlike Jane Austen, had carried on Fanny Burney's tradition of the broad comedy of eccentricity which she inherited from the eighteenth-century picaresque novel. George Moir in a review of Susan Ferrier's works in the *Edinburgh Review*, January 1842, deplored 'this tendency to the grotesque which few who have possessed the power of successful humourous delineation have ever been able to resist'[15] (he cites Shakespeare, Smollett, Scott and Fanny Burney), but he still sees it as an excess of comic characterization, rather than a distinct kind of its own. Critics of this opinion could hardly distinguish Jane Austen's wit from such humour except by a careful choice of epithets. They speak of her 'sly humourous touches', or, like Sara Coleridge, of 'the delicate mirth, the gently-hinted satire, the feminine decorous humour',[16] but these are terms which inevitably underplay the force of her comedy, and confuse the gentility of her settings with the real nature of her art.

A reaction was inevitable against this picture of subdued sweetness, and, ironically, the publication of the *Memoir* occasioned it. Margaret Oliphant, reviewing the Memoir in *Blackwood's Magazine*, March 1870 found that Austen-Leigh 'throws out of his dim little lantern a passing gleam of light upon the fine vein of feminine cynicism which pervades his aunt's mind.'[17] The stress is still on femininity; Mrs. Oliphant uses words like 'soft' and 'gentle' to modify the scepticism she detects, but she feels that the amiable tolerance of Jane Austen's attitude has 'none of the sweetness which proceeds from the highest Christian graces'—it is not charity. Charity, like sympathy, could be connected with humour; Thackeray had delivered a lecture in tribute to Dickens on one of his American tours called 'Charity and Humour'. But the temper Mrs. Oliphant describes in Jane Austen has neither.

> She is not surprised or offended, much less horror-stricken or indignant, when her people show vulgar or mean traits of character, when they make it evident how selfish and self-absorbed they are... She stands by and looks on, and gives a soft half-smile, and tells the story with an exquisite sense of its ridiculous side, and fine, stinging yet soft-voiced contempt for the actors in it. She sympathizes with the sufferers, yet she can scarcely be said to be sorry for them; giving them unconsciously a share in her own sense of the covert fun of the scene, and gentle disdain of the possibility that meanness and folly and stupidity could ever really wound any rational creature...... Miss Austen is not the judge of the men and women she collects round her. She is not even their censor to mend their manners; no power has constituted her her brother's keeper. She has but the faculty of seeing her brother clearly all round as if he were a statue, identifying all his absurdities, quietly jeering at him, smiling with her eyes without committing the indecorum of laughter.[18]

The account of Jane Austen's early burlesques in the *Memoir* shows us she says, how soon she

> commenced the amused, indifferent, keen-sighted, impartial inspection of the world as a thing apart from herself, and demanding no excess of sympathy which is characteristic of all the work of her life.[19]

Mrs. Oliphant claims to think none the worse of Jane Austen for her cynicism, but in *Pride and Prejudice* the dispassionate clarity, the love of fools for their extreme ridiculousness, obviously unnerves her. Jane Austen seems to her too harsh in her treatment of Mr. Collins, who, coming nearest to a 'humourous' character, appears to have had a particular attraction for nineteenth-century readers:

> Whether it is not too cruel to make the wife of this delightful Mr. Collins share so completely her creator's estimate of him is a different matter. 'When Mr. Collins could be forgotten there was really a great air of comfort throughout, and by Charlotte's evident enjoyment of it Elizabeth supposed he must often be forgotten' the unflinching narrative goes on.[20]

She says of the Bennet family 'we acknowledge its truth and yet we rebel against this pitiless perfection of art', and she finds *Emma* the greater book because 'though there is scarcely one character in *Pride and Prejudice* for whom we can feel any kindly sympathy', in *Emma* 'there is nobody to hate'.[21] But few readers fail to feel kindly sympathy with the Gardiners, Jane Bennet and Bingley, and there is nobody to hate in either book; Mr. and Mrs. Elton are as absurd as Mr. Collins and Lady Catherine, but Jane Austen's fools are to be delighted in, not detested. The sentimentalizing of Mr. Collins and the moral earnestness revealed here, like the descriptions of Jane Austen's wit as gentle, feminine, decorous humour, are interesting examples of the coarsening of comic sensibility in the nineteenth century. Her fineness and pointed accuracy of taste, of moral descrimination and observation seemed to them either a minor, womanly skill, or a limitation, not a gift comparable to Chaucer's or Molière's.

Mrs. Oliphant's pieces of unflinching narrative from *Pride and Prejudice* are a characteristic example of Jane Austen's wit. The epigrammatic brilliance of this early work relates it in tone to the eighteenth century, as does the characterization. Mr. Bennet, for example, is essentially the eighteenth-century man of wit, a type we might expect to find in Goldsmith or Sheridan. Like Mr. Burchell he is sardonic, like Honeywood, the Good-Natured Man, he shows the dangers as well as the merits of his foible. But he is used as a focal character throughout the book, and only two people, the hero and heroine, are allowed to increase in stature beside him. Because he loves a fool he increases our delight in them: Mrs. Bennet, Mr. Collins and Wickham are all funnier because of his comments on them, and he thus sustains and increases the comic tone of the book. His relationship to Elizabeth is beautifully contrived. As a figure of wit he is Jacques to her Rosalind, and with all Jacques's irresponsible detachment; but he is used to reveal her nature, too. She alone sees his folly in allowing Lydia to go to Brighton, and at least once her deeper nature is revealed when she goes beyond him again. To her question, has he any objection to Darcy? Mr. Bennet replies:

> 'None at all. We all know him to be a proud, unpleasant sort of man; but this would be nothing if you really liked him.'
> 'I do, I do like him', she replied with tears in her eyes. 'I love him. Indeed he has no improper pride. He is perfectly amiable. You do not know what he really is; then pray do not pain me by speaking of him in such terms.'

(ch. 59)

Elizabeth's response, which for a moment puts her love for Darcy above her life-long confederacy with her father, is a stroke of great tact and subtlety. To Jane's question, how long she has loved Darcy? she answers in the old style: 'It has been coming on so gradually that I hardly know when it began; but I believe I must date it from my first seeing his beautiful grounds at Pemberley'. But with her father she is reduced to seriousness, to something more than the wit he stands for and she shares. So the implicit censure of Mr. Bennet's inertia in the novel must be balanced against his important function. He sets the scale of criticism though he is criticized himself, and it is in relation to him that we recognize the heroine's good sense and her real feelings.

Mrs. Oliphant was astonished to learn from the *Memoir* how warmly Jane Austen felt about Darcy and Elizabeth. To her Darcy was 'a very ordinary young man', and Elizabeth's wit no more than 'a certain sharp smartness'. She could not see why the author felt such pride in her heroine when 'our beloved Mr. Collins... evidently goes for very little with his maker'. Yet one of the most difficult achievements in comic fiction is to keep the hero and heroine central, to attach our interest to them throughout and to allow the minor characters only so much independent vitality as distinguishes them from the main pair in a relationship of contrast and support. This is less difficult to manage in drama than in the novel: Beatrice and Benedick, Millamant and Mirabel easily maintain their position. But Fielding alone resisted the temptation in the picaresque comic novel to allow minor figures to proliferate at the expense of the hero; it is this that gives its classical proportions to the plot of *Tom Jones* and constitutes its ingenuity. The 'humourous' novel of the nineteenth century had developed from the eccentricity of a lesser writer—Smollett—who could not prevent a complete shift of interest from the hero to the supporting cast where every individual oddity is allowed an independent growing life of its own. Jane Austen's dramatic presentation of character, her construction and her sense of balance and proportion all prevented this in her work. But the classic poise which relates her to the comic dramatists, the moral essayists and even the satirists of the eighteenth century, hindered an appreciation of her art at a time when the tradition of comic fiction had developed from Smollett through Scott and Dickens.

There was another aspect of her work which prevented her from becoming truly popular in the nineteenth century—her lack of any recognizeably romantic qualities. Scott had gently reproved her for the prudential attitude to marriage he found in *Emma*, and Whately had produced *Persuasion* as the answer to this. But Lewes thought *Persuasion* her weakest work, and Mrs. Oliphant disliked in it 'the old imperfection which renders every character a fool except the heroic pair who hold their places in the foreground'.[22] Neither saw in it the romantic elements some twentieth-century readers have found, but their idea of the romantic was perhaps more distinct than ours. Lewes associates it with description, and misses in Jane Austen that essentially romantic power of embodying the inner spirit in a unique outer form. The nineteenth-century passion for the visual as a physical correlative of insight or vision lies behind his remark that if the reader has to image for himself without any help from the author, he may 'miss many of the subtle connections between physical and mental organization'.[23] He finds Jane Austen deficient, too, in poetry and passion, and concludes that her genius

> with no power over the more stormy and energetic activities which find vent even in everyday life, can give her a high rank among great artists... when it is admitted that she never stirs the deeper emotions, that she never fills the soul with a noble aspiration or brightens it with a fine idea, but, at the most, only teaches us charity for the ordinary failings of ordinary people, and sympathy with their goodness, we have admitted an objection which lowers her claims to rank among the greatest benefactors of the race; and this sufficiently explains why, with all her excellence, her name has not become a household word.[24]

Greater men than Lewes had felt the same. Sara Coleridge tells us

> My uncle Southey and my father had an equally high opinion of her merits; but Mr. Wordsworth used to say that though he admitted that her novels were an admirable copy of life, he could not be interested in productions of that kind; unless the truth of nature were presented to him clarified, as it were, by the pervading light of imagination, it had scarce any attractions in his eyes; and for this reason, he took little pleasure in the writings of Crabbe.[25]

Newman in 1837 wrote to Anne Mozley

> I have been reading 'Emma'. Everything Miss Austen writes is clever, but I desiderate something. There is a want of *body* to the story. The action is frittered away in over little things. There are some beautiful things in it. Emma herself is the most interesting to me of all her heroines. I feel kind to her whenever I think of her. But Miss Austen

has no romance—none at all. What vile creatures her parsons are! She has not a dream of the high Catholic ἦθος. That other woman Fairfax is a dolt—but I like Emma.[26]

No imagination, and no romance; these are severe charges. A surviving memory of them perhaps accounts for the present tendency to elevate *Persuasion* above her novels, not so much for itself, but as a sign that Jane Austen was changing her manner to suit the subtler sensibility of a more complex age. It is an assumption that needs some modification, especially since the last fragment *Sanditon*—though that, too, has been represented as a new departure—is in so many ways a return to the earlier spirit of comedy.

There is no doubt that *Persuasion* seems different in kind from the other novels. Jane Austen herself is on record as saying only one thing about it—that the heroine was almost too good for her. Certainly Anne Elliot is as carefully guarded from the play of wit as Fanny Price (though, like her, she is susceptible to it: we are told that Wentworth was witty and rash). Her situation is more sympathetic than Fanny's but also more static; less can happen to her. The retrospective position in which she finds herself can hardly help the narrative forward, and seems therefore to require a new kind of structure. Professor Wright has pointed out the dual time scheme of the book, how the past elucidates the present, but Jane Austen had not developed any new technique for dealing with it. Her sense of place and mood—already strong in *Emma* where the hot day at Donwell Abbey, the wind despoiling the shrubbery at Hartfield, and the fine morning after, all support the changes of feeling and action—has more scope in this static tale. The scenes crystallize, and an autumnal suspension of time in character and season gives unity to a book which is unusually clumsy in some of its narrative devices.

We have now, in Professor Wright's valuable edition of *Persuasion*, the cancelled tenth chapter of Volume II, which Jane Austen clearly found too flat and repetitive, but the real weakness of the book lies in the long and unalleviated exposition in Chapter 9—Mrs. Smith's exposure of Mr. Elliot's character. Its dullness is related to the shadowiness of Mr. Elliot himself, of whom we have no very clear picture. He is allowed only two brief pieces of serious dialogue—one of which (his remarks in Chapter 5, Volume II, on the difference between good company and the best) faintly echoes Henry Crawford's intelligence and wit. But the comparison indicates the change at once; in contrast to Henry Crawford we hardly know Mr. Elliot. We realize him as little as we realize Mrs. Smith, Mrs. Clay, or even Lady Russell, though we are told more about all of them than is usual in any of the previous novels. In no other work of Jane Austen's does the self-sufficiency of the characters falter: here it barely exists. Anne and Captain Wentworth themselves come to life partly through our extensive knowledge of their past. The people we get to know in the present, the Elliots, the Musgroves and the Crofts are lightly sketched in, real enough—especially the Musgroves —in a day-to-day fashion, but often needing commentary from the author.

On the whole, wit is absent. After a promising opening in the old style, it flickers and gradually dies. Sir Walter and Elizabeth Elliot and Mrs. Clay soon cease to amuse. In the emotional, barely comic light of the conclusion, Mary Musgrove's acceptance of Anne's marriage because it is late and does not eclipse her own, is regrettable rather than entertaining, and we feel Anne's grief at her family's stupidity far more seriously than Elizabeth Bennet's because we have never laughed whole-heartedly at them. The sharpness of the author's comment on Mrs. Musgrove's 'large fat sighings over the destiny of a son, whom alive nobody had cared for' scarcely fits Professor Wright's admonition to listen carefully here to the convinced and formidable moralist. Straight-faced criticism in Jane Austen is often less convincing than witty ridicule. She felt it herself, for the sentence is followed by a quite unprecedented explanation and excuse:

> Personal size and mental sorrow have certainly no necessary proportions. A large bulky figure has as good a right to be in deep affliction, as the most graceful set of limbs in the world. But, fair or not fair, there are unbecoming conjunctions, which reason will patronize in vain—which taste cannot tolerate—which ridicule will seize.
>
> (ch. 8)

This is the apology of wit not morality, but had the wit been working well enough there would have been no need for it. Jane Austen recognized the note of irritation which, had she allowed it to rise naturally as Anne's nervous reaction to her absurd situation, separated from Captain Wentworth on a small sofa by a large lachrymose woman, would have passed as a touch of comedy. But though Emma would have been permitted to think it, Anne had been conceived as 'too good' for such a response, and there was no outlet for the author's exasperated taste but this peevishly obtrusive comment.

The predominance of hero and heroine in *Pride and Prejudice* is an element of high comedy and requires the perfect inter-relating of the subsidiary characters. Here it is an intense centre of feeling from which all the surrounding characters are shut out. There is much more discussion of feeling, and much less demonstration of attitude in action. But since Jane Austen had chosen to retain the old kind of structure, this inner intensity throws the devices of plot into awkward relief and makes it even more necessary that they should be handled with great tact. Yet after the Lyme episode, when the suspense of Captain Wentworth's apparent feeling for Louisa has been resolved, we wait too long and with too little interest for the denouement. Mr. Elliot does not convince us as a rival since Anne is never moved by him. The interest in Bath flags heavily, and the introduction of Mrs. Smith is a crude way of precipitating the conclusion.

There are, of course, many fine touches in *Persuasion* particularly in the treatment of the heroine's feelings. But by the standards we have used to judge her other works, it is a failure, and we have to use these standards because Jane Austen clung to the outlines of the old form, the contrived denouement, the pattern of suspense and resolution. But these bare bones of comic structure obtrude awkwardly, and when we admire *Persuasion* we are not thinking of the form but of the feeling, the mood; the happy ending is 'the more delayed, delighted' in a deeper than structural sense. It is a reconciliation piece, like one of Shakespeare's romances, but so much more difficult to achieve in prose without the help of artifice and fantasy, in the bounds of that naturalistic setting Jane Austen had so perfectly adjusted to classic comic schemes. We are forced to think that had she gone on wanting to write thus, she would inevitably have looked for a more suitable form for her content.

But she did not want to. *Sanditon* shows a deliberate return to the comic spirit of the earlier works. It is dangerous to deduce intentions from an unrevised fragment, but as it stands it shows the taste for burlesque reviving under a diet of new material, romanticism, land speculation, the passion for the spa and fashionable hypochondria (a favourite eighteenth-century theme) which is used here as a comic physical counterpart to a yet more fashionable sickness, Byronism. There is a topographical emphasis in *Sanditon*, but it is only bolder, not more important than in *Emma*, where, as Mrs. Oliphant remarked, Highbury is 'a perfect piece of village geography'. More striking is the return to wit, the sense of the ridiculous which informs the narrative, the dialogue and the commentary. Sir Edward Denham in his liberal praise of Burns elicits at least one epigram from the prudent Charlotte: 'I have not faith in the *sincerity* of the affections of a Man of his description. He felt & he wrote & he forgot'. And Jane Austen cannot conceal her delight in describing Sir Edward himself. Byronism had roused her sense of the ridiculous as strongly as the taste for the Gothic, and her tone is a mixture of the old youthful exuberance, and a maturer wit as she exposes the complacent would-be Don Juan:

> Sir Edw:'s great object in life was to be seductive.—With such personal advantages as he knew himself to possess, and such Talents as he did also give himself credit for, he regarded it as his Duty.—He felt that he was formed to be a dangerous Man—quite in the line of the Love-laces.—The very name of Sir Edward he thought, carried some degree of fascination with it . . . . . . but it was Clara alone on whom he had serious designs; it was Clara whom he meant to seduce. Her situation in every way called for it. She was his rival in Lady D's favour, she was young, lovely dependant.—He had very early seen the necessity of the case, had now been long trying with cautious assiduity to make an impression in her heart, and to undermine her Principles.— Clara saw through him, and had not the least intention of being seduced—but she bore with him patiently enough to confirm the sort of attachment which her personal Charms had raised.—A greater degree of discouragement indeed would not have affected Sir Edw:— He was armed against the highest pitch of Disdain and Aversion.—If she could not be won by affection, he must carry her off. He knew his Business.[27]

This is far from the tone of *Persuasion*, indeed the whole idiom of *Sanditon* suggests that Jane Austen still felt that her true form was comedy and her natural expression wit. She dearly loved a fool, and she worked with the greatest happiness and ease in the medium of ridicule. Swift, Pope and Johnson would have understood her attitude better than Wordsworth and Newman. The pitiless perfection of art, the intellectualism of art for art's sake which the nineteenth-century critics found in her was nothing more than the traditional genius of comedy unrecognized in a more solemn period.

Our own is not always more sympathetic. If their ambiguous use of the word 'humour' hinders their criticism of comedy, so does our use of 'irony', which is equally confused and confusing. Our idea of Jane Austen's moral consciousness, too, is further from the mark than Mrs. Oliphant's view that she considered herself neither her brother's keeper nor his censor, but was content, rather, to be the amused observer who could herself amuse. Thus she maintained the spirit of comedy which needs innate confidence in absolute standards, standards an ordered society comes nearest to representing in an imperfect world, but which exist outside that society and are ideally reflected in the form of the work. Jane Austen benefited as a comic writer both by being a Christian, and by inheriting many eighteenth-century attitudes, among them that folly and knavery can never be radically reformed, but that they may be laughed out of countenance. From her letters we find that she was an admirer of Johnson, that she knew *Tom Jones* and *Tristram Shandy*, that she was amused by the eighteenth-century plays she saw at the theatre in London, admired Cowper's restrained sentiment, and of all modern poets preferred Crabbe. The backwater world she inhabited was as near in spirit to the preceding age as a vicarage in the first decade of the twentieth century probably was to the nineteenth. Since we cannot share her attitude, it is as hard for us as it was for her nineteenth-century critics to avoid reading our own into her work. A good preventative against this is to think of her in company with Goldsmith and Sheridan rather than George Eliot and Henry James. But she is a greater artist than either, and like Lewes, though more confidently, we may find ourselves comparing her to Shakespeare and Molière, for her achievement is not really related to any period, but to an attitude of mind, a type of genius which naturally expresses itself in the ageless form of comedy.

## NOTES

1. *Persuasion*, ed. Andrew Wright (1965), p. xv.
2. *Quarterly Review*, Vol. XIV, p. 197.
3. *Minor Works*, p. 434.
4. *ibid*, p. 438.
5. *Quarterly Review*, Vol. XXIV, p. 363.
6. *ibid*., p. 366.
7. *Edinburgh Review*, Vol. LI, pp. 448–9.

8. *Blackwood's Magazine*, vol. LXXXVI, p. 105.
9. J. A. Bayley, *Tolstoy and the Novel* (1965).
10. *Memoir and Correspondence of Susan Ferrier*, ed. J. A. Boyle (1898) p. 128.
11. *Minor Works*, p. 434.
12. *Quarterly Review*, vol. XXIV, p. 360.
13. *Blackwood's Magazine*, vol. LXXXVI, p. 105.
14. *Edinburgh Review*, vol. XCI, p. 172.
15. *Edinburgh Review*, vol. LXXIV, p. 500.
16. *Memoir and Letters of Sara Coleridge*, 2nd edition (1873) vol. I, p. 75.
17. *Blackwood's Magazine*, vol. CVII, p. 294.
18. *ibid*, pp. 294–5.
19 *ibid*, p. 295.
20. *Blackwood's Magazine*, vol. CVII, p. 300.
21. *ibid*, p. 303.
22. *ibid*., p. 304.
23. *Blackwood's Magazine*, vol. LXXXVI, p. 106.
24. *ibid*, p. 113.
25. *Memoir and Letters of Sara Coleridge, loc. cit.*
26. *Letters and Correspondence of Newman*, ed. Anne Mozley (1891) vol. II, p. 223. I am indebted to this reference to Miss Lascelles, who in turn had it from Professor Kathleen Tillotson.
27. *Minor Works*, p. 405.

# X

## THE NEIGHBOURHOOD OF TOMBUCTOO: CONFLICTS IN JANE AUSTEN'S NOVELS

*Angus Wilson*

---

'I DOUBT', wrote Jane Austen's nephew in his *Memoir*, 'whether it would be possible to mention any other author of note whose personal obscurity was so complete.' Virginia Woolf in her essay of 1923 quotes this passage and adds, 'Had she lived a few more years only, all that would have been altered. She would have stayed in London, dined out, lunched out, met famous people, made new friends, read', [it is difficult to see why Virginia Woolf should have supposed that Jane Austen would or could have read more than she did] 'travelled and carried back to the quiet country cottage a hoard of observations to feast upon at leisure'. She goes on to predict that had this happened Jane Austen's 'sense of security would have been shaken. Her comedy would have suffered. She would have trusted less to dialogue and more to reflection to give us a knowledge of her characters. ... She would have devised a method ... for conveying, not only what people say, but what they leave unsaid; not only what they are, but what life is. She would have stood farther away from her characters, and seen them more as a group, less as individuals'. The greater part of Jane Austen's more serious admirers today would, I think, be amused, even perhaps a little disgusted at the sound of 'dined out, lunched out, met famous people'; here, they might feel, is Bloomsbury at its most 'social' and metropolitan. It is worth recalling, however, Mrs. Woolf's deep, if tragic understanding of the traditional English country values as shown in *Between The Acts;* only by so doing can we fully estimate the extraordinary comprehension that allowed her (almost uniquely among English novelists with such traditional loyalties) to celebrate London (a city as a source of life and energy) and, in the course of that celebration, to engage with worldly values without succumbing to them. For this reason, I can think of no other novelist so equipped justifiably to criticize Jane Austen on this score. Such criticism conflicts markedly, it seems to me, with the almost universal acceptance by modern writers on Jane Austen of her preferred range of artistic concern, as expressed in her letter to her niece Fanny of 'three or four families in a country village'. For some novelists, no doubt, this limitation would be a valuable discipline; for her, I believe, the constriction, however inescapable, was a deforming one; it distorted the balance between the two views of life whose conflict made her art. If only they would admit this, modern critics would feel less compelled to tie themselves into knots in order to give a moral unity to the continuous contradiction that exists not only between her different novels but also within each of them.

To approve Virginia Woolf's speculation and the criticism implied in it is not necessarily to accept her conclusions. The changes that she suggests might have taken place in Jane Austen's art, though meaningful, bear, as with most novelist-critics, a suspiciously close appearance to an analysis of her own artistic ambitions. It is after all also perfectly possible that had Jane Austen seen more of the world, she might have finally retired more fully into her country values, have produced as movingly stoical a novel as *Mansfield Park* but with a deeper compassion. I doubt if this is what Virginia Woolf either hoped or supposed. On the other hand greater acquaintance with the world might have led Jane Austen to produce as splendid a defence of freedom, of personality and energy as *Pride and Prejudice* without it striking her as too 'light, bright and sparkling'. Or perhaps she would have continued to oscillate between her two views of life—life which does not always instruct so singly as modern literary criticism seems, as its most dogmatic, to demand. However, I do not believe she would again have employed the wonderful complexity of her irony and the fineness of her moral discrimination on a resolution of her conflict so ultimately diminished and depressing as that of *Emma*.

To dispose of what however useful, is after all only a speculation, let it be said at once that whatever effect a further acquaintance with the great world might have had on Jane Austen, it does not seem very likely that such an acquaintance would have come about, despite her growing fame. Though young to die, she was hardly by the standards of her day of an age to change her way of living. Her refusal to meet Madame de Staël is perhaps insufficient evidence to tell us how she would have reacted to further overtures from literary society, but it is not promising. Family attachment, far beyond any contemporary convention I think, was of her essence. She had always depended for her periodic tastes of metropolitan life upon her merchant brother Henry and his Henrietta Street mansion. After his bankruptcy and appointment to a curacy at Bentley near Alton, not only was her only London family centre gone, but she writes that 'London is become a hateful place' to her brother. The 'three or four families', it seems, might well have been even more the horizon of her fame than they had been of her obscurity. And even if they had not been so, though, as Mrs. Woolf suggests her powers might have deepened, the dichotomy in her nature would surely have remained. *Persuasion*, despite its wider horizons—not only of Bath, the Italian opera and Mrs. Smith's poverty, but more importantly of its hero's fuller experience—does not resolve the old dilemma. Prudence chides Louisa's impetuosity at Lyme; even the fuller prospect of her marriage to Wentworth does not permit Anne to throw over her former acceptance of Lady Russell's disastrous prudential advice. In *Sanditon*, with its shift to a 'modern' phenomenon—a seaside resort —there is, as Mr. Tony Tanner in his illuminating introduction to *Mansfield Park* suggests, promise of a further declaration in favour of rest and of resistance to the new century's demands of clamorous individualism. Unresolved temperamental conflict would surely have remained the source of Jane Austen's creative powers. Professor Wright, recognizing the fundamental contradictions in her work tries to elevate them into 'a conception of the total personality', something Olympianly above ordinary moral choice. For me this is an injustice done to her continuous serious moral concern for solution, for some resting point between the two extremes of her nature; just as many other critics' identification of her oscillations as her final convictions—allowing her to be claimed in recent years by Anglicans, materialists, Marxists, vitalists, quietists and sceptics—ignores the masterly artistry and pervasive irony with which she hedges her bets. To accept her uncertainties as much as her desire to resolve them and to admit the degree to which her search is limited by her material may save her from a half hidden inflation of her creative contribution that will surely end in undeserved hostile reaction.

Ever since Victorian critics, rightly impressed by her comic genius, murmured 'Shakespearean comic characterization' with the same breath that they treated of her limited range, a curious dual process has gone on of proclaiming aloud her small world and at the same time nudging her into the ranks of the very few greatest masters of the novel. The motives for such promotion by stealth are very clear: her extraordinary intelligence appeals to the many critics, for whom intelligence is the first necessity of greatness; her undoubted inner warmth compels admiration because of the rare sincerity with which its limits are announced; the pioneer complexity of her artistry demands recognition from every discerning reader, above all the pioneer complexity of her irony demands tribute from the vast army who now judge the novel by Jamesian canons—a tribute given with an added, piquant, rebellious flavour because the Master himself failed to rise above the less discerning standards of his time in his judgement of her; let me add to all these respectable reasons that her wonderful entertainment is a lawful feastday for those who are under vows to deny themselves such fare. In short her charm, always so potent among certain middlebrow readers, operates quite as effectively among kindred spirits of higher intellectual pretensions. To this must be added a natural desire among Anglo-Saxon critics to advance the international claims of a first class English writer who largely resists translation, and a wish, in my opinion less respectable, to canonize the foundress of the religion of the English novel, meaning by that religion a regard for all the qualities which the English novel does not share with the great novels of other countries. Not that I should care to deny the justification of this canonization, for through Jane Austen was transmitted to her English heirs Richardson's brilliant Grandisonian care for minutiae and mistrust of worldliness; while foreigners preferred Clarissa, Lovelace and passion; to be fair to the English tradition, the loss, I should say, was only a shade less theirs than ours. But it is not only to critics defending a literary tradition that she appeals; social traditionalists (often but not always the same as the literary ones) find her defence of prudence, reflection, good sense and custom peculiarly delightful because they are offered with a wit and a liveliness that are not always to be found associated with conservative counsels; yet lovers of energy, boldness, and freedom and the vital spirit can also claim allegiance to her and find in her a seriousness (but not any dowdy earnestness), a taste and a discretion that are not always the mark of life-enhancing art. The former, perhaps, may make light of Catherine Morland's youthful vitality, and quote Jane Austen's own words in moderate disparagement of *Pride and Prejudice*; the latter may only succeed in swallowing Fanny and Edmund after extraordinary displays of acrobatic distortion; both parties will probably join together in saluting the complex artistry of *Emma*, though the traditionalists will dwell on the virtues of the best of Highbury and the vitalists on the energy of Emma herself even in her regenerate ending. As to the trickle of critics hostile to Jane Austen, from Victorian times onwards they have been either temperamentally off key like Charlotte Brontë, Mark Twain, or Lawrence, or insufficiently informed like Professor Garrod, or critical only partially like Mr. Amis in his unwillingness lightly to undertake inviting Mr. and Mrs. Edmund Bertram to dine; her less intelligent, more fulsome admirers have been more an embarrassment to her high reputation than her hostile critics. On the whole after her scurvy treatment by Crosby, the purchaser of 'Susan' (*Northanger Abbey*)—possibly one of the most consequential blows to a great writer by the trade when we consider her many years of comparative inactivity after 1803 that may have lost us masterpieces —the progress of her reputation has been continuous. The Victorians established her genius without making much of how far it was tutored; three eminent scholars in the 'thirties established once for all her extensive conscious artistry; in the last two decades many of the best English and American scholars and critics have sought in her work the conscious moral unity (something at a higher level than the merely didactic) which modern criticism demands of the greatest novelists. I have no doubt that she, too, sought it both in her creative work and, more importantly to her, in her life, but I doubt if she attained it. To trace her contradictions, ambiguities and attempted resolutions may do more to illustrate her great richness than to force her (whatever else, no first Mrs. Rochester) into any sort of straitjacket.

The dilemma in her work may be given many names—one, she herself contributed, sense and sensibility; or we may say head and heart, prudence and impulse, rest and motion, or wit and plain speech, or country and town, though once we use symbols we become aware that the opposing parts are themselves ambiguously represented in her novels. The contradictions lie deep in her temperament; whether either or both sides of her nature were congenital it would, I suppose, be impossible even to guess at now, although the allied question of whether she herself believed in original sin or in man as a blank sheet on which environment traces character is one of the most interesting ambiguities in her novels. Certainly we may feel sure that she had no belief in man's primitive benevolence, Shaftes-buryean or Rousseauistic alike; although I should like to note in passing that even so exact a scholar as Chapman seems to imply the probability of her having read *Caleb Williams* and *St. Leon* only from the dates of their publication and from her right-thinking jest that Mr. Pickford 'is as raffish in his appearances as I would wish every disciple of Godwin to be'. Her family certainly contributed environmentally as much to her wit (although she was the leader of the childhood revels) as to her seriousness; we may guess her eldest brother James, perhaps, Mr. Knight Austen and Cassandra, to have been on the prudential side, Henry lamentably not, save no doubt in retrospect after his fall, and her two admiral brothers splendidly to have united risk with good sense. For the many who have read between the lines of her letters that her Mother with her hypo-chondriac nature was a trial to Jane, it is worth noting that Mrs. Austen's preference was decidedly for *Pride and Prejudice* over *Mansfield Park*.

Her reading, which I shall return to, though clearly so central to her development, is so hedged round by ironies and jests in her references that it is often difficult to know exactly what were the final moral influences upon her even of her 'dear Doctor Johnson' or of Cowper, let alone of Richardson and his lesser successors in novel writing.

Born, acquired, or both, her contradictions gained a definite flavour fram the *form* of her novels. I mean by this not the pervasive irony, for that is simply the covering of the contradictions, but the general manner of her plots. Here the influence of Richardson is in-controvertible. The careless guardians descend through Miss Burney from the inadequate Reeves, guardians of Harriet Byron, and the bad parents descend from the Harlowes. The plausible seducers, too, and all their mechanism which disturbs Professor Mudrick and other modern critics, are Richardsonian, although if they rise above the stagey level of Sir Hargreaves Pollexfen, they fall miles short of the splendour of Lovelace. But the most important effect of her plotting was her reversal after *Northanger Abbey* of the usual Richardson–Burney scheme. Following *Clarissa* and more still Harriet Byron's story in *Grandison*, Fanny Burney had plunged her unprotected or ill-protected heroines into the dangers of the wicked London world of masquerades. In all the useful talk about Plato and simulation with which modern critics have illuminated the amateur theatricals in *Mansfield Park*, the parallel with the dangerous masquerades in *Pamela*, *Grandison* and Miss Burney's novels seems to have been overlooked. Masqueraders at the London pleasure gardens seem to have assumed exactly these dangerous amorous roles that destroyed Maria Bertram. Edmund makes as clear a distinction between professional acting and this aristocratic country house party stuff as Richardson does between the professional theatre (although Mr. B. is a little severe on this too) and the masquerades of the London *bon ton*. Incidentally it is often said that Jane Austen had no dislike for amateur theatricals as such, only for the particular events of *Mansfield Park*. Is there any proof of this? The amateur theatricals in her family home are connected with the Comtesse de Feuillide's visits in Jane's girlhood. We can't tell how she may have looked back on them. This general theme of the orphan abroad is satirized in *Northanger Abbey*, with Mrs. Allen as the embodiment of an insufficient guardian. But with *Sense and Sensibility* the pattern changes, though a touch of the old satire is kept when vulgar Mrs. Jennings turns out to be far from a careless guardian in London. From the heroine abroad we turn now to the heroine's home invaded, and invaded by London or, at any rate, worldly types. Willoughby, Wickham, the Crawfords, Mr. William Elliot threaten the stability of certain dearly held values; Frank Churchill offers the same threat in a less virulent, more juvenile form. It is not always possible to match the threatened moral citadel with a particular country home. This is partly for the simple reason that heroines, being women, expect to change their homes on marriage—Longbourn (in any case, a village, not a house) is threatened by plausible rogues and aristocratic insolence, it is very poorly defended by Mr. and Mrs. Bennet, but it is not the final repository of the values Elizabeth seeks to defend. Pemberley will be this. For all the sentimental attachment that makes Elinor deplore the cutting down of the walnuts at Norland as much as Fanny does the threatened avenues at Sotherton, neither place is the heroine's home. Only in *Mansfield Park* and *Emma* does the identification of house and value work exactly to typify the besieged citadel. Fanny, settling at last at Mansfield Parsonage, finds it as dear as everything else associated with Mansfield Park. Emma settles for Hartfield followed by Donwell—but Highbury, of which she herself has been the careless guardian, remains always the citadel of values. I shall return in my conclusion to the effect this identification of place and value has upon those two novels. Meanwhile what kind of values are embodied in Mansfield Park, Donwell, Pemberley or Kellynch?

They are, of course, in some degree, social. Jane Austen was a realist; she could hardly find interest in the sort of social fantasy or social rarity (for Richardson's conscious realism would allow him only to paint from nature) of Mr. B's marriage to a serving maid. Such romantic notions are held up to ridicule in Emma's dreams about Harriet's birth. She accepted the social values of her world, but I am sure that Dr. Arnold Kettle is right in thinking that she did so with some impatience, even at times distaste. She was, on the whole, like Richardson anti-aristocratic (a good part of her mistrust of worldliness comes from this). She stood by the professional classes from which she came—by the Navy, the Church and the respectable counting houses. The leavening is peculiarly marked in *Pride and Prejudice* and in *Persuasion*. 'Mr. Gardiner was a sensible, gentlemanlike man, greatly superior to his sister, as well as by nature as by education. The Netherfield ladies would have had difficulty in believing that a man who lived by trade, and within view of his own warehouse, could have been so well bred and agreeable.' Mrs. Gardiner's bourgeois friends at Lambton could only give hearsay evidence about the Darcys, for they were 'the inhabitants of a small market town where the family did not visit'. Surely this social barrier must have been overturned when Lizzie became mistress of Pemberley, and 'with the Gardiners, they were always on the most intimate terms'. The arrogance of birth and inherited property are never so lightly dismissed as by the admirable Admiral Croft—'the baronet will never set the Thames on fire, but there seems no harm in him.' Mansfield Park may seem at times a more socially grand background, but Sir Thomas is a merchant, his interests are trade rather than land. All in all this championship of the active, professional, dutiful and expanding section of society saves Jane Austen from class rigidity, and hence from many of its less trivial companion evils. The limits, however, are marked: Mr. Knightley espouses Mr. Robert Martin's cause, but the paternalistic form of this friendship is always clear—'You laugh at me about William Larkins, but I could quite as ill spare Robert Martin.' The professional classes Jane Austen identifies with have become associated with the land. Except for the Gardiners I can think of no purely city people or even purely professional people (Fanny's brother William has still to make his way), for in *Persuasion*, with the war over, even the sailors—Harville, Croft, Wentworth—have their eyes on country gentleman-like pursuits. True, save for Bingley and Darcy, the professional element is never far away—Mr. Weston's roots are in trade, Mr. Knightley's brother is a London lawyer, Mrs. Jennings to Lady Middleton's disgust keeps her city friends, but her daughters, like the elder Bennet girls, have married landed gentlemen. The fusion, as I have noted, preserves Jane Austen from taking social divisions too seriously, but it has some evils.

One of these is not, I think, as Mr. Auden and others have said, a concern for money. Lord David Cecil's intended praise for Jane Austen's commonsensical attitude towards moneyed marriage has done her great disservice. She never allows friendship let alone love to be touched by prudential considerations; and those who do so are, like Mrs. Bennet, or the Steele sisters, or Mrs. Norris, judged with the utmost severity. Far more serious, it appears to me, is the touch of philistinism that descends from the alliance of the English country gentry and the English professional classes. Here her distrust of the London world is deforming. Dislike the fact though we may, the amateur painting, even the home music of Jane Austen's heroines, is largely rubbish (think with what contempt such stuff is treated by George Eliot). There are double ironies, it is true, in Emma's statement to Harriet of what her life will be at fifty if she remains single—'Woman's usual occupations of eye and hand and mind will be open to me then as now. . . . If I draw less I shall read more; if I give up music I shall take to carpet work.' But the reality is not so remote from this—'taking likenesses'; making collections of elegant riddles, music seen solely as rivalry in execution. Reading is a different matter, from Catherine onwards the heroines' love of reading is real and valuable; but only Marianne, that highly attractive half-concession to Romanticism, appears to have any true passion for music. Indeed I suspect that Jane Austen found the triviality of the concern for the arts in her world repulsive and so substituted for it an honest philistinism—hence Elinor's treatment of music as a useful cover for private gossip on public occasions and Lizzie's 'knowing nothing of the art' of painting and being only interested therefore in portraits of people she knew. (Jane Austen's own attitude is evidenced by her remarks in 1816 on the London galleries). The feeble caricature of Mary Bennet is the only *Punch* humour in all her work, and it is directed at a 'highbrow'; phoney though Mary's pretensions may have been. Of course, I am not suggesting that an injection of a trivial London modish regard for the arts (Mary Crawford's 'something clever to be said at the close of every air') would have been an improvement, but the Philistinism and the confinement of area in her work do seem intimately connected. We seem to breathe a different and more exalting air at once when Anne Elliot attends the Italian Opera at Bath; as in some passages of the Bath world of *Northanger Abbey*. But fear of the contamination of the trivial, the unprincipled, the smartly second rate (the whole Crawford ethos which Jane Austen catches so beautifully with such deadly severity) seems peculiarly to hang around most of the heroines' visits to London. True, Elinor, Jane Bennet, and Marianne are lovesick at Mrs. Jennings's and Aunt Gardiner's, but is it impossible that they (and alas the authoress on their behalf) are pleased to forego the life of the town which they might have otherwise enjoyed? The most noted Londoner of her novels, Mr. John Knightley, is also safely the most anti-gregarious. Here, at any rate, and for once, the Jane Austen of the letters seems more open to life than the novelist. The merchant interest and the country interest, in fact, join puritanism to philistinism, as anyone who lives among businessmen turned country gentry in England today can still detect. And both these attitudes to life fight with the elan and wit that not only are Jane Austen's first impetus to writing, but, so paradoxical is the whole situation, obviously marked most of the Austen family.

We might hope that in this country world what is lost in concern for the arts might be made up for by a feeling for Nature. And so in part, it is. It is sometimes said that there is no poetry in Jane Austen; this view takes no regard for the essential atmosphere of her novels —an instinctive response to those basic realities of nature, the weather and the seasons. If we seek for any conscious concern for nature, we get either the Gilpin textbook stuff of *Northanger Abbey* or the 'thoughts from the poets' of Fanny or Anne Elliot. But being alive (not necessarily being healthy, for Fanny and Anne are not so) is never absent from the texture of the thoughts of her heroines.

If her hostility to aristocracy and town (London or Bath) is ambiguous, and her allegiance to the solid professional classes turned gentry has its contradictions, towards another aspect of social life she is surely quite determined. The triviality of Meryton, the small town, is the most corrupting force in the Bennet world. Suburbanism, small town life she detests. There is even some snobbery in this, that makes her merciless to Mrs. Elton, and uses Mrs. Elton to attack the trivial snobberies of Emma herself. For it is not enough emphasized how that very model of small towns, Hartfield, is itself very nearly, even in those times, a suburb. Against this small town cruelty and triviality and silliness and insensibility to privacy is directed the most part of what Professor Harding has called her 'regulated hatred'. It is Meryton or Hartfield far more even than the countryside around Northanger that are Henry Tilney's 'neighbourhood(s) of voluntary spies'. It is this above all that makes Emma's ending so forlorn.

But if there is no escape (although I do not really accept this either for the author or for most of her heroines) what are the alternatives? One—it is, of course, the meaning of *Mansfield Park*—lies in a quietism that can live among the spies and yet be untouched by them. Professor Trilling has suggested the half-mockery with which Lady Bertram's inertia offers a refuge to Jane Austen. In the same fascinating essay however, speaking of Sir Thomas, he writes: '... of all the fathers of Jane Austen's novels, Sir Thomas is the only one to whom admiration is given.... The fathers of the heroines of *Pride and Prejudice*, *Emma*, and *Persuasion*, all lack principle and fortitude; they are corrupted by their belief in their delicate vulnerability —they lack apatheia.' Unless we are to judge on purely intellectual grounds (and it is not by intellect that the leechgatherer's wisdom must be assessed) Mr. Woodhouse is a most reverend man. In point of intellect—'Mr. Woodhouse, only half comprehending' etc.—he must be judged an idiot, but there is a touch of the nineteenth century divine idiot in him. Not only are his courtesy, his thoughtfulness and, above all, his warmth of heart constantly dwelt upon, but everyone feels easily able to give him the respect due (but alas not usually paid for in the novels) to parents. His life is the perfect Cowper recipe for living—a few friends at the same hour, habit, the same moderate enjoyments whether of whist or of gruel, the same charities, attachment to the customary, horror for the new. Of course, he is absurd as Lady Bertram is, but his mistrusts are so often instinctively right—'That young man is not at all the thing', he says of Frank Churchill. And his statement that 'the sooner every

party breaks up, the better' is proved true again and again. If Mr.
Woodhouse had had his way Emma would never have been to the
ball where she voiced her monstrous fancies about Jane to Frank
Churchill, Harriet would have attended no ball to be snubbed by Mr.
Elton, there would have been no improvised strawberry gathering
to pain Jane Fairfax's feelings or explorations to Box Hill where
Emma could hurt Miss Bates. In point of the good life as conserv-
ation of energy, caution and limitation, Mr. Woodhouse is a more
central value than Lady Bertram, for his egotism is less permissive.
There just couldn't have been theatricals in a house ordered by Mr.
Woodhouse; no one, not even Mr. Yates, could have ventured
to propose it. It seems doubtful if Mr. Woodhouse's health and
feelings could have permitted the unfortunate trip to Lyme, even if
there had been no suggestion of his being party to it.

This joining of Cowper to Wordsworth is one of the chief marks
of Jane Austen's most important writing. It is clearly Christian;
some remarks in her later letters to her niece Fanny about Evan-
gelicalism and the famous accusation against Mr. Elliot have led
people to attribute it to her attraction to that new Church movement.
The whole question is a very difficult one because we know comparatively little about Jane Austen's religious life, nor, if she had
any intense private religious life (which I am inclined to believe, at
any rate in her later years) would she or Cassandra have allowed
it ever to become a matter of public knowledge. Her three prayers
that have been conserved do not seem more than conventional; their
only at all unusual note is a special plea not to hurt others (Miss
Bates?). Her early references to religion are anti-enthusiastic, the
latter ones more favourable. She deplores that Sir John Moore did
not make a more Christian end at Corunna; Marianne, after her illness, says, 'I wonder at my recovery—wonder that the very eager-
ness of my desire to live, to have time for atonement to my God,
and to you all, do not kill me at once' (ch. 46). Fanny, hearing of
Tom Bertram's grave illness, 'without any particular affection for
her eldest cousin, her tenderness of heart made her feel that she
could not spare him; and the purity of her principles added yet a
keener solicitude, when she considered how little useful, how little
self-denying his life had (apparently) been.' (ch. 13). These, above
all the bracketed word denying the right to public judgement, leaving it to God's judgement, suggest an apprehension of Death some-
where in accord with those of her admired Cowper and Dr. Johnson.

Her description of the tranquillity of expression on the face of her Father's corpse belongs to the same tradition. On the other hand the deaths of the foolish or the reprobate are sometimes the subject of mockery in her letters, as they are in the treatment of Mrs. Churchill's death, or, to me rather repulsively, the death of young Musgrave (a callousness I find more repulsive than the lack of taste so often deplored in ridiculing fat Mrs. Musgrave's grief). All this may be no more than a healthy contempt for pietistic hypocrisies about the deaths of people unknown to their conventional mourners; but, however healthy its cause, such unconcern for reprobate death marries strangely with the other examples I have given. On the whole the balance of evidence suggests that Jane Austen was poised (as in everything else) between two religious viewpoints: the more awful orthodoxy of Cowper, Johnson or Richardson, and a more secularized Christianity resting upon works, social duty, the high calling of the clergy, the place of the Church in a properly established social order. Certainly this latter is the view of a great number of her Anglican readers, for when in a series of lectures on 'Evil in the English Novel' published in *The Listener*, I, an agnostic, attempted to give the ethics of *Mansfield Park* what seemed to me a deeper foundation by suggesting that the 'limited life' was like Cowper's at Olney deliberately cultivated to give fuller time to an inner spiritual life, I received a great number of angry letters from Anglicans protesting at my attributing such vulgar enthusiasm to the author. The habit of mockery which she cultivated in the schoolroom to protect herself from the division of her feelings remained with her all her life, I think; and a notable example relates to this very subject: in a letter of her last years to Cassandra, where speaking of William, a servant of her London brother Henry who had given notice, she says, 'He has more of Cowper than of Johnson in him, fonder of Tame Hares & blank Verse than of the full tide of human Existence at Charing Cross.' The mocking shorthand is of the same wonderfully funny kind as she used long before in 'Love and Friendship', but the aspects of her two great mentors that she mocks are the tranquil and crowded lives that each selected in part as his remedy against terrible religious agonies.

The protective quality of her irony sometimes leads her to a more complacent view of the civilized nature of her times than is surely justified. In Henry Tilney's famous protest that dispels Catherine's horrid imaginings about the General, Professor Harding has rightly pointed to the bitterness of 'a neighbourhood of voluntary spies', but even if we accept that she mocked her respect for contemporary social order with such discernment of its cruel gossip, is the rest of Henry Tilney's ecomium so justified? Were murders by arrogant, tyrannical husbands, even successfully concealed murders only possible in the Alps and the Pyrenees or 'the northern and western extremities' of our islands that Catherine, if pursued, would have yielded? One thing, we know, although with L.S.D. and heroin now our own central concerns we can no longer be so indignant as ten years ago, laudanum pervaded the England Jane Austen lived in, for all Mr. Tilney's assurance that 'neither poison nor sleeping potions [are] to be procured, like rhubarb, from every druggist.' 'Let other pens dwell upon guilt and misery. I quit such odious subjects as soon as I can.' There have been critics quick to point out that, of course, she doesn't quit them. This, I believe, is the virtue of the seduction motif she kept from the eighteenth century. Colonel Brandon's story of his distinguished relative in the sponging house may seem to come from the pages of *Amelia*, yet we have only to think of Edith Dombey if she had not had Cousin Feenix to sustain her in her disgrace. Seduction with all its terrible consequences for unemancipated, rightless women was still almost as terrible a blow in Victorian times as in the days of Clarissa. What is disturbing is not Jane Austen's inclusion of such stories—this is realism—but her toning down of them. But then, if as her nephew said, 'Every circumstance narrated in *Sir Charles Grandison*, all that was ever said or done in the cedar parlour, was familiar to her; and the wedding days of Lady L. and Lady G. were as well remembered as if they had been living friends', she may have known as well but she certainly did not regard so highly Mother Sinclair's house or the raping day of Clarissa. Sir Edward in *Sanditon* is set to be a figure of absurdity, 'for his fancy had been early caught by all the impassioned, & most exceptionable parts of Richardsons ... With a perversity of Judgement, which must be attributed to his not having by Nature a very strong head, the Graces, the Spirit, The sagacity & the Perseverance, of the Villain of the Story [presumably Lovelace] outweighed all his absurdities & his Atrocities with Sir Edward', and again, 'he felt a strong curiosity to ascertain whether the Neighbourhood of Tombuctoo might not afford some solitary House adapted for Clara's reception;—but the Expence alas! of Measures in that masterly style was ill-suited to his Purse.' This is a splendid hit at Richardson's fantasy; and yet were middle class girls so absolutely free from the arrogant sexual designs of their aristocratic social superiors in Regency times, let alone in the days of *Evelina* or, more still, of Clarissa? And, if they were more secure, what about their lesser sisters—shopkeepers' daughters, landladies' daughters, farmers' daughters, to sink no lower? It was hardly necessary in 1860, let alone in 1810, to go to Tombuctoo to find brothels, complaisant Sinclairs, and the possibilities of sexual violence. As to the preference for Lovelace's superiorities we can be happy that only weak-minded Frenchmen from Prévost and Diderot through Laclos to Balzac found any inspiration in them.

But I only state this case against Jane Austen's assurance of propriety and civilized decorum to admit that it is not a serious defect, only a pointer to a conflict that was too often met by avoidance. The extremes of religious feeling as the extremes of evil passion she probably avoided. Yet one is still forced to ask her what was her view of human nature. Her novels are mainly novels of education in which the heroes and heroines learn better; environment, though never accepted as an excuse (see the Prices in Portsmouth or the Crawfords in London) is recognized as a cause of evil; Mrs. Norris, she admits, might have done far better in her sister Price's position, and so on. All this suggests a view of human nature as open to improvement, a blank page, like Fielding's, on which life will write its results. Richardson, too, professed this view, but he was evidently bound to an older conception of Original Sin. There is much to suggest that Jane Austen believed something similar, at any rate sometimes. Mr. Gardiner is saved, Mrs. Bennet not; Lizzie and Jane have some essential good that their sisters do not share; Anne, too, is superior to her sisters. Education and environment are certainly not all. Fanny resists Sir Thomas's failure to imbue right principles into his charges, so almost does Edmund. Nor does the explanation lie in folly—Mrs. Bennet's crime is stupidity as is Lydia's, but stupidity saves Miss Bates and sets Mrs. Jennings and Mrs. Palmer above Lady Middleton; no amount of intelligence can help Mr. Elliot or the Crawfords. The distribution of Nature's saving graces is arbitrary.

For this reason one is always left in some perplexity about the hopes for the future that lie beyond the endings of Jane Austen's novels. It is easy enough to say that the wedding bells endings are a mere convention, but they are solutions and, what is more, solutions that cast back a light upon the stories that is often the final illumination. Thus I should say that the union of Fanny and Edmund gives promise both to their future *and also to their past*. It may not be possible to find evidence for any deep inner spiritual life from Fanny's communing with the evening sky, but even though the Edmund Bertrams's Christianity may be a secularized one—of duty, respect for profession, limited social usefulness, a somewhat second-hand culture—the fact is that there is something hopeful about their compatibility, their powers to endure, the very obstinacy of their priggishness, if you like. They are not of the stuff to entertain us at dinner—Mr. Amis is quite right; but as we look back from their union we surely see a more real account of love—both Fanny's for Edmund, and Edmund's for Mary—than elsewhere in the novels. Edmund is a stick, but he is a real stick that suffers, not a dream like Darcy or Knightley. Mr. and Mrs. Bertram, though not 'our sort of people,' are made for one another. And this is important when we think where incompatibility in marriage has landed Mr. Bennet and Sir Thomas, where compatibility has elevated the admirable Gardiners and the more than admirable Crofts. But the somewhat dusty union of Fanny and Edmund is not the only compatible marriage in her novels; there are more lively ones, unions more to our taste. In her first novel, when conflicting views weighed less heavily on her spirits, Jane Austen joined Catherine Morland and Henry Tilney. They are young, of course; their author was young. But Henry Tilney was invented when Jane Austen did not mistrust charm as a mark of confidence tricksters like Wickham, or as a sign of triviality as with Willoughby and Crawford, or a failure in manliness like Churchill. Henry Tilney radiates charm and kindness, and a slightly absurd seriousness of a very young man, and humour, and a care for aesthetic enjoyment. Catherine as she grows, bids fair to equal him. It may be a young author's Eden but it is very palatable. And, strange to say, we are not so far away when we arrive at the autumn of *Persuasion*. Only Anne's pious certainty that she was right to respect Lady Russell's opinion in her youth jars; otherwise we have a hero as charming, lively and kind as Tilney, but more manly, and what is most important a travelled man, experienced outside the parish pump. Anne, too, is the most serious and the most genuinely cultivated of the heroines. If there is any teasing it will be from him, but they are an essentially compatible couple. We may be sure that a man whose delightful and loved sister declares, 'I hate to hear you talking so, like a fine gentleman, and as if women were all fine ladies, instead of rational creatures. We none of us expect to be in smooth waters all our days', will expand his wife's horizons. But Anne's sights are already half there, as her determination to revisit Lyme despite its sad associations shows. Mr. Tony Tanner in his essay on *Mansfield Park* (p. 184 above) wrongly cites Anne's attitude to Lyme as though it were conservative and backward looking, when it is, in fact, a sign of her courageous independence. What other of her novels dares to end with so accepted a threat as 'she gloried in being a sailor's wife, but she must pay the tax of quick alarm.'

Anne can do so because the compromise between her and Wentworth has not been large; they promise to become Crofts. Only disseminated depression following her serious illness can give one hope that Marianne will find happiness with the estimable Colonel Brandon. But it is the compromise of the two major novels that most fails to convince me. Lizzie, perhaps, may teach Darcy how to be teased. They will at least be removed from Longbourn; Pemberley lies among lofty mountains. In any case Lizzie is so real and Darcy so unreal that we cannot take the compromise seriously. *Emma* is the tale I cannot swallow despite all its great artistry, its reverberating intricate ironies. For what has Miss Woodhouse learned? That she cannot make up daydreams of grandeur to sugar the pill of Highbury's pettiness. What sort of future awaits her? No removal from Highbury. The visits of a brother-in-law who never goes out in London; of Mrs. Suckling; occasionally of Jane and Frank with Miss Bates in tow. Mr. Knightley, so much admired by modern critics, seems to me pompous, condescending and a bore. His manliness consists in the looming spectre of a Victorian paterfamilias, authoritative on every subject, lecturing, always being in the right. As a landowner he may be excellent, as an employer model, to be praised as a thoughtful and tactful provider of apples for Miss Bates; but what sort of a husband will he make for Emma's untutored high intelligence? What will she do all day while he is busy, healthily walking about in all weathers? What has he learned but to treat her as 'the little woman', 'my Emma', who has made him think better of spoiled children. It is a sad sort of father-daughter marriage that has been achieved—Rochester and Jane Eyre without the passion. And what will Emma do now? I think most modern critics today, following the concern of Mr. E. M. Forster, will point out that she will never again be cruel to Miss Bates. This cruelty to Miss Bates has become a central point to the worshippers of *Emma*—this, in little, they imply, is the concentration camp, the knout and the whip. Of course, no one wishes hurt to Miss Bates, but if the price of all Emma's high spirits, her wit, her natural impetuosity is that Miss Bates should know that Emma does not like her, I cannot object to the price. For that's the truth of it—from the start of the book as she tells Harriet, Emma, though appreciating Miss Bates' sterling qualities of the heart, does not like her. It is not only, I think, that Miss Bates bores her—though this is understandable; it is that Miss Bates's gabbling gratitude towards those who condescend to her, towards all those—Westons, Knightleys, Coles, Woodhouses, and Eltons—who are 'kind' to a foolish spinster in straightened circumstances is repellent to Emma, as I am sure it must have been to Jane Austen. Emma hates Hartfield where nevertheless all her affections lie, all her limited young life has been spent. She knows that it is a neighbourhood of voluntary spies, not, as Miss Bates, whose battle is lost, asserts, 'such a happiness when good people get together—and they always do.' Only regulated hatred—regulated now by the lessons Mr. Knightley and Jane Austen have taught her—can reconcile Emma to Hartfield, where her affections and her roots lie. It is a sad ending, a depressing compromise. I am not persuaded by Professor Shorer that 'Emma's individual being, as she has discovered it, will make that society better', although I am sure that he is right to add 'but it will not make it different.'

# INDEX

Absentee, The, 55
Acting and theatricals, 43–4, 150–6
Adams, Henry, 55
Addison, Joseph, 118
Amelia, 195
American criticism, 9–10
Amis, Kingsley, 137, 186, 197
Anna Karenina, 3, 16–17
Aristotle and Aristotelian school of moralists, 114–15, 118–22, 135, 168
Arnold, Matthew, 55
Arnold, Thomas, 139
Aspects of the Novel (Forster), 16, 123
Auden, W. H., 190
Austen, Caroline, 28
Austen, Cassandra, 23, 27, 29, 30, 37, 38, 187, 193, 194; letter from JA on Pride and Prejudice, 41–2
Austen, Charles, 31, 150, 168
Austen, Francis, 23
Austen, George (brother of JA), 27, 31
Austen, George (father of JA), 30–1, 37
Austen, Henry, 31, 43, 45, 187, 194; bankruptcy of, 29, 183; London life, 183
Austen, James, 31, 187
Austen, Jane: and education, 33–6, 51–2; and Evangelicals, 44, 194; and tradition, 123–35; artistic economy, xiv; character and caricature, 83–105; conflict in her psychology, 25–26, 184; cynicism, 171–2; devices of construction, 168–70; fictional method, 12; inability to spell, 35; invention of characters, 12–17, 167–9; Letters, 104–5; limitations, xii–xiii, xv; moral ideas and systems, 115–22; modesty, xii; on Wisdom and Wit, 42, 157; Prayers, 105; problem of ridicule, 104–5; reading, 187; religious upbringing and Christian principles, 105, 131, 180, 193–4; wit and humour, 170–1, 173, 177–8
Austen, Mrs., 23, 29–31, 33, 37, 187
Austen-Leigh, J. E., 29, 30, 152, 162, 171, 182
Austen-Leigh, M. A., 35

Balzac, 167, 196
Bayley, John, 167
Beast in the Jungle, The, 48
Bellow, Saul, 136
Between the Acts, 183
Bostonians, The, 4, 12
Blake, William, 53
Bradley, A. C., 166; on JA, 3
Brontë, Charlotte, 13, 171: on JA, xiv, 186
Brontë, Emily, 15
Browning, Elizabeth Barrett, on JA, xiv
Brydges, Sir Egerton, 29
Burnet, Bishop, 49, 51: on Improvement, 53
Burney, Fanny, 115, 124, 163, 171, 187–8
Butler, Bishop, 45, 49, 118, 119, 121, 171
Byron and Byronism, 139, 178–9

Caleb Williams (Godwin), 187
Calvinistic school of moralists, 114–115, 117, 119
Camilla, 55
Cannan, Gilbert, 125
Carswell, Catherine, 126

Castration symbolism, 27
Cecil, Lord David, 190: Leslie Stephen Lecture (1935), xi–xiii
*Cecilia*, 55
Cervantes, 128
Chapman, George, 55
Chapman, R. W., 128, 187: Index to the Letters, 23
Character and caricature in JA: borderline, 85–102; contrasts, 95–9; different handling of caricatures, 88–9; differentiation, 91–9; intention of satire, 85–9; likeable caricatures, 90–1; natural portraiture, 84–85; preliminary description of characters, 84; ridiculous caricatures, 89–90
Charm in JA's novels, 45–6, 130, 185
Chaucer, 173
Chawton, JA's cramped feelings at, 28–30
Chekhov, 55
Chesterfield, Lord, 45
*Clarissa Harlowe*, 148, 188
Clark, Rev. W., xii
Class and snobbery, 11–13
Clergy, status of, 44–5
Cobbett, William, 138
*Cocktail Party, The*, 52
Coleridge, Samuel Taylor, 175
Coleridge, Sara, 171, 175
*Collection of Letters*, 34
Conflicts in JA's novels, 182–99: and the arts, 190–1; appeal to traditionalists, 185–6; attitude to money, 190; canonization of JA, 185; championship of professional classes, 189–90; constriction of JA's life, 183; country values, 183; detractors of JA, 186; dichotomy in JA's nature, 184; dilemma in JA's work, 184, 187; dislike of small town life, 192; family attachment, 183; feeling for nature, 191; form of novels, 187–189; influence of Richardson, 187–8; quietism, 192–3; religious feeling, 193–4, 196–7; social values, 189–91; unresolved temperamental conflict and search for solution, 184–5; values, 189–91; Victorian view of JA, 185, 186; view of human nature, 196
Congreve, 170

Conrad, Joseph, xii, xiii, xvi, 2, 125, 126
Cooper, Edward, 23, 37
Cowper, William, 42, 53, 125, 193–4: JA admires, 180, 187, 193; religious orthodoxy of, 194
Crabbe, George, JA admires, 180
*Culture and Anarchy*, 55

Dallas, E. S., xiv
*Daniel Deronda*, 4
D'Arblay, Madame, *see* Burney, Fanny
de Feuillide, Eliza, 43, 188
Descartes, 119
de Staël, Madame: JA refuses to meet, 184
Dickens, Charles, 84, 166, 171, 174: characters drawn from real life, 12
Diderot, 153, 196
Dostoevsky, 3
du Barri, Madame, 33

Edgeworth, Maria, 171
Education, JA and, 33–6, 51–2
*Education of Henry Adams, The*, 55
Eliot, George, xii, xiv, 1–13, 13, 14, 126–7, 133, 165, 180, 190: characters drawn from real life, 12; fictional method, 12; on JA, 127; outlook, 7; portrayal of society, 8, 9, 15
*Emma*, xii, 2–3, 5–7, 9–15, 17–19, 35, 36, 39–42, 47, 70, 121, 127, 131–4, 175–7, 179, 183, 186, 188–9, 198–9: acceptance of misunderstanding, 7; character and caricature, 85–9, 91, 94–5, 97–9, 102–5; completely matured art, 72; construction of, 169–170; harmony between sadness and joy, 18–19; irony in, 40–1; JA's masterpiece, 62; learning experience, 60–2, 72–81; Newman on, 175–6; opening paragraphs, 84; review by Scott, xiii, xiv, 163–5, 168, 174–5; theme-notion of influence and interference, 110–12
Epicurus and the Epicureans, 118, 119
Evangelicals, JA and, 44, 194
*Evelina*, 55, 196

Farrer, Reginald, 2–3, 15
*Felix Holt*, xiv
Ferrier, Susan, 168, 171

Fielding, Henry, 119, 124, 128, 165, 169–71, 174, 196
Flaubert, 15
Ford, Ford Madox, 160–1
Forster, E. M., 16, 123, 198
*Fragments in the Theory and Practice of Landscape Gardening* (Repton), 52
*Frederic and Elfrida*, 36
French Revolution, the, 139
Freud, 23, 75, 133, 135

Garrick, David, 165
Garrod, H. W., 1, 130, 186
Godwin, William, 139, 187
Goethe, 139
*Golden Bowl, The*, 8, 150
Goldsmith, Oliver, 53, 118, 173, 180: *History of England* and *Abridgement*, 30, 32, 37: JA's tilt at, 22
Gore, Mrs., 163, 164

Halévy, Elie, 44
Harding, D. W., 2, 8, 158, 192, 194: JA as astringent figure, 39, 40
Hastings, Warren, 139
Hawthorne, Nathaniel, 10
Herbert, George, 160
Heroines, JA's, 131–5, 137–8
*History of England, The*, (Jane Austen), 21–2, 24–7, 30–6: arbitrariness, 21–2; faith in education, 33–6; gothick metaphor, 31–2; JA on every losing side, 25; Lambert Simnel joke, 25–6; Mary Queen of Scots, 24–6, 30, 33; resistance of own romantic fantasies, 32; sarcasms against babies, 33; side-swipes, 22; vindication of Stuarts, 245, 30; wronged Austens and wronged Stuarts, 30–1
*History of England and Abridgement* (Goldsmith), 22, 30, 32, 37
*History of England* (Hume), 22, 32, 37
*History of England in the Nineteenth Century* (Halévy), 44
Hobbes, Thomas, 46, 119
Homosexuality, 25–6
*Howard's End*, 53
Hume, David, 22, 32, 118, 119, 121
Hutcheson, Francis, 49, 118, 119

*Idler, The*, 119
'Improvement', 52–5, 57, 150–2; im-

provements of estates, 52–5, 150–2; moralists and, 53
Inchbald, Mrs., 124
Industrial Revolution, the, 139
Irony, 40–1, 185, 187, 194–5
*Irony as Defence and Discovery* (Mudrick), 41
'Irresponsibility' of JA, 1–20: acceptance of misunderstanding, 7; affinity with Tolstoy, 16–19; American criticism, 9–10; class and snobbery, 11–13; definition, 4; fictional method, 12; harmony between sadness and joy, 18–19; invention of character, 12–17; liberation from morality, 8; living inside community, 5–7; living with characters, 16; necessities of resignation, 18; 'plasticity', 4; portrayal of society, 8–12

*Jack and Alice*, 22–4, 26, 37
James, Henry, xii, xiii, 1–2, 16, 48, 55, 125–7, 130, 133, 148, 150, 180, 185: characters drawn from real life, 12; fictional method, 12; on American society, 10; on character, 13; on JA, 3–4, 39; portrayal of society, 8–9, 15
James, William, 45
*Jane Austen: A Depreciation* (Garrod), 1
*Jane Eyre*, 154
Johnson, Rev. Augustus, 23–4: JA's fantasy revenge on, 24, 30
Johnson, Samuel, 44, 115, 118, 134, 139, 179; JA admires, 180, 187, 193; religious orthodoxy of, 194
Jonson, Ben, 53
*Jude the Obscure*, 136
Juvenilia, JA's, 21–7, 30–6, 101, 172, 194

Kettle, Arnold, 189
Kipling, Rudyard, 127–8, 162
Knight, Edward (Austen), 28, 31
Kott, J. A., 2
Kotzebue, 124

Laclos, 196
Lascelles, Mary, 128
Lawrence, D. H., xii, 2, 17, 123, 125, 126, 186
Learning experience and change,

60–82; and 'Sense', 61–2; *Emma*, 60–62, 72–81; *Mansfield Park*, 60–1, 67–70, 74; *Persuasion*, 80–2; *Pride and Prejudice*, 60–2, 70–2, 81; *Sense and Sensibility*, 60–7, 69, 70, 74, 80; success and failure, 60–2
Leavis, F. R.: and 'Great Tradition', 2; on JA, xii, xvi, 131–3, 135
Leavis, Mrs., 128
Leigh family, 23, 32, 34, 36
*Le Rouge et le Noir*, 136
Letters of JA, 104–5
Lewes, G. H.: article on JA, xiv, 163, 165–6, 175, 180; indebtedness to other authors, 168–9; lacks sense of JA's wit and humour, 170–1; on JA's construction, 168–9
Lister, T. H.: account of JA's work, 163–5; explanation of her naturalism, 165
Litz, A. Walton, 8, 20
Locke, John, 53, 119
*Longest Journey, The*, 123
*Lovers' Vows*, 43, 124, 125, 134, 155

Macaulay, Lord, xiv, 2, 55, 163, 165
Mackenzie, (Sir) Compton, 125
*Madame Bovary*, xii
Mandeville, Bernard, 46
*Mansfield Park*, xii, 3, 13, 18, 19, 25, 39–59, 71, 110, 114, 137–61, 164, 168, 183, 184, 187–9, 194, 198: character and caricature, 85–6, 90; character of Fanny Price, 137–8, 148–9; characters' inner qualities revealed by actions, 149–50; complications, 169; covert preaching, 196; Edmund's choice of priesthood, 44–5, 157; education, 51–2; Fanny's love for Edmund, 44–5; fraternal and conjugal ties, 112–13; game of Speculation, 56–8; general background, 138–9; grandeur to poverty, 28–9; guardians of Mansfield Park, 143–6; 'improvement', 52–5, 57, 150–2; interlopers, 146–8; JA as moralist, 132–5; JA's most committed novel, 44; learning experience, 60–1, 67–70, 74; local irony, 39–40; moralists and the moral sense, 49–52, 55–7; preservation of moral consciousness against selfishness of society, 157–9; 'quietness' and 'repose', 144; relationships of characters with Mansfield Park, 143–9; stable values and new forces, 158–61; subject of ordination, 44–5, 157; temptation of charm, 45–6; temptation of selfishness, 45–9; theatricals, 43–4, 52, 144, 150–6; traditional rural life, 138–9; Wisdom, Truth and moral sense, 42–3, 45
*Marmion*, 125: JA's parody of, 2
*Marriage of Heaven and Hell, The*, 53
Marvell, Andrew, 53
Mead, George, 134
*Memoir of Jane Austen* (Austen-Leigh), xiii, 29, 152, 162, 171–2, 174, 182
Meredith, George, 170
*Middlemarch*, 8, 16
Moir, George, 171
Molière, 169, 170, 173, 180
*Mont Saint-Michel and Chartres* (Henry Adams), 55
Moore, Sir John, 193
Moralists and the moral sense, JA and, 49–53, 55–7, 106–22, 131–5: abstract nouns as titles, 106–10; aesthetic terms, 117–18; Aristotelian school, 114–15, 118–22; Black-White dichotomy, 114–16; Calvinistic school, 114–15, 117, 119; comparative character-delineation, 108–9; fraternal and conjugal ties, 112–13; influence and interference, 110–12; influence of Shaftesbury, 118–22; JA's moral ideas and system, 115–22; persuadability, 109–10; problems about human nature, 106–7; solicitude, 110; use of 'Mind', 121; vocabulary of Shaftesbury and JA, 119–21
Mozley, Anne, 175
Mudrick, Marvin, 5–6, 20, 41, 60, 67, 68, 74, 187
*Mysteries of Udolpho, The*, 114

Napoleonic wars, 138
Newman, John Henry, 175–6, 179
Nicolson, Sir Harold, 132
Nineteenth century and JA's comedy, 162–80: devices of construction, 168–70; early critics, 163–71; her creation of characters, 167–9; her cynicism, 171–2; her wit and humour not appreciated, 170–1; lack of

recognizable romance, 174–6; re-action against picture of subdued sweetness, 171–3; supposed absence of plot, 168

*Northanger Abbey*, 32, 41, 43, 47, 55, 102, 116–17, 131, 186, 188, 191: no abstract ethical theme, 113–14

Oliphant, Mrs. Margaret on JA, 171–175, 179, 180: and *Persuasion*, 175; and *Pride and Prejudice*, 172–3; JA's 'vein of feminine cynicism', 171–2

*On Translating Homer* (Arnold), 55

*Pamela*, 188

*Parade's End*, 160

*Peopled Landscape, A* (Tomlinson), 53

*Persuasion*, 18, 19, 36, 41, 42, 45, 46, 55, 62, 106, 110, 116, 117, 121, 128, 159, 162, 175–9, 184, 189, 190, 197: absence of wit, 177–8; character and caricature, 85, 102; characters lacking in self-sufficiency, 177; dif-ference in kind from JA's other novels, 176; fine touches in, 178; harmony between sadness and joy, 18, 19; learning experience, 80–2; opening paragraphs, 84; predomi-nance of hero and heroine, 178; theme-notion of persuadability, 109–10

Plato, 118: objection to acting, 153

*Plumed Serpent, The*, 123

Pope, Alexander, 118, 121, 179

*Portrait of a Lady*, 136, 140

Prayers of JA, 105

Prévost, 196

*Pride and Prejudice*, 4, 34, 35, 45, 46, 106, 107, 110, 116, 158, 172–4, 183, 186, 187, 189: character and carica-ture, 83, 85, 88–90, 99; epigram-matic brilliance, 173; JA's com-ments on, 41–2; learning experi-ence, 60–2, 70–2, 81; predominance of hero and heroine, 178; theme-notion of persuadability, 109

*Princess Casamassima, The*, 8

Professional classes, JA's champion-ship of, 189–90

Proust, xii, 3

Quietism and the 'Quiet Thing', 136–161, 192–3

Rabelais, 171

*Rambler, The*, 115, 119, 124

*Rameau's Nephew* (Diderot), 153

Read, Sir Herbert, 129

Regency London, 138, 142

Repton, Humphrey, 52, 53

Richardson, Samuel, 133, 185, 195–6; influence on JA, 187–8; religious or-thodoxy of, 194, 196

*Rise of the Novel* (Watt), xiii

Ritchie, Lady (Anne Thackeray), 162

Romantic poets and Romantic move-ment, 139, 153

Romantic self-projections, 14–15

*Romola*, 8

Rousseau, 187

Ruskin, John, xiv, 53

*St. Leon* (Godwin), 187

*Sanditon*, 41, 46, 158–9, 176, 178–9, 184, 195: return to comic spirit of earlier works, 178

Sartre, Jean-Paul, 158

*Scenes of Clerical Life* (George Eliot), 165

Scott, Sir Walter, 42, 128, 139, 171, 174: on JA's realism, 163; review of *Emma*, xiii, xiv, 163–5, 167, 174–5

Selfishness in JA's novels, 45–9: pun-ishment of, 46–7

*Sense and Sensibility*, 41, 42, 44–7, 55, 106–8, 110, 114, 116, 121, 131, 133, 134, 188: character and caricatures, 83, 85, 91–4, 99–101; learning ex-perience, 60–7, 69, 70, 74, 80; moral-izing, 106

Sexual morality, 132–4

Shaftesbury, Lord, 3, 8, 13, 44, 49, 53, 187: Deism of, 118; direct or indirect influence of JA, 118–22; use of 'Mind', 121; vocabulary, 119–21

Shakespeare, 5, 7, 55, 76, 128, 154, 171, 178: comparison with JA, xiv, 2–4, 164–7, 170, 180

Shelley, 135

Sheridan, 173, 180

*Shirley*, 171

Shorer, Professor, 199

Simpson, Richard, xiii, xv, 19

*Sir Charles Grandison*, 188, 195

Smith, Adam, 44, 49, 51

Smollett, 128, 171, 174

Society, JA's portrayal of, 8–12

*Sons and Lovers*, 125, 136
Sophocles, 169
Southey, Robert, 139, 175
*Spectator, The*, 119
Spinoza, 119
Sterne, Laurence, 167
Stoics, the, 118
Strindberg, 55
Stuarts, JA and the, 21–38: awareness of homosexuality, 25–6; castration symbolism, 27; faith in education, 33–6; *History of England*, 21–2, 24–7, 30–6; *Jack and Alice*, 23–4, 26; JA's family as distressed aristocracy, 27–30; overcoming absolutism of daydream, 36; physiological dethronement of girls, 26–7; resistance of her own romantic fantasies, 32; transportation from grandeur to poverty, 28–9; unfair social rules, 27; vindication of the Stuarts, 24–5
Swift, 171, 179

Tanner, Tony, 184, 198
*Task, The*, 53
Thackeray, Anne (Lady Ritchie), 162
Thackeray, W. M., 171
Theophrastus, 108
*Theory of Moral Sentiments* (Adam Smith), 49
*Three Sisters, The*, 55
Tolstoy, xii, 7: affinity with JA, 16–19; comparison with JA, xv, 5, 167
*Tom Jones*, 136, 174, 180
Tomlinson, Charles, 53
*To the Lighthouse*, 135
Tradition and Miss Austen, 123–35; 'charm', 130; her books as solace and refreshment, 128; her detractors, 128–9; impossibility of synoptic view, 123–4; 'intense moral pre-occupation', 131–2; irony, 130–1; play of moral feelings, 135; seen through her heroines, 131–5; sexual morality, 132–4
*Treatise on Education* (Locke), 43
Trilling, Lionel, xii, 120, 128: essays on JA, 3, 9–12, 15, 67, 68, 70, 74, 80, 132–5, 148, 152, 157, 192
*Tristram Shandy*, 167, 180
Trollope, Anthony, 12
Twain, Mark, xi, 186

*Ulysses*, 1, 76

*Vanity Fair*, 136
*Vicar of Wakefield, The*, 115

Walpole, Horace, 3
Walpole, (Sir) Hugh, 125
*War and Peace*, 16–19
Ward, Mrs. Humphry, 133
Watt, Ian, xiii
Wells, H. G., xiii, 125–6
Wharton, Edith, 125
Whately, Archbishop Richard: early admirer of JA, xiv, 163–5, 175; on devices of plot, 168; on JA's realism, 164
Whitman, Walt, 153
Wilson, Edmund, 3, 20
Wiltshire, John, xiii
*Wings of the Dove, The*, 148
*Women as they Are* (Mrs. Gore), 163, 164
*Women in Love*, 123
Woolf, Virginia, 182–4
Wordsworth, William, 53, 139: and JA, 175, 179
Wright, Andrew, 162, 176, 177, 184
*Wuthering Heights*, 15

Yeats, W. B., 13